Politics wi

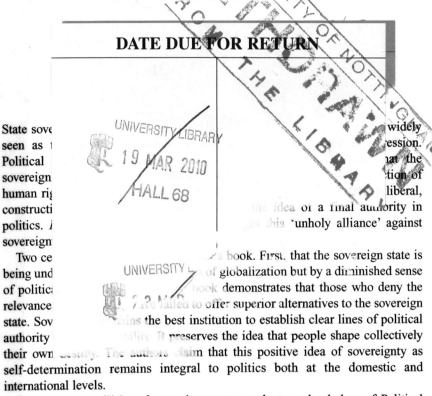

State sove   widely
seen as   ession.
Political   at the
sovereign   tion of
human ri   liberal,
constructi   the idea of a final authority in
politics.   his 'unholy alliance' against
sovereign

Two ce   book. First, that the sovereign state is
being und   of globalization but by a diminished sense
of politic   book demonstrates that those who deny the
relevance   have failed to offer superior alternatives to the sovereign
state. Sov   ins the best institution to establish clear lines of political
authority   ility. It preserves the idea that people shape collectively
their own destiny. The authors claim that this positive idea of sovereignty as
self-determination remains integral to politics both at the domestic and
international levels.

This key text will be of great interest to students and scholars of Political
Science, International Relations, Security Studies, International Law,
Development and European Studies.

Christopher J. Bickerton, St John's College, University of Oxford, UK.

Philip Cunliffe, King's College London, UK.

Alexander Gourevitch, Columbia University, USA.

Politics without Sovereignty

A critique of contemporary international relations

**Edited by
Christopher J. Bickerton,
Philip Cunliffe and
Alexander Gourevitch**

UCL
PRESS

UNIVERSITY COLLEGE LONDON PRESS

First published 2007
by UCL Press
The name of University College London (UCL)
is a registered trade mark used by
UCL Press with the consent of the owner

Taylor & Francis
2 Park Square, Milton Park, Abingdon, Oxon OX14 4RN

Simultaneously published in the USA
by UCL Press
270 Madison Ave, New York, NY 10016

*UCL Press is an imprint of the Taylor & Francis Group,
an informa business*

© 2007 UCL Press

Typeset in Times New Roman by
Newgen Imaging Systems (P) Ltd, Chennai, India
Printed and bound in Great Britain by
Biddles Ltd, King's Lynn

British Library Cataloguing in Publication Data
A catalogue record for this book is available from the British Library

Library of Congress Cataloging in Publication Data
    Politics without sovereignty: a critique of contemporary international
relations / edited by Christopher Bickerton, Philip Cunliffe and
Alexander Gourevitch.
        p. cm.
    Includes bibliographical references and index.
    1. Sovereignty. 2. International relations. I. Bickerton, Christopher.
II. Cunliffe, Philip. III. Gourevitch, Alexander.

    JC327.P63 2007
    320.1'5–dc22   200619933

ISBN10: 0–415–41806–2 (hbk)
ISBN10: 0–415–41807–0 (pbk)

ISBN13: 978–0–415–41806–5 (hbk)
ISBN13: 978–0–415–41807–2 (pbk)

100524935 X T

Praise for *Politics without sovereignty*

Echoing Churchillís famous aphorism about democracy, *Politics without Sovereignty* argues that the sovereign state is the worst form of governance except for all others. In a forceful post-revisionist critique, the editors and contributors contend that only the sovereign state allows both collective agency and political accountability. Bemoaning the slide into global civil society or global governance, only sovereignty, they claim, allows peoples to shape their destinies in progressive ways. This volume is a powerful challenge to current theory in international relations and requires all of us to think deeper about the virtues and necessity of global political change.

(David A. Lake, University of California, San Diego, USA)

This multi-sided onslaught on fashionable notions and theories about the decline and the mischiefs of state sovereignty is not likely to convince all readers, but the authors' central point, about the fact that political accountability and agency require state sovereignty, is one that needs to be faced rather than evaded out of distaste for the excesses and liabilities of sovereignty.

(Stanley Hoffmann, Harvard University, USA)

Critical international relations theory has generally used its cutting edge against traditional realist notions of sovereignty. An orthodoxy has emerged which portrays the notion of sovereignty and its embodiment in practice as a block to human emancipation. The essays in this book reappraise the wisdom of this. Its chapters provide bold, closely argued and provocative normative evaluations of the notion of state sovereignty. The arguments here will start a number of hares that will run and run. The book is the culmination of an intellectual project that has been going for over a year, the chapters in it have been refined in seminars and conferences. The editors are skeptical of the idea that the withering away of the state would usher in a utopia of cosmopolitan politics. Instead, they argue that there is a close link between individual agents, sovereign states and human liberty. The ideas in this book will be tested in the vigorous reaction which will undoubtedly follow its publication.

(Mervyn Frost, King's College, UK)

In recent years the concept and practice of state sovereignty have been subjected to searching analytical and normative critique. Not only is sovereignty not what IR scholars long assumed it to be, but the taken for granted equation of sovereignty with security and justice has been severely questioned. Curiously, the defense of state sovereignty has so far amounted to little more than the bland reassertion of analytical state-centrism. *Politics without Sovereignty* lifts this defense to a higher plane. Together, the editors and contributors advance a defense of sovereignty that is at once analytical, normative, and deeply political. It is a volume that will confront and provoke, and in so doing fuel debate and, in turn, insight.

(Chris Reus-Smit, Australian National University, Australia)

Contents

Contributors

Christopher J. Bickerton is co-convenor of the Sovereignty and its Discontents (SAID) working group of the British International Studies Association. He is a D.Phil. candidate at St John's College, University of Oxford, and is currently researching the foreign policy of the European Union. <www. said-workshop.org>

Chris Brown is Professor of International Relations at the London School of Economics and the author of, amongst other works, *Understanding International Relations* (third edition, 2005), *Sovereignty, Rights and Justice* (2002) and co-editor of *International Relations in Political Thought: Texts from the Greeks to the First World War* (2002).

David Chandler is Professor of International Relations at the Centre for the Study of Democracy, University of Westminster. He is the editor of the *Journal of Intervention and Statebuilding* and author of, amongst other works, *Empire in Denial: The Politics of State-building* (2006) and *Constructing Global Civil Society: Morality and Power in International Relations* (2004).

Philip Cunliffe is co-convenor of the SAID working group. He is a PhD candidate in the Department of War Studies at King's College London. He is currently researching developing countries' involvement in peacekeeping operations. <www.said-workshop.org>

James Der Derian is a Watson Institute Research Professor of International Studies and Director of the Institute's Global Security Program. Der Derian also founded and directs the Global Media Project and the Information Technology, War, and Peace Project at the Watson Institute. His most recent book is *Virtuous War: Mapping the Military-Industrial-Media-Entertainment Network* (2006).

Michael W. Doyle is the Harold Brown Professor at Columbia University in the School of International and Public Affairs, Columbia Law School and the Department of Political Science. His publications include *Making War and Building Peace* (2006) and *Empires* (1986). He served as Assistant Secretary-General and Special Adviser to United Nations Secretary-General Kofi Annan.

Alexander Gourevitch is co-convenor of the SAID working group. He is a PhD student at Columbia University, and is currently researching the theory of democratic representation in American politics. He is also co-editor of 'Against the War on Terror'. <www.againstwot.com>

James Heartfield is a writer and lecturer based at the Centre for the Study of Democracy, University of Westminster. He is researching the process of European integration. His *The 'Death of the Subject' Explained* was published in 2002. <www.heartfield.org>

David Kennedy is the Manley O. Hudson Professor of Law at Harvard Law School, and Director of the European Law Research Center. He is also founder of the New Approaches to International Law project. He has practiced law with various international institutions, including the United Nations High Commissioner for Refugees and the Commission of the European Union.

Tara McCormack is a PhD candidate in International Relations at the Centre for Study of Democracy, University of Westminster. She is currently researching aspects of post-Cold War security theory and policy.

John Pender is an independent researcher. His previous publications include 'Empowering the Poorest? The World Bank and the "Voices of the Poor" ', in David Chandler (ed.) *Rethinking Human Rights: Critical Approaches to International Politics* (2002).

Michael Savage is an investment banker. He is researching how the changing relationship between politics and law, and between politics and economics, is limiting the scope for political action today.

Jack L. Snyder is the Robert and Renée Belfer Professor of International Relations in the political science department and the Saltzman Institute of War and Peace Studies at Columbia University. His books include *From Voting to Violence: Democratization and Nationalist Conflict* (2000); and *Myths of Empire: Domestic Politics and International Ambition* (1991).

Foreword

I am not sure who was responsible for the generic name for the project out of which this volume arose – 'Sovereignty and its Discontents' – but, in any event, it was a stroke of near genius. Apart from generating a catchy acronym, SAID, the name focuses attention on the two most salient features of international relations – and International Relations (IR) theory – in our time, the centrality of the notion of sovereignty, and the widespread discontent this centrality provokes. As the editors remark (p. 7) there is 'a broadly based antipathy to the idea of a final, absolute authority in political life – namely the sovereign state', but, as these chapters also demonstrate, this same idea remains more or less analytically indispensable, and, for many, politically desirable. We (some of us) can not live with it, we (most of us) can not think without it.

It was ever thus. Some recent writers manage to give the impression that the meaning of state sovereignty was stabilized sometime in the seventeenth century, perhaps at 'Westphalia' in 1648, and has only recently been put into question by the emergence of complex interdependence, globalization, global civil society and the idea that states should be held responsible for their actions towards their own citizens – 'sovereignty as responsibility'. Not so; sovereignty has always been a contested concept and, as Stephen Krasner has pointed out, the Treaties of Westphalia actually imposed more limitations on state sovereignty (e.g. with respect to the protection of minorities) than the Peace of Augsburg in 1555, or than the common practice 100 or 200 years after 1648. In the realm of theory, Hobbes's account of sovereignty was different from that given by, say, Pufendorf, but even Hobbes was less 'Hobbesian' than assumed by the IR scholars of an earlier generation.

In fact, in 1945 an attempt *was* made to stabilize and fix the notion of sovereignty as part of the post-war settlement, but the attempt failed because of its internal contradictions. The new normative framework for IR was based on the United Nations (UN) Charter which, on the one hand, limited the sovereign rights of states by outlawing the use of force unless authorized by the UN Security Council or in immediate self-defence, but, on the other hand, set in place a very strong doctrine of non-intervention that appeared to strengthen the sovereign state's claim to at least domestic jurisdiction, that is, to a 'final, absolute authority in political life'. All states, and not simply the powerful, would, in principle, be free from external interference in their domestic affairs. The problem was, and is, that the UN Charter also asserted the existence of various universal human rights, which were codified in the Universal Declaration of 1948, and in extensive international treaty law thereafter. The result was that, on the one hand, all states were given the right to follow their own sense of the 'Good' domestically, but, on the other, they were immediately told that, actually, and at least in principle, their scope for being different was to be severely limited, that there were certain standards to which all states should conform, even if these standards contradicted the kind of common life they wished to promote.

The potential contradiction here was realized very quickly, with newly independent India leading the camp of those who believed that South Africa should not be allowed to defend its policy of *Apartheid* on the basis of the domestic jurisdiction clause of the UN Charter (Article 2.7) – a view that soon became near-universal – but for most of the next 40 years the Cold War actually suppressed the argument. In the context of East–West conflict, other normative frameworks faded into the background. Partly because of this, when the Cold War ended and the contradiction between the sovereignty norms and the human rights norms of the system came to the surface, some observers thought they were seeing something genuinely new, and, as Nicholas Wheeler has demonstrated, some commentators, and even some states, began to play with the idea that internal domestic arrangements could simply, in and of themselves, constitute a threat to international peace and security. Kofi Annan has argued that there are now two concepts of sovereignty, one associated with absolute internal freedom, the other conditional on good governance and respect for human rights. It would be more accurate to say that both of these notions have been around a long time, and both are supported by the Charter of the institution of which he is Secretary-General.

In normative terms, sovereignty involves a state's *right* to govern itself, to shape its own destiny, and this is inevitably constrained by the notion of universal rights; some states, for example, in the European Union (EU), have accepted this constraint and internalized international standards – but others, especially in Asia, but also including for most purposes the United States, have rejected the idea on the basis that self-determination (let alone constitutional and responsible government) requires a strong doctrine of sovereignty. But, irrespective of the right of states to be self-governing, in practical terms the state's *capacity* to govern itself is also at stake, and, once again, always has been. Today's global economic and social forces clearly impose some limits on the capacity of states to exercise what Robert Jackson has called 'positive sovereignty', but although some of these forces are undoubtedly new, the idea that states are constrained by the existence of forces outside their control is by no means simply a feature of this age. States have always existed in such a context – only states without an 'outside' could be genuinely and purely 'self-determining', or, to put it another way, only a genuine world-empire could ignore its external environment, because, of course, it wouldn't have one.

In short, a central feature of international relations has always been the assessment of costs and benefits associated with particular policies and strategies, and this assessment has always been shaped by the external environment of the state. What would be interesting, and different, would be if the people of particular states no longer valued 'their' sovereignty, and carried out cost–benefit analyses without seeing loss of sovereignty as a cost. Is this actually happening? I think the answer here is a resounding 'no'. In some parts of Western Europe the political class may have lost faith in their own ability to govern and look to buttress their position by enhancing the authority of the EU, but, even here, when they have been asked, the people generally express support for sovereignty, albeit often in a confused and messy way. In the rest of the world, the situation is much clearer. The USA, the emerging BRICs (Brazil, Russia, India, China) and the rest of Asia are staunch defenders of a very traditional conception of state sovereignty – they may be delusional in thinking that this is obtainable nowadays, but the desire is clearly there. And this desire, it seems to me, is not based on an archaic traditionalism which refuses to accept that things have changed, but rather reflects the perfectly logical view that 'politics' in the old sense of the term – ruling and being ruled in turn – is possible only in societies which are, in some sense, sovereign. Political accountability requires identifiable, responsible agents, and amorphous formations, such as 'global civil society', cannot fill this particular gap; the much-praised non-governmental organizations that do exercise agency of a kind are in no sense democratic or subject to the popular will. If publicly accountable agency is what we are interested in – and I believe it should be – then, for all its inadequacies, the sovereign state remains the only game in town.

One of the many strengths of this collection is that most of the authors represented here have a strong sense of the political and of the centrality of issues of agency – they can see what the question is, even if they disagree sometimes over the answer. The range of subjects covered defies easy summary, and no 'party line' emerges though the volume. This is as it should be – what the editors have demonstrated by putting together this collection is that sovereignty is a live issue, a contested concept that is, and should be, at the heart of many of the most important debates in public discourse and IR theory. We are in their debt.

Chris Brown
London School of Economics
May 2006

Acknowledgements

The chapters in this volume came out of many discussions, seminars and conferences across the last few years. For that reason it would be nearly impossible to thank everyone who contributed to sharpening the ideas contained herein.

However, we would especially like to thank the British International Studies Association for their financial and moral support of the 'Sovereignty And Its Discontents' working group. At Columbia University, we would like to thank the following institutions for their generous funding: the Political Science Department, Columbia University Political Science Students' Association; Columbia University Presidential Initiative Fund; the Council for European Studies; the Institute for the Study of Europe, and the Center on Global Legal Problems. At Oxford University, we would like to thank the Centre of International Studies and the Department of Politics and International Relations for their equally generous support. Our thanks go out to the staff of both departments.

We would also like to thank the following individuals who have either supported the SAID working group or helped to ensure that the conferences and seminars have run smoothly, and sometimes both at once: Kay Achar, Lisa Anderson, Jason Bello, Helen Fisher, Nicholas Frayn, Mervyn Frost, Forrest Heidel, Andrew Hurrell, Lee Jones, Andrew Nathan, Nhu-Y Ngo, Micaela Ordahl, Emily Prince and R.B.J. Walker.

We would also like to thank the following people who took the time to read and provide feedback on the manuscript: David Bickerton, Chris Brown, David Cunliffe, Nicholas Frayn, Peter Gourevitch, James Heartfield, Tom Ogg, Peter Ramsay and Suke Wolton. Last but not least, we would like to thank our editors, who helped bring this manuscript to completion – Briar Towers, Heidi Bagtazo and Harriet Brinton.

Introduction

The unholy alliance against sovereignty

Christopher J. Bickerton, Philip Cunliffe and Alexander Gourevitch

In this book, we argue that the current movement against state sovereignty participates in the degradation of political agency at both the domestic and international levels. The case against sovereignty is generally cast as a way of opening up our political imagination to new understandings of power and new possibilities for organizing the world. But its substance is to limit our sense of political possibility, and to sever the relationship between the exercise of power and political responsibility. As a consequence, there is little that is progressive about the current retreat from state sovereignty. The result is that we endure all the negative aspects of sovereignty, and enjoy few of its potential benefits. The sovereign state, however imperfect, still provides the best framework for the organization of collective political life. That, at least, is what we aim to show in this book.

No discussion of international affairs can avoid discussing sovereignty, and everyone has something to say about it. The intellectual productivity around the concept has been enormous. Political scientists Stephen Krasner and David Lake have published a number of books and articles examining the logical coherence and empirical relevance of the concept. Liberal theorists Fernando Tesón and Robert Keohane have looked at the concept in relation to human rights and humanitarian intervention. Postmodern theorists, such as Richard Ashley and Jens Bartelson, have traced the genealogy of sovereignty, while international lawyers, such as Martin Loughlin and Gerry Simpson, have outlined the basic tenets and historical movements of the concept.[1] What is more, sovereignty is a concept that escapes the dry arguments of academics and international lawyers into the wider realm of public debate. Major states and international organizations have published standard-setting treatises on the topic, such as *The Responsibility to Protect*, the Report of the International Commission on Intervention and State Sovereignty (2001), whose suggestions were incorporated in the United Nations' reform report *A More Secure World: Our Shared Responsibility* (2004). Prominent public figures feel obliged to take a stand on sovereignty. US President George W. Bush has repeatedly defended the invasion of Iraq on the grounds that he 'restored sovereignty to the Iraqi people'.[2] Former UN Secretary-General Kofi Annan tried to develop 'two concepts of sovereignty'.[3] But in all these theories and political discussions, the understanding of sovereignty is one sided. As we shall see, state sovereignty is in retreat on all fronts, and even its proponents are not what they seem (on the latter, see Christopher Bickerton's, Alexander Gourevitch's and John Pender's chapters). All of which has led us to ask, what is politics without sovereignty?

In this introductory chapter, we seek first to demonstrate the breadth and depth of what we call the unholy alliance against sovereignty. We suggest that this unholy alliance explains the striking expansion of international theory in recent years. Insofar as this new international theory builds over the ruins of state sovereignty, it plays a key role in helping us to understand the political possibilities beyond the sovereign state. But how successful is it in this task? That is a question for the book as a whole. The second section of this introduction develops the conceptual relation between modern politics and sovereignty. Instead of providing an idealized conception of sovereignty to hold up against its critics, we pursue a different tack. We show that our central concern is the possibility for politics. This emphasis gives us good reason to appreciate the constraints of sovereignty, but also good grounds to judge theoretical and practical alternatives to the sovereign state. That is to say, alternatives must be assessed by the extent to which they expand our political and moral horizons in international affairs. Thus the second section of the introduction provides a theoretical frame for the rest of the book, which subsequent chapters will develop by investigating various alternatives to the sovereign state in different domains of international life. The cohering message of this book is that today's politics without sovereignty is a constrained and evasive politics, marred by a limited sense of political possibility, and organized around the increasingly unaccountable exercise of power.

An unholy alliance

The sovereign state was the enabling concept of traditional International Relations (IR) scholarship. If sovereignty means supreme authority over a particular territory, it also implies its antithesis: international anarchy, the absence of a higher authority above the sovereign state. But if sovereignty carves out a sphere for IR theory, the sovereign state is also a profound constraint, as Martin Wight observed in his famous essay 'Why Is There No International Theory?' Wight argued that the division between international and domestic politics reflected the fact that the sovereign state is the exemplary achievement of human will and creativity in politics. For this reason, the sovereign state 'absorbed almost all the intellectual energy devoted to political study. It has become natural to think of international politics as the untidy fringe of domestic politics'.[4] As there is no overarching authority within the international domain, the ever-present possibility of war threatens to shatter any design for a more humanized social order between states. 'International politics is the realm of recurrence and repetition' and, consequently, international theory a brutalized 'theory of survival'.[5] So long as political life remained constrained by the sovereign state, international theory, too, would remain limited.

In light of these limits identified by Wight, it is logical to infer that international theory should proliferate on the back of the critique of sovereignty. What is more, this proliferation should indicate an expansion of creative human energies into the international sphere.[6] Indeed, one could even go as far as to inverse the places assigned to domestic and international politics by Wight. With the decline of ideologically charged party politics in the domestic sphere, the substance of government in many countries has increasingly been transformed into a mundane process of dreary administration (see Alexander Gourevitch's and James Heartfield's chapters in this volume). If anything, it seems that it is the politics of the domestic realm that is afflicted by 'recurrence and repetition' while it is the global realm that appears open to new possibilities.[7] Indeed, a whole generation of Western youth have had many of their defining political experiences forged around international questions, rather than domestic issues emanating from within their own societies, including, for example: mobilization against the Iraq war, solidarity with the Palestinians, activism in defence of sustainable development, human rights and global cooperation to tackle climate change. School leavers and university students participate in far-flung NGO (non-governmental organization) projects throughout the developing world – developments that are discussed and criticized in David Chandler's chapter in this volume.

Recent developments in IR theory have appeared to extend and confirm the logic of Wight's intuition. Echoing Wight, R.B.J. Walker has argued that the study of international relations has been constrained by its exclusive concern with interactions between states:

> theories of international relations affirm a claim that only within the secure borders of territorial states is it possible to engage in a serious politics, a politics that aspires to some kind of moral status on the basis of some kind of community...Politics, real politics, they suggest, can occur only as long as we are prepared – or able to – live in boxes.[8]

Thinking 'outside the box', as the management jargon goes (the box, in this case, being the sovereign state), means that the bottom effectively drops out of the discipline, and its intellectual prejudices dissolve. This shift is reflected in the grasping for a new conceptual vocabulary – 'global', 'globalized', 'transnational', 'cosmopolitan' – words that try to shift us beyond the restrictive idea of political, legal and economic relations between states, connoted by the more traditional term 'international'. The sheer range of ideas, issues and theoretical approaches that have battered down the walls of a previously isolated and self-contained discipline is truly dizzying. New theories of global justice, international community, cosmopolitical democracy, global civil society, environmental justice, humanitarian intervention, neo-trusteeship, world constitutionalism, global capitalism, empire and imperialism and world citizenship have rapidly gained a foothold in mainstream debates. The result, as described by one academic, is an 'intellectual Somalia', by which he means the fragmentation of the discipline into warring academic clans based around competing theories – constructivism, neo-realism, critical theory, feminism, post-structuralism, normative theory and international society.[9] In contrast, we intend to show here that this diversity is belied by an underlying consensus: a distrust of state sovereignty. This shared antipathy towards a final authority in politics is the unifying, driving force informing most theoretical arguments today. Almost all of these international theories are convinced of the morally dangerous, conceptually vacuous or empirically irrelevant character of sovereignty, and of the need to discard or at least recast the concept in light of new global imperatives.

To be sure, it is the critical schools of thought in IR that have most vigorously established themselves by laying siege to sovereignty (see further our discussion in Chapter 1). Richard Devetak summarizes why state sovereignty draws so much fire from critically tempered IR theories:

> State sovereignty is the foremost target in international relations because it is predicated on an exclusionary political space...ruled by a single, supreme centre of decision-making which claims to represent a single political community or identity. Sovereign statehood...claims to trump all other competing levels of decision-making or representation. The sovereign state may well be the dominant mode of subjectivity in international relations today, but it is questionable whether its claim to be the primary and exclusive ethical and political subject is justified.[10]

In other words, what makes the sovereign state so appealing a target is not merely that it arbitrarily restricts the boundaries of political life ('an exclusionary political space'). It is also that the sovereign embodies a unique concentration of power, combined in a single, self-sufficient entity: 'The sovereign, by the mere fact that it is, is always all that it ought to be' as Rousseau put it.[11] This 'terrifying image', in the words of William Rasch,[12] not only exercises supreme power, but brazenly proclaims its unfettered right to do as it pleases; it defines its own limits. The sovereign is not only supreme but also rational. In Rousseau's words: 'the general will is always rightful and always tends to the public good'.[13]

The problem for various radicals therefore, is that sovereignty is not just repressive, but that it shuts down our collective imagination by limiting politics to a monolithic 'terrifying image' of unity, rather than plurality and possibility. Post-modernist Richard Ashley considers sovereignty a 'metaphysical conceit', in step with Walker's dismissal of sovereign states as mere 'boxes'.[14] The surprisingly popular Michael Hardt and Antonio Negri's *Empire* rejects even the most democratic form of sovereignty – popular sovereignty – as 'really nothing more than another turn of the screw, a further extension of the subjugation and domination that the modern concept of sovereignty has carried with it from the beginning'.[15] Not to be outdone, critical theorists, such as Andrew Linklater, argue that 'achieving the aims of critical theory requires the reconstruction of the state...and the introduction of post-nationalist conceptions of citizenship'.[16] Similarly, 'feminism...questions the very core of conventional international relations practice, namely the supreme value of sovereignty'.[17]

Imagining themselves to be rebels against the consensus, the radicals and post-modernists are in fact the champions of a new consensus. Liberals and humanitarians have also ardently attacked sovereignty as a morally regressive concept. International lawyer George Robertson luridly denounced the 'great play of sovereignty, with all its pomp and panoply' that 'can now be seen for what it hides: a posturing troupe of human actors, who when off-stage are sometimes prone to rape the chorus'.[18] Ken Booth condemns 'Westphalian sovereignty' as a 'tyrant's charter'.[19] The Executive Director of Human Rights Watch, Kenneth Roth, has argued that 'sovereignty cannot be used as an excuse to avoid human rights commitments' and has 'praised the decision to overrule the claims of tyrants and war criminals to be protected by the cloak of national sovereignty'.[20] Liberal political theorist Fernando Tesón has radicalized the human rights critique of sovereignty and demanded that the concept be wholly redefined so that 'gross violation of human rights is not only an obvious assault on the dignity of persons, *but a betrayal of the principle of sovereignty itself*' (original emphasis).[21] Tesón means to substitute a new concept of sovereignty in place of the old one, as is discussed in Philip Cunliffe's chapter.

The moral and political critiques stand shoulder-to-shoulder with what we might call more empirical critiques. For globalization and cosmopolitan theorists, such as Susan Strange, David Held and Daniele Archibugi, sovereignty is not just politically atavistic, but also historically outdated. Susan Strange's *The Retreat of the State* (1997) is the most well known of a raft of books and articles arguing that the rise of global financial networks, multinational corporations, regional trading blocs and expansion of the world economy has rendered the nation-state obsolete. David Held argues that the internationalization of communication and culture has pushed not just economic processes but political identities themselves beyond the state:

> any assumption that sovereignty is an indivisible, illimitable, exclusive and perpetual form of public power – entrenched within an individual state – is now defunct...the boundaries between states, nations and societies can no longer claim the deep legal and moral significance they once had.[22]

'Cosmopolitical' theorist Daniele Archibugi echoes Held's assessment, arguing that 'state sovereignty is not called into question by armies, missiles and armoured cars, but by elements which spontaneously escape national government control'.[23] He takes the argument to its logical conclusion – world government. 'The state is too large for small issues, too small for bigger ones. It is here that pressures arise for a new form of world governance, more potent than anything that exists.'[24] Sovereignty is, on this account, not only an impediment to thinking the world anew, but also to seeing the current world as it is. In other words, sovereignty is not only morally dangerous but also politically impotent. Even if one does not share the progressive and emancipatory goals of more radical critics, these thinkers suggest we must jettison sovereignty if we wish to keep control over those elements – human rights, economic and social policy, cultural identity and defence of the environment – that are already accepted as general concerns.

Even from the more traditional and mainstream thinkers sovereignty has taken a battering. Liberal Robert Keohane thinks that the indivisible and inalienable right of sovereignty has been transformed into something that can be traded away: sovereignty 'is less a territorially defined barrier than a bargaining resource for a politics characterized by complex transnational networks'.[25] Realist Stephen Krasner believes sovereignty has always been a kind of 'organized hypocrisy', in which formal sovereign status fails to correspond with actual respect for sovereignty.[26] Krasner's edited collection *Problematic Sovereignty* (2001) addresses a number of case studies (China–Taiwan relations; the protectorate in Bosnia Herzegovina, Palestinian state-building) that are designed to explore how we might find solutions to crises, if only we are willing to move beyond our attachment to the traditional notion of sovereignty as supreme authority over a particular territory and population. The creation of semi-autonomous entities offers a way of sidestepping the problems that arise from bitter struggles to resolve competing claims to supreme political authority over a given territory – an argument he has pressed with even greater force in more recent writings on 'shared sovereignty'.[27] Realist scholar David Lake argues, 'sovereignty is far more problematic than recognized in the classical model' because it represents international politics as relations among equals, thereby blurring hierarchical relations of power that exist today.[28] This not only hampers our ability to see power at work, it also impedes effective conflict resolution: 'To the extent that states find the norm of juridical sovereignty attractive, showing that practice differs systematically and frequently from this norm undermines its salience and its utility as a justification for other practices.'[29] Better, thinks Lake, to accommodate our 'norms' to reality, than to operate with redundant concepts. Here we see political scientists like Krasner and Lake converging with normative theorists and human rights advocates who argue, for example, that the colonial-era institution of trusteeship[30] is a moral necessity, needed to tackle the misery prevailing in 'failed states', as discussed further in Christopher Bickerton's chapter. This gives us some idea of the extent to which hostility to sovereignty cuts across the various schisms in IR theory.

But as we have already observed, the assault on sovereignty goes far beyond the academy. In a trendsetting document for the post-Cold War era, former UN Secretary-General Boutros Boutros-Ghali wrote, 'The time of absolute and exclusive sovereignty . . . has passed; its theory was never matched by reality.'[31] His successor, Kofi Annan, carried the torch with his own pronouncement that 'state sovereignty, in its most basic sense, is being redefined'.[32] Former US Secretary of State Madeleine Albright agreed, saying that 'Sovereignty carries with it many rights, but killing and torturing innocent people are not among them.'[33] Former British Foreign Secretary, Jack Straw, has argued for 'pooling sovereignty' because '[i]t is at the supranational level that we can achieve our goals in a way which is no longer possible at the national level'.[34] In the words of the renowned Czech intellectual Vaclav Havel, 'Human liberties constitute a higher value than State sovereignty. In terms of international law, the provisions that protect the unique human being should take precedence over the provisions that protect the State.'[35] An article in the *Economist* magazine, evocatively titled 'Taming Leviathan', brought together the advance of human rights alongside recent economic and technological developments:

> sovereignty is no longer absolute, but conditional...Eventually, a government's claim to sovereignty may depend on whether it respects the basic human rights of its citizens. That is the way in which international law is slowly moving. Other forces are pushing in the same direction. Global economic integration, the growth of international broadcasting, telecommunications and travel will all make it more difficult in future for repressive regimes to go about their business unhindered by outside influence.[36]

The erosion of state sovereignty does not just apply to poor and weak states that are unable to enforce their authority or resist the armies mobilized under the banner of the international community. Francis Fukuyama traces many of our prevailing attitudes towards sovereignty to the integration activities of the European Union over the last half-century. From its inception in the post-war cross-border economic arrangements within western Europe, integration has been defined according to Fukuyama by the impulse 'to embed those sovereignties [of Europe] in multiple layers of rules, norms and regulations to prevent those sovereignties from ever spinning out of control again [...] a kind of antisovereignty project.'[37] These public statements demonstrate that there is a broadly based antipathy to the idea of a final, absolute authority in political life – namely the sovereign state.

But perhaps this unholy alliance is weaker than we make it out to be. Indeed, a counter-offensive has already been launched by the so-called new sovereigntists, a 'group of academics – many of whom are highly credentialed and attached to prestigious institutions or conservative Washington think tanks'.[38] The foreign policy of the Bush administration is believed to be undermining the transnational achievements of the 1990s. The new passion for state-building that has so exercised the United States and various European governments seems to herald a return of active support for the idea of independent statehood. Yet, as the chapters by Christopher Bickerton, John Pender and Philip Cunliffe show, the new champions of the state are not what they seem. Initiatives such as state-building are wholly within, and even presuppose, a deeper and more profound antipathy to the self-determination and political autonomy once enshrined in sovereignty. Nor is the United States as straightforwardly 'sovereigntist' as it is made out to be, as Alexander Gourevitch demonstrates in his chapter.

But if the hostility to state sovereignty is real and profound, perhaps we should not set too much store by it. The sceptic would point out that the discipline of IR itself was born amidst speculation about the imminent demise of the sovereign state. In one of the discipline's founding texts, *The Twenty Years Crisis*, E.H. Carr was only one among many on the eve of the Second World War to muse whether the nation-state would 'survive as a unit of power'.[39] Indeed, the Second World War saw virtually all the historic nation-states of Europe overrun or overthrown in conquest. Though the sovereign state was restored after the war, it never fully recovered.[40] Its perceived weakness and illegitimacy was such that, even nearly 30 years later, Hedley Bull observed that liberalism, the political doctrine that gave birth to the sovereign state, could only survive in the era of imperialism by mutating into the search for world government or other similar, second-best solutions:

> The feeling of unease about the system of sovereign states ... exists not only among those who explicitly espouse the elimination of this system, but also where we might least expect to find it, in pronouncements of the servants of sovereign states themselves ... These pronouncements often betray a sense of inadequacy of the ... system, a lack of confidence in its situations, a tendency guiltily to disguise their operation of the system or to apologise for doing so. The League of Nations and the United Nations we are invited to see not as diplomatic machinery in the tradition of the Concert of Europe, but as first steps towards a world state. Military alliances, in this manner of speaking, become regional security systems; exclusive political groupings, like ... the British Commonwealth, experiments in world order; war, police action.[41]

But if the sovereign state has been called into question at different points throughout the twentieth century, each time it was in a different context. Though the sovereign state remains the predominant unit of political organization throughout the world, and though its numbers continue to grow,[42] it would be wrong simply to ignore the cacophony of claims questioning the reality or desirability of state sovereignty. However exaggerated some of these claims may seem, this does not exonerate us from the task of thinking through what is historically distinctive about the way in which sovereignty is being attached today. It is untangling the relationship between the historical context and the reigning political ideas at any particular moment that is the challenge. It is to this challenge that this volume is addressed. As we have seen, the unholy alliance exists along a spectrum of opinion, ranging from those who think sovereignty must be modified, restrained or qualified, to those who see it as a totalitarian monolith in need of deconstructing. But they all agree that the idea of sovereignty with which we have worked in the past must be rethought. It must be rethought so that we can deal with the realities of our world in a more appropriate way, or even to realize new possibilities on a global scale. But what form of politics is supposed to replace sovereignty?

Sovereignty and modern politics

Whether the sovereign state is in decline, and possibilities for global cooperation on the rise, is the question for the book to answer as a whole. In the final part of the introduction, we seek only to lay some intellectual markers that will help orient the reader to subsequent chapters. Each of the chapters will try to answer the question 'what is politics without sovereignty?' by investigating the retreat of state sovereignty in relation to specific domains of world politics, such as security, international law, European integration and so on. Alternatives to the state tend to gain more acceptance from the way they share in the disenchantment with sovereignty than from proving their merits on their own terms. Yet assessing them on their own terms, as the chapters in this volume do, does not relieve us of the burden of giving our own account of sovereignty. If we are to judge the alternatives to sovereignty according to their ability to provide a superior form of politics, we must understand what kind of political form sovereignty is, and how it is related to modern society.

Sovereignty, as supreme public power, has traditionally been counterposed to property, or private right. The distinction can be appreciated through contemporary discussions of the decline of sovereignty. Consider the stylized argument that 'Westphalian' sovereignty, defined by Krasner as the 'exclusion of external actors from domestic authority',[43] is being gnawed away by globalization. As globalization liberates social relations from their territorial restrictions, this undermines the ability of a quintessentially territorial organization – sovereignty – to regulate these densely interwoven, globalized social links. But there are two sleights of hand in this stylized argument. The first is the rhetorical sleight of hand in the reference to Westphalian sovereignty. The emergence of this idea is usually associated with the Peace of Westphalia in 1648, which is taken to have ushered in the modern state system. The suggestive power of the idea that *Westphalian* sovereignty is fading today insinuates that, by the early twenty-first century, a 350-year-old institution is redundant by default. This is conveyed in the politely sneering language of UN reports ('Whatever perceptions may have prevailed when the Westphalian system first gave rise to the notion of State sovereignty... '[44]). In fact, the idea of sovereignty that is fading today is of more recent origin: the liberal, constitutional sovereign state ('nation-state') that can be usefully dated to the 1789 French Revolution. Indeed, the revolutionary French state was inspired by *philosophes* who excoriated the Westphalian states for their egotistical power struggles that sustained the domestic rule of the parasitic 'plundering classes', in the words of Tom Paine.[45] The *philosophes* argued that political authority had to be based on the ends of individuals in civil society, rather than on the caprice of belligerent sovereigns.[46] This is important insofar as we need to be clear about the nature of the sovereignty that is being eroded – in this case, the idea that government should flow from the will of the people, and not the absolutist conception of sovereignty connoted by the term 'Westphalian'.

The second sleight of hand involves the role played by globalization. The implication of globalization is that sovereignty is essentially 'parasitic' on a certain set of social relations, and when these change, sovereignty simply shrivels away.[47] But this is to misunderstand the nature of sovereignty. Sovereignty is a *political* concept, and as such cannot be reduced to material factors. While private, economic power involves ownership and control over material resources, political power is more narrowly the product of a relationship among individuals, the power that emerges when people form an association for the purposes of action.[48] The autonomy of politics is enshrined in the idea of sovereignty, as it forms public power by uniting the wills of all citizens. This establishes the general will in opposition to the private will of any particular individual. By virtue of its claim to embody ultimate authority based on consensual relations between citizens, sovereignty is at once supreme and collaborative, thereby endowing modern states with historically distinctive efficacy and power. This is illustrated by G.W.F. Hegel in his discussion of the difference between modern valour and the valour of the medieval knight or robber. Specifically, Hegel argues that modern valour renders violence and courage impersonal. Alluding to the success of British colonial conquest in India, Hegel writes that

> the true valour of civilized nations is their readiness for sacrifice in the service of the state, so that the individual merely counts as one among many. Not personal courage but integration with the universal is the important factor here. In India, five hundred men defeated twenty thousand who were not cowards, but who simply lacked the disposition to act in close association with others.[49]

The impersonal nature of modern valour grows out of the fact that it embodies a joint effort, whereby the individual *willingly* helps to enact the activity of a greater whole, rather than merely pursuing his own private gain.

It is important to be specific about the claim here. It is not that politics *always* takes the form of sovereignty. Rather, it is that in capitalist societies based on relations between contracting individuals, sovereignty is the form that collective activity for public purposes takes. In societies defined by contractual associations between formally free and equal individuals pursuing private gain, the pooling of common human purposes can only be made effective if it is distinct from the routine bustle of social life. As Martin Loughlin puts it, politics is achieved 'through the establishment of a governing authority that can be *differentiated* from society and which is able to exercise an *absolute* political power' (emphasis added).[50] Paradoxically, then, the consciousness of society as a collective endeavour between people can *only* exist in a form raised over and above society, as David Runciman indicates:

> It is states that go to war, not peoples, and it is the existence of the state that allows peoples to know when they are at war, when the war is over, and whether they have won. Otherwise war would not be war, but chaos. It is, in other words, the state that enables peoples to know whether they are up or down.[51]

The point of this abstract discussion is to be clear about what is at stake in the narrative of the eclipse of sovereignty. Globalization theory asserts the unravelling of the sovereign state. But the autonomy of the political indicates that economic expansion and new technologies alone are insufficient to eclipse politics. Political power has an intangible quality, given that it is founded on mediated relationships between individuals. It involves both material capacity in its institutionalized forms, such as the public power of the state, *and* the subjective will of every citizen; it is reducible to neither.

As James Madison put it

> If it be true that all governments rest on opinion, it is no less true that the strength of opinion in each individual, and its practical influence on his conduct depend much on the number which he supposes to have entertained the same opinion.[52]

In other words, the agency of the sovereign is internally related to the agency of the individual. Modern society does not spontaneously act upon itself. All socially purposive activity is mediated through various social spheres and institutions, which help to steer society in particular directions. Sovereignty, by virtue of its totalizing claims, is the pre-eminent sphere, to which all others are subordinate. The alienation of the state from society gives it the potential to exercise tyranny over society. But the totalizing claim of the sovereign is a vivid reminder of the fact that society is a product of human agency. By rooting itself in the consent of citizens, sovereignty contrasts human will to divine power, private morality and economics. For this reason, sovereignty means that an individual or group of individuals can always be held responsible for the political order. To act as sovereign is to claim the mantle of responsibility. To lose grasp of sovereignty, then, is potentially to lose grasp of society as the conscious creation of individuals. Without sovereignty, there is little left that stands in opposition to all that is merely mechanical or spontaneous in social development. At the very least, it is up to the alternatives to sovereignty to demonstrate how they better keep sight of the way society is, or at least can be, the product of human will and agency. Political progress must be measured by the degree to which that ideal collective potential is made real.

If individuals must look beyond their private differences to participate in politics, it is also apparent that political passions and interests are always rooted in society. The 'political' and the 'social' are not two ontologically distinct spheres. Critics of sovereignty are of course right to say that politics pushes up against the limitations of the sovereign state. As the representative of its citizens' general will, the sovereign state is universal, in that it allows all of its citizens to participate in politics within its own borders. Within the protective shelter of the sovereign state, all citizens are free to build the good life as they see fit. But the sovereign also violates his own promise, by limiting this universalizing impulse. Political self-assertion in international affairs often means one nation pitting itself against another. Thus the expression of collective political agency, when expressed in the form of the sovereign state, ends by dividing humanity against itself. Universalism becomes mired in national particularism.[53] It is precisely because of these hazards and limits of state sovereignty that we shall assess the alternatives to state sovereignty from the viewpoint of politics and agency: do the practical alternatives to state sovereignty lay the ground for greater political possibilities than the sovereign state provides? Does the new international theory enhance our understanding of these new possibilities? The critics of state sovereignty cannot be allowed to earn their progressive credentials simply by attacking the limited political form of state sovereignty.

There are limits to any abstract, logical analysis of a concept. Its meaning only really comes alive in relation to the ideas against which it is counterposed. The brief, foregoing analysis of sovereignty prepares the ground for the chapters that ensue. But it does provide us with at least a preliminary conclusion about the political significance of the unholy alliance, and the explosion of international theory.

First, it is not straightforward that the critique of sovereignty and the proliferation of alternative views of international politics are the sign of an enhanced sense of political possibility on the global stage. We shall, indeed, argue that, at present, what we find is the opposite. The retreat of state sovereignty has coincided with diminished political possibilities throughout the world. Second, the concept of sovereignty is bound up with a particular idea of responsibility. The idea of a supreme power, subject to no higher law, articulates the idea that human beings are the authors of their own destiny. Power is always exercised by an agent representing the supreme power of the collective, an agent who, in claiming that power, is therefore at least in principle accountable for that act. Although many critics of sovereignty claim to be making power relations more visible by jettisoning the vexing abstraction of sovereignty, we argue that the result of this is that one form of power – collective power – is rendered more oblique, and the exercise of power is made less accountable. If it is not inevitable, it is nonetheless not surprising that the reorganization of political theory and practice around a fragmented, divisible conception of sovereignty serves to separate the relationship between power and responsibility. That is to say, political activity still exists, and collective power is still exercised, but in a mystified and more unaccountable way.

The 'mixed condition' of twenty-first century politics

Understanding the limits of international politics is always important for understanding the limits of politics more broadly. Tom Paine observed that the wars fought between absolutist states in late-seventeenth-century Europe buttressed the *ancien régime* in its rule at home. Warfare abroad perfected the 'art of conquering at home'.[54] Slavoj Žižek has made a similar point about the Iraq war today:

> We should . . . be very careful not to fight false battles: the debates about how evil Saddam was, even about the cost of the war, and so forth, are red herrings. The focus should be on what actually transpires in our societies, on what kind of society is emerging *here and now* as the result of the 'war on terror'. The ultimate result of the war will be a change in *our* political order.[55]

But discussions about sovereignty are about more than how international politics may buttress the limits of domestic political systems. The idea of sovereignty is integrally bound up with the most fundamental concepts of modern politics, such as freedom and democracy. The natural rights theorists of the seventeenth century observed the English, French and Dutch determinedly pursuing their commercial and colonial self-aggrandizement with little regard for the theological constraints of medievalism. Hugo Grotius and Thomas Hobbes were inspired to propose a new model of society and politics, based around the self-determining, reflective individual, rationally pursuing his own ends. This model of nations robustly pursuing their own interests would, via the doctrines of the natural rights theorists, eventually suffuse all of society, reflecting modern societies centred on notions of autonomy, individuality and rationality.[56] The ebbing away of a vigorous idea of the sovereign state reflects the ebbing of a wider model of robust, determined political individuals, pursuing their idea of the good life in a more rational social order. The limited sovereign state of the day mirrors the depleted, withdrawn individual of contemporary society.[57] In the words of Richard Tuck:

> There has been a much greater willingness on the part both of philosophers and the general public to accept the existence of a wide range of moral constraints on the principles which can govern a civil society – the idea of sovereignty is unpopular both in politics and ethics, and the dangers of the unpoliced international realm are seen as mirroring the dangers of the unpoliced civil society.[58]

We began this essay by observing how fashionable it is to damn what the critics misleadingly call 'Westphalian sovereignty'. Of the original critics of the pre-1789 Westphalian system, Rousseau is perhaps the most eloquent. Troubled by the wars of the latter half of the eighteenth century, Rousseau pondered whether the civil peace within society was bought at the expense of wars between them. How could 'the perfection of the social order' be reconciled with wars between states?[59] This prompted Rousseau to observe that

> by living both in the social order and in the state of nature, we are subject to the inconveniences of both without finding security in either...the mixed condition in which we find ourselves [is] the worst state possible.[60]

Here Rousseau is pointing, once again, to the sovereignty/anarchy paradox. But Rousseau is, with the idea of a 'mixed condition', also going deeper, by eyeing this paradox from the viewpoint of the individual subject. The individual who sacrifices certain liberties in order to benefit from the security of living under a sovereign loses all these benefits by being dragged into the wars between sovereigns. The sovereigns, having no overarching power above them, exist in a state of nature themselves. What is worse, the wars fought between sovereigns are vastly more destructive than any conflict among individuals in the state of nature, outside of society. Thus 'everywhere the vain name of justice only serves as a shield for violence'.[61] The 'mixed condition' that results from submitting to the sovereign means that we cannot enjoy either the pristine liberty outside of society (the state of nature), nor the safety allegedly provided by the sovereign (the social order). Thus, we endure insecurity that is much worse than the insecurity outside of society (wars between states), while we are simultaneously burdened by the constrictions of having entered society (the alienation of liberty to the rule of law). The result is 'the worst state possible'.

Rousseau's analysis of the 'mixed condition' blighting eighteenth-century European politics could be justifiably levelled against today's states system. While we have watched the political substance of sovereignty ebb away, we now find ourselves in a situation where we still endure all of the worst features of state sovereignty, and yet derive none of its benefits. The world is still fragmented into different peoples; the freedom of movement is still impeded by borders and barbed wire; the state still exists as a 'body of armed men with prisons, etc., at their command' as Lenin tersely put it;[62] militarism still propels states into war with each other; liberties are still trampled in the name of security. All this is endured without any of the benefits that sovereignty should impart. If agency is still exercised in all those repressive, divisive ways, with the shift from 'government' to 'governance', we have lost the ability to formulate a general will that can bend the institutions of public power to sovereign ends. Sovereignty has been lost, but no more universal form of political organization has emerged to replace it.

As we saw earlier in this essay, what makes the power of sovereignty distinct is its rootedness in human agency; it is a force that is only sustained by conscious human will. Individuals must be able to abstract themselves, look beyond their differences and find the common basis for collective action. The ability to direct oneself only emerges in the self-creative process of acting politically. For all its historical imperfections, and however attenuated it may be today, the framework of the sovereign state remains the best means of organizing and sustaining the process of politics, in opposition to all that is offered in its place.

If at one level the critics of sovereignty express a rather limited view of politics, at another level, they reflect a politics that attempts to conceal its own existence. This change, which we label a 'politics without sovereignty', is a politics that is at odds with itself. The essential feature of 'politics without sovereignty' cannot be logically deduced from the critique of sovereignty alone, but made apparent only through an investigation of the alternatives that constitute it. We conclude with a brief outline of the rest of the book.

The structure of this volume

Each chapter focuses on a discrete realm of global politics. The first chapter of the book, collectively authored by the editors, provides a critique of two 'reflectivist' schools of international theory – constructivism and post-structuralism. Both of these theories have explicitly counterposed themselves to traditional IR theories by advancing criticisms of sovereignty. This makes both of these schools useful barometers of changing ideas of state sovereignty. In addition, in their criticisms of state sovereignty, both of these theories claim to be establishing theoretical foundations for the exercise of greater political agency in international politics. In this chapter, we will contest that claim, criticizing both of these schools for offering impoverished ideas of agency in place of the sovereign state. Being unable to offer a coherent account of agency leaves these theories unable to root international relations in political will.

In Chapter 2, 'Sovereignty and the politics of responsibility', Philip Cunliffe analyses one of the most influential new ideas of sovereignty – the 'sovereignty as responsibility' doctrine, which aims to shift sovereignty away from supremacy to responsibility. Cunliffe argues that, theoretically speaking, the doctrine has nothing to offer, in that sovereignty already gives us a coherent theory of political responsibility. In practice, by pulling apart responsibility (enshrined in the sovereign) and ultimate authority (enshrined in the international community) 'sovereignty as responsibility' only means that the exercise of power is that much more distant and unaccountable to a state's citizens. In Chapter 3, 'National Insecurities: the new politics of the American national interest', Alexander Gourevitch analyses the national interest in US political history. America is usually identified as the archetypal great power, jealously guarding its sovereignty and aggressively pursuing its interests. Against this, Gourevitch argues that the traditional, reified concept of an 'objective' national interest made sense when it stood above the contested field of domestic politics. As political contestation in the domestic realm has declined, so the traditional 'national interest' has nothing to define itself against. Just what the national interest is has therefore proved increasingly difficult to identify. Building on the theme of security, in Chapter 4, 'From state of war to state of nature: human security and sovereignty', Tara McCormack analyses the shift from state-centred conceptions of national security to 'human security'. Rather than establishing security policy on a more humanistic basis, McCormack argues that taking the viewpoint of the isolated individual rather than the state has, perversely, multiplied security problems by assimilating more and more social issues under the rubric of security. But the more social issues are transformed into existential questions of security, the less they are open to political debate.

In Chapter 5, 'State-building: exporting state failure', Christopher Bickerton analyses the internationalization of state-building in post-conflict regions and further afield around the world. Bickerton argues that policies designed to strengthen governance in weak and failing states exacerbate the very problem that they set out to solve. The products of state-building are frail because they derive their authority from their relationship with international organizations, rather than a political relationship with their own societies. The technocratic approach of state-building is rooted, Bickerton argues, in the misconceived theory of state failure, which he criticizes. In Chapter 6, 'Country ownership: the evasion of donor accountability', John Pender analyses how the new politics of aid are changing the role of the state in development policy. Through a case study of Tanzania, Pender investigates the shift to 'post-conditionality' forms of development. In place of openly coercive structural adjustment, today's development policy seeks to 'empower' poor countries to wrest control of development back from international organizations. Against this, Pender argues that the rhetoric of empowerment and autonomy is belied, first, by the reality of wider international influence in developing countries, and, second, because the rhetoric of empowerment makes it more difficult to hold aid donors to account for their policies. In short, talking up the agency of poor countries makes them responsible for policies that are set by outside powers.

In Chapter 7, 'European Union: A process without a subject', James Heartfield argues that the dynamic driving the European Union cannot be reduced either to the *realpolitik* scheming of a great power, nor to any intrinsic dynamism of the organization itself. Rather, argues Heartfield, the Union's haphazard forward momentum derives from the political involution of its member states, who hand over sovereign responsibilities to the Union. He concludes by suggesting that, instead of seeing the Union's institutions as unfinished stepping stones to a fully fledged superstate, these semi-formed institutions are the product of an integration process that has no coherent, centrifugal agency driving it. Chapter 8, 'Deconstructing sovereignty: constructing global civil society' by David Chandler, assesses critically 'global civil society', the new model of transnational politics that claims to pioneer new solidarities beyond the sovereign state. Chandler argues that, under the cover of renouncing state-based politics, global civil society activists are also renouncing the democratic accountability and formal representation that goes along with territorially based politics. This in turn reflects a deeper disenchantment with mass politics. This disenchantment is at once the precondition for the articulation of global civil society, while also throwing up intrinsic barriers to the realization of its own political goals. In Chapter 9, 'Legalizing politics and politicizing law: the changing relationship between sovereignty and international law', Michael Savage scrutinizes international law, which has often been upheld as a means of 'taming' state sovereignty. Savage examines the extent to which the substance of international politics has been assimilated to the formal framework of international law in the post-Cold War period, and the implications of this development. Savage argues for the disentanglement of international law and politics, in so far as both spheres would be strengthened by using them as distinctive tools for steering international affairs.

As should be apparent from this overview, there are common themes that are repeated, refreshed and reinforced throughout this book. The key theme is to describe how the decline of state sovereignty crystallizes in different domains of international politics, and to analyse what this can tell us about the contemporary exercise, and understanding, of human agency. The final chapter, 'How should sovereignty be defended?', is the transcription of a round table discussion that took place in late 2005 among Professors James Der Derian, Michael W. Doyle, Jack L. Snyder and David Kennedy. This chapter not only provides an overview of the thought of these leading scholars, but also has them probing each other's ideas in relation to concrete issues of world politics, such as terror, nationalism and globalization. As such, Chapter 10 brings together four dominant and distinctive approaches to the contemporary problems of international politics.

Notes

1 S.D. Krasner, *Sovereignty: Organized Hypocrisy*, Princeton, NJ: Princeton University Press, 1999; S. Krasner (ed.), *Problematic Sovereignty: Contested Rules and Political*

Possibilities, Chichester: Columbia University Press, 2001; D. Lake, 'The New Sovereignty in International Relations', *International Studies Review* 5, 2003, pp.303–323; Fernando Tesón, 2003, 'The Liberal Case for Humanitarian Intervention', in J.L. Holzgrefe and R. Keohane (eds), *Humanitarian Intervention: Ethical, Legal and Political Dilemmas*, Cambridge: Cambridge University Press, 2003, pp.93–129; R. Keohane, 2003, 'Political Authority After Intervention: Gradations in Sovereignty', in Holzgrefe and Keohane, *Humanitarian Intervention*, pp.275–294; R.K. Ashley, 'Untying the Sovereign State: A Double Reading of the Anarchy Problematique', *Millennium: Journal of International Studies* 17:2, 1988, pp.227–262; J. Bartelson, *A Genealogy of Sovereignty*, Cambridge: Cambridge University Press, 1995; M. Loughlin, 2003, 'Ten Tenets of Sovereignty', in N. Walker (ed.), *Sovereignty in Transition*, London: Hart Publishing, 2003, pp.55–86; G. Simpson, *Great Powers and Outlaw States: Unequal Sovereigns in the International Legal Order*, New York: Cambridge University Press, 2004.

2 G.W. Bush, speech delivered 28 June 2005 at Fort Bragg. Online. Available at HTTP: <www.americanrhetoric.com/speeches/wariniraq/gwbushiraq62805.htm> (accessed 30 May 2006).

3 K. Annan, 'Two Concepts of Sovereignty', *Economist*, 18 September 1999.

4 M. Wight, 1966, 'Why is There No International Theory?', in J. Der Derian (ed.), *International Theory: Critical Investigations*, London: Macmillan, 1995, p.20.

5 Ibid., p.25.

6 P. Cunliffe, 'Why is There So Much International Theory?', paper presented at Millennium 35th Anniversary conference, LSE October 2006.

7 Ibid.

8 R.B.J. Walker, 2002, 'International Relations and the Concept of the Political', in K. Booth and S. Smith (eds), *International Relations Theory Today*, Cambridge: Polity Press, 2002, p.307.

9 Peter Vale, cited in K. Booth, 1996, '75 Years on: Rewriting the Subject's Past – Reinventing its Future', in S. Smith, K. Booth and M. Zalewski (eds), *International Theory: Positivism and Beyond*, Cambridge: Cambridge University Press, 1996, p.331.

10 R. Devetak, 1996, 'Critical Theory', in S. Burchill C. Resus-Smit, M. Paterson, J. Donnelly, J. True, R. Devetak, A. Linklater (eds), *Theories of International Relations*, London: Macmillan Press, 1996, p.201.

11 J.J. Rousseau, *The Social Contract*, London: Penguin Books, 1968 [1762], p.63.

12 W. Rasch, *Sovereignty and its Discontents: On the Primacy of Conflict and the Structure of the Political*, London: Birkbeck Law Press, 2004, p.116.

13 Rousseau, *Social Contract*, p.72.

14 Ashley, 'Untying the Sovereign State', p.250.

15 M. Hardt and A. Negri, *Empire*, London: Harvard University Press, 2000, p.102.

16 A. Linklater, 1996, 'The Achievements of Critical Theory', in Smith, Booth and Zalewski, *International Theory*, p.295.

17 Cited in F. Halliday, *Rethinking International Relations*, London: Palgrave MacMillan, 1994, p.19.

18 G. Robertson, *Crimes Against Humanity: The Struggle for Global Justice*, New York: Free Press, 1999, p.347.

19 K. Booth, 'Human Wrongs and International Relations', *International Affairs* 71:1, 1995, p.116.

20 Human Rights Watch, 'Human Rights Trump Sovereignty in 1999', *Human Rights News*, 9 December 1999.

21 Tesón, 'Liberal Case', p.110.

22 D. Held, 2003, 'Violence, Law and Justice in a Global Age', in D. Archibugi (ed.), *Debating Cosmopolitics*, London: Verso, 2003, pp.189–190.

23 D. Archibugi, 2003, 'Cosmopolitical Democracy' in Archibugi, *Debating Cosmopolitics*, p.3.

24 Ibid., p.4.

25 R. Keohane, 'Hobbes's Dilemma and Institutional Change in World Politics: Sovereignty in International Society', in H.H. Holm and G. Sørensen (eds), *Whose World Order? Uneven Globalization and the End of the Cold War*, New York: Westview Press, 1995, p.177.
26 Krasner, *Sovereignty*.
27 S.D. Krasner, 'The Case for Shared Sovereignty', *Journal of Democracy* 16:1, 2005, p.80.
28 Lake, 'New Sovereignty', p.304.
29 Ibid., p.320.
30 Indeed, the call for softening sovereignty and creating 'neotrusteeship' now emanates as vigorously from rationalists, squarely on the 'scientific' side of the IR discipline, as it does from the normative theorists, for example, J.D. Fearon and D.D. Laitin, 'Neotrusteeship and the Problem of Weak States', *International Security* 28:4, 2004, pp.5–43.
31 B. Boutros-Ghali, *An Agenda for Peace, With the New Supplement and Related UN Documents*, New York: United Nations, 1995, p.44.
32 Annan, 'Two Concept of Soverignty'.
33 M. Albright, 'Opening Remarks to Press Conference on release of Country Reports on Human Rights Practices', 25 February 2000.
34 J. Straw, 'Full Text: Jack Straw's Speech', *Guardian*, 1 October 2003.
35 V. Havel, 'Address to the Senate and House of Commons of the Parliament of Canada', 29 April 1999.
36 *Economist*, 'Taming Leviathan', 3 December 1998.
37 F. Fukuyama, *State Building: Governance and World Order in the Twenty-First Century*, London: Profile Books, 2004, p.152.
38 P.J. Spiro, 'The New Sovereigntists: American Exceptionalism and Its False Prophets', *Foreign Affairs* 79:6, 2000, p.9.
39 E.H. Carr, *The Twenty Years' Crisis, 1919–1939: An Introduction to the Study of International Relations*, Basingstoke: Palgrave, 2001, p.211.
40 See J. Heartfield, 'The War in Europe: What Really Happened?' Online. Available at HTTP: <www.heartfield.pwp.blueyonder.co.uk/WWII/WWII_8.htm#4> (accessed 30 May 2006)
41 H. Bull, 1966, 'Society and Anarchy in International Relations', in Der Derian, *International Theory*, p.76.
42 Montenegro is the world's newest state as of 22 May 2006.
43 Krasner, *Sovereignty*, p.9.
44 United Nations, *A More Secure World: Our Shared Responsibility, Report of the High Level Panel on Threats, Challenges and Change*, A/59/565, 2004, p.17.
45 Cited in J. Macmillan, *On Liberal Peace: Democracy, War and the International Order*, London: I.B. Tauris, 1998, p.35.
46 Ibid.
47 A. Gamble, *Politics and Fate*, Cambridge: Polity Press, 2000, p.5.
48 Loughlin, 'Ten Tenets of Sovereignty', p.62.
49 G.W.F. Hegel, in Allen W. Wood (ed.), trans. H.B. Nisbet, *Elements of Philosophy of Right*, Cambridge: Cambridge University Press, 2000, p.364.
50 Loughlin, 'Ten Tenets of Sovereignty', p.56 in N. Walker (ed.), *Sovereignty in Transition*.
51 D. Runciman, 2003, 'The Concept of the State: The Sovereignty of a Fiction', in Q. Skinner and B. Stråth (eds), *States and Citizens: History, Theory and Prospects*, Cambridge: Cambridge University Press, 2003, p.34.
52 Madison, cited in Loughlin, 'Ten Tenets of Sovereignty', p.64.
53 I. Hont, 'The Permanent Crisis of a Divided Mankind: "Contemporary Crisis of the Nation state" in Historical Perspective', *Political Studies* 42:SI, 1994, pp.166–231.
54 Cited in Macmillan, *On Liberal Peace*, p.35.

55 S. Žižek, *Iraq: The Borrowed Kettle*, London: Verso, 2004, p.19.
56 R. Tuck, *The Rights of War and Peace: Political Thought and the International Order from Grotius to Kant*, Oxford: Oxford University Press, 2001.
57 See further J. Heartfield, *The 'Death of the Subject' Explained*, Sheffield: Sheffield Hallam Univesity Press, 2002.
58 Tuck, *Rights of War and Peace*, p.234.
59 Ibid.
60 J.J. Rousseau, 'The State of War', in V. Gourevitch (ed.), *Rousseau: The Social Contract and Other Later Political Writings*, Cambridge: Cambridge University Press, 2006, p.162.
61 Ibid., p.163.
62 V.I. Lenin, *The State and Revolution: The Marxist Theory of the State and the Tasks of the Proletariat in the Revolution*, London: Junius, 1994, p.9.

1   Politics without sovereignty?

Christopher J. Bickerton, Philip Cunliffe and Alexander Gourevitch

It is standard fare to open a book on International Relations (IR) with a critique of realism, the theory of geopolitical rivalries and the balance of power. In this chapter we turn this convention around. We aim to deepen our theoretical investigation of the unholy alliance against sovereignty identified in the Introduction by isolating a particular strand of international theory for special attention, namely 'reflectivism'.[1] We shall focus in particular on constructivist and post-structuralist theories. Both of these reflectivist schools of thought have established themselves by offering critiques of state sovereignty. Indeed, the rapid advance of these theories in the discipline indicates just how out of step with world politics realist theories of IR have become. It is for this reason that we believe it is time to begin theoretical reflection with reflectivist, and not realist theories. The putative purpose of the reflectivist critiques is, first, to enhance our understanding and appreciation of change in international affairs, and, second, to open up the possibility for new political actors to enter the global stage. Both of these theories claim that changing our understanding of international affairs is crucial to opening up new political possibilities. A further reason why we focus on these theories and their claims is that, given their recent origins, they are ostensibly best positioned to provide new insights into changing circumstances. Moreover, as we discuss in the Introduction, we agree with their basic premise that sovereignty is a constrained form of political activity. In keeping with the aims and methods of the book as a whole, then, we ask: How successful are new reflectivist theories at pointing to new forms of political creativity after having abandoned the sovereign, self-determining state? This is the question that we shall seek to answer in this chapter.

Despite their promising theoretical starting point, we believe reflectivist criticisms of state sovereignty miss the mark. Far from providing new conceptions of political agency, their theoretical claims do little more than reflect the attenuation of the already limited model of political agency embodied in the sovereign state. We open the chapter with a discussion of how these new theories are bound up with the end of the Cold War, which raised the pressing need to theorize change in international politics. We show how, in trying to theorize a greater role for change and political creativity in international relations, reflectivist theories are inexorably led to a critique of sovereignty, which has hitherto been the fundamental mode of political interaction in international affairs. We then pursue the theories of constructivism and post-structuralism, exploring how the nature of their critique of the sovereign state leaves them unable to grasp human agency in international politics. After that, we take a step back and provide two wider criticisms of reflectivist theory as a whole. The first is that it tries to recapture agency without sovereignty by elevating fluidity and change. The second criticism is that, as a consequence of its inadequate grasp of the role of human agency, reflectivist theorizing is left without a causal theory, and is forced to import external, objective factors to explain change. As we shall see, the desire to discipline political agency among reflectivist theorists eventually leads some of them even to fall back on the sovereign state as a way of constraining political possibilities. We demonstrate this by reference to Andrew Linklater's critical theory. The presentation of our argument necessarily means that the differences between these various reflectivist theories are overlooked, doubtless to the detriment of their case. But this is made possible because of the common hostility across these theories towards agency and the sovereign state. A serious examination of reflectivist theories on their own terms shows, we argue, that the reflectivist critique of sovereignty neither improves our understanding of change, nor expands our sense of political possibilities.

Theorizing agency after the Cold War

Much of the thrust of reflectivist theorizing emerged as an attempt to inject conceptions of agency, contingency and historical context into a discipline dominated by the arid structuralism of Kenneth Waltz's seminal 1979 work *The Theory of International Politics*.[2] Waltz's neo-realism fixed on the structural arrangement of the international system, rather than states that make it up. It was the system, Waltz claimed, rather than the actions of any particular state that explained the dynamics of international politics, and in particular the recurrence of war. The defining aspect of this structure was the absence of any overarching authority – the states system is anarchic, thereby inhibiting the development of social order. Waltz described the concealed structure of international politics as functioning like the hidden hand of the market, which intercedes between the action of individual agents to generate common outcomes from vastly divergent inputs: 'A market constrains the units that comprise it from taking certain actions and disposes them toward taking others.'[3]

This emphasis on structure was coupled with a tight link between IR theory and the practical concerns of the Cold War. Cold War historian John L. Gaddis observes that much of the political science that was forged in American academies during the Cold War was shaped by the political needs of the American state, grasping for an intellectual apparatus that would help it to steer the world under American hegemony. The result was an intense focus on prediction: predicting the decisions of Soviet leaders; predicting the outcomes of nuclear rivalry and nuclear exchanges; predicting the outcome of development – capitalism or communism in the decolonized world. This affinity for prediction influenced Waltz's own work: 'Theory explains regularities of behaviour and leads one to expect that...outcomes produced by interacting units will fall within specified ranges.'[4] This entrenched tradition of prediction meant that the failure to foresee the end of the Cold War was acutely felt:

> The abrupt end of the Cold War...astonished almost everyone, whether in government, the academy, the media and the think tanks. The end of the Cold War...was of such importance that no approach to the study of international relations claiming both foresight and competence should have failed to see it coming.[5]

The end of the Cold War therefore powerfully strengthened the case for more flexible conceptions of international politics that better incorporated the possibility of change. What is more, since this change seemed to be the product of purposive action – popular movements in Eastern Europe, human rights campaigns and so on – it was felt that new theories had to incorporate human intentionality, rather than fixate on structure. In an article assessing the declining use of realism as an explanatory theory in scholarly journals across the years 1970 to 2000, Thomas C. Walker and Jeffrey S. Morton observe that with the 'end of the Cold War, the expansion of democracy, and the increasing importance of global trade and international organizations, the world is no longer neatly suited to realist concerns'.[6]

While critical IR theories were already incubating in the discipline throughout the 1980s,[7] the end of the Cold War gave them a dramatic new opening to seize the initiative. Critically minded theorists responded to this opportunity by putting forward arguments that challenged the deterministic emphasis on the structure of the states system, pointing instead to the importance of historical context and the interrelationship between ideas and structures. These arguments militated for an emphasis on change rather than stasis. Alexander Wendt, one of the first to try to systematize reflectivism, mobilized the insights of structuration theory, injecting a much-needed dose of intellectual sophistication into the entire discipline. This brought the discipline of IR more into line with a wave of theoretical restructuring that had occurred earlier throughout the social sciences, and allowed for greater theoretical ambition while also not drifting too far from empirical research.

This theoretical reorganization brought to the fore theories concerned with human agency and reflexivity in world affairs, as a way of trying to grapple with change. Robert Keohane coined the term reflectivism, because they all allegedly 'emphasize the importance of human reflection for the nature of institutions and ultimately for the character of world politics'.[8] As John Gerard Ruggie, former UN Assistant Secretary-General and one of the first to introduce reflectivist thinking to mainstream IR wrote, 'constructivism is about human consciousness and its role in international life'.[9] The ostensible purpose of this emphasis on reflexivity was to call into question what seemed natural and given, thereby pointing towards its potential for change. Wendt claimed that the point of these new theories was to 'denaturalize' human institutions: 'constitutive or critical theory reminds us that social kinds like the international system are ideas authored by human beings'.[10]

As efforts to inject the discipline with a greater sense of agency, these reflectivist theories unavoidably converged on a discussion of the prime actor in international affairs: the sovereign state. As with their critique of structure, the reflectivist strategy was to call into question what had been taken for granted. Wendt's work again was instrumental in opening up a far-ranging discussion about the nature of the state, which had hitherto been taken for granted as the key actor in international affairs.[11] Writing with James Fearon, Wendt argued 'rather than taking agents as givens or primitives in social explanation...constructivists are interested in problematizing them, in making them a dependent variable'.[12] Calling the state into question pushed against the boundary that defined, some would say confined, the discipline.[13] This was intellectually liberating. As post-structural theorist R.B.J. Walker, points out 'Many [intellectual] differences...arise far more from disagreements about what it is that scholars think they are studying than from disagreements about how to study it.'[14] Instead of oscillating between power politics (realism) and the possibilities for greater international cooperation (idealism), the floodgates opened to a whole slew of 'awkward philosophical themes' that traditionally had been bracketed under other disciplines – ontology, ethics, ideology and relations between theory and practice.[15]

Reflectivist theories were correct that agency had been understood as something self-evident in international relations, requiring little theoretical reflection. Historian A.J.P. Taylor exemplified this attitude when he defensively qualified what he meant in referring to 'Great Britain' or 'Russia' in his celebrated textbook of international history, *The Struggle for Mastery in Europe 1848–1918:*

> I have written throughout this book as though states and nations were monolithic units, with defined personalities [as if implying] every Englishman and every Russian...The meaning is obvious enough, though no doubt technically indefensible. Nevertheless, there was something like a national outlook on foreign questions in each country, despite the indifference and the disputes.[16]

Leading realist scholar and political economist Robert Gilpin cheerfully admitted:

> Of course, we 'realists' know that the state does not really exist...Only individuals really exist, although I understand that certain schools of psychology challenge even this...we do write as if some particular social or political entity really does exist and acts. It is a matter of convenience and economy to do so.[17]

Gilpin's and Taylor's blitheness about the role played by the agency of the state partially reflected the fact that this agency was relatively self-evident. The analyst could go quite far in international politics simply thinking in terms of the 'Russians did that' and the 'British did this'.

The great virtue of reflectivist theory, then, is that it asks higher order questions, with a good deal more theoretical sophistication, about the nature of political agency in international relations and about the possibilities for change. By posing these questions directly, and by developing their intellectual apparatus around them, reflectivist theories seem to be better positioned to grasp what is distinctive about the contemporary phase of international relations than theories, such as realism, that developed in a different set of circumstances. What is more, in alerting us to the contingent nature of international relations, and in pushing beyond sovereignty, reflectivist theories seek to avoid the realist apologia for power politics, and to open up whole new realms of political possibility that once seemed unimaginable. As Ruggie, puts it, ' "making history" in the new era is a matter not merely of defending the national interest but of defining it ... '.[18] But this begs the question. How successful are reflectivist theories at presenting a theory of agency without the sovereign state? Let us begin with constructivism.

Constructivism: social but not political

Constructivism has been one of the schools of thought that has been most instrumental in loosening the dead hand of neo-realism. Alexander Wendt, perhaps its most influential exponent, explicitly set out to use constructivism to breathe new life into the tradition of liberal internationalism, in order to accomplish its original goal – pacifying the anarchic international order by building institutions and international organizations.[19] For too long, argues Wendt, liberal international theory conceded too much to realism. Liberal internationalism hobbled itself by refusing to acknowledge the way in which interaction between states may accumulate sufficient momentum that it tips over into something new, inaugurating a qualitative shift in the international order that is deep enough to penetrate and transform states themselves. Anarchy is not an immutable structure, but 'what states make of it'.[20] Wendt is saying that interaction, if properly theorized, offers the tantalizing promise of ameliorating the depredations of international anarchy.

If Wendt set about updating the old liberal argument about cooperation between states, constructivism is not reducible to this impulse. At bottom, Wendt's argument against the overbearing structures of neo-realism is about validating agency.[21] When Wendt penned his seminal 1992 article 'Anarchy is What States Make of It: The Social Construction of Power Politics', he tightly lashed his ideas to the unfolding dissolution of the Cold War order, thereby giving his argument the force of immediacy and practical applicability:

> The substantive issue at stake in debates about social theory is what kind of foundation offers the most fruitful set of questions and research strategies for explaining the revolutionary changes that seem to be occurring in the late twentieth century international system.[22]

So how faithful is constructivism to its promise of giving greater theoretical scope to agency in international politics? Consider Wendt's discussion of how power politics is 'socially constructed'. Wendt argues that anarchy is insufficiently powerful as a causal nexus to set in motion the competitive dynamics of power politics seen in the Cold War. In other words, there is a conceptual gap between the absence of any central authority in the states system (anarchy), and the way states behave in ensuring their security and self-preservation (self-help). Realists have it that self-help forces other states to behave in a similar fashion, thereby setting in motion the competitive dynamics of power politics. As it is self-help, rather than anarchy per se, that bears the burden of generating power politics, Wendt spies a way of moving beyond power politics without needing to argue for world government.

Wendt argues that as the identities of states cannot be considered independently of context, it is possible that the process of interaction between states can gradually transform their identities, and by changing their identities, change their interests. Thus, Wendt points out that there is no such thing as agency independent of socialization; anarchy cannot presuppose actors that somehow exist prior to the system. Wendt argues that egotistical, power-hungry states could only become like this from the way they set themselves against other states:

> [such] claims presuppose a history of interaction in which actors have acquired 'selfish' identities and interests; [but] before interaction... they would have no experience upon which to base such definitions of self and other. To assume otherwise is to attribute to states in the state of nature qualities that they can only possess in society.[23]

Identity and agency is therefore brought into being through a mutually constitutive, relational process dependent on context. Wendt demonstrates this by pointing out the difficulty that the United States and former Soviet Union had in formulating conceptions of national interest at the end of the Cold War: 'without the cold war's mutual attributions of threat and hostility to define their identities, these states seem unsure of what their "interests" should be'.[24] Wendt concedes that this 'may all seem very arcane, but there is an important issue at stake'[25]; namely, the possibilities for change within the international order. Thus what determines the political character of an anarchical system is not the balance of power – but rather the extent to which states' conceptions of themselves enable them to identify with each other: 'if the United States and Soviet Union decide that they are no longer enemies, "the cold war is over". It is collective meanings that constitute the structures which organize our actions.'[26]

Thus even the most fundamental institutions of political order, such as state sovereignty, need not be regarded as immutable and fixed, but as social artefacts, open to change. While Wendt acknowledges that sovereignty has provided protection for weak states, it has also helped to 'harden territorial' identities, producing a spurious association between arbitrary national borders and security,[27] a doctrine of 'territorial property rights' that 'functions as a form of "social closure" that disempowers nonstate actors'.[28] Change occurs as the process of interaction is gradually sedimented over time.

But Wendt's apparent elevation of agency over structure is deceptive. In his attempt to socialize structure, and to open it up to change, agency slips through Wendt's fingers. For having taken out any notion of agency as being in some sense over and above the flux of interaction, Wendt is unable to specify a moment at which agency is decisive, or logically prior to something else. Wendt tears causality away from anarchy, but instead of placing it onto states, he endows *process* with agency. For if there is no agency prior to social interaction, what is it that sets a process of social interaction into motion? Here it becomes impossible to grasp hold of subjectivity, submerged as it is in the flux of communication. Drawing on symbolic interactionist sociology and its conception of the 'looking glass self', Wendt uses the analogy of two mirrors facing each other to try to describe the process whereby agency emerges through a reciprocal process of identification. But a mirror reflecting a mirror is reflecting nothing; no matter how long they face each other, no image will spontaneously emerge.[29]

Identities determine states' interests, argues Wendt, but these identities are only acquired from being slotted into a predetermined role, allocated within intersubjective frameworks of meaning. Agency has no constitutive power of its own. Rather, it belongs to formal legal rules and international agreements that are the contingent products of continuous interaction between international actors. In Wendt's terms, 'sovereignty is an institution, and so it exists only in virtue of certain intersubjective understandings and expectations'.[30] In a sense, constructivism returns us to a hollow, legalistic conception of sovereignty, entirely defined by agreements external to sovereignty itself (see further Michael Savage's chapter in this volume). Sovereignty, on this account, becomes not a concept identifying the key actor in international affairs, but a legal instrument by which political actors are defined. But state sovereignty involves both recognition *and* self-assertion. Constructivism sacrifices the latter at the expense of the former. The difference can be teased out through Hegel's discussion of the sovereignty of revolutionary France, the archetypal modern nation-state, when France challenged the absolutist, dynastic states of pre-Napoleonic Europe:

> When Napoleon said before the Peace of Campo Formio 'the French Republic is no more in need of recognition than the sun is', his words conveyed no more than that strength of existence which itself carries with it a guarantee of recognition.[31]

Here, Hegel's equation runs from 'strength of existence' (subjectivity) to recognition, and not vice versa, as with constructivism. The refusal of the absolutist states to recognize revolutionary France did not stop their armies being crushed and their consequent need to sue for peace. The sovereignty of revolutionary France was constituted through self-assertion and force of arms – not through formal recognition or lack thereof.

To be sure, there are cases where sovereignty seems to be more artificial and dependent on the international order, rather than bubbling up from below. Writing in 1964, Andrew Boyd recounts, for example, how the survival of Jordan after the withdrawal of British troops was ensured by the United Nations:

> Jordan was still there in 1963, the British having left in November 1958. Nobody was quite sure why; but [United Nations Secretary-General Dag] Hammarskjöld's three weeks of very quiet diplomacy...in Amman, Cairo, and other capitals...had something to do it. His only tangible creation was a UN office in Jordan...Yet this modest installation...[a]t critical moments...had a steadying effect.[32]

In cases like that of Jordan, we must ask why such a fictitious political entity had to be granted independence. Or in other words, why could British power in the Middle East no longer be exercised in the direct form of empire? The reason 'nobody expected' Jordan to survive the withdrawal of British troops was the strength of the centrifugal force of pan-Arabism at that point in time. Pan-Arabism was a political movement that sought to unite the Arab peoples by transcending the arbitrary grid of national borders inherited from colonial administrators. It was the strength of this very same nationalist movement, emanating principally from Egypt, which made imperialist power in the Middle East so illegitimate, forcing the granting of independence to states such as Jordan. The point is that even states that seem to be simply fabricated by international diplomacy are ultimately dependent on the existence of a constituted, self-organizing political power, even if this power exists elsewhere.

But by dissolving structure into intersubjectivity, Wendt is unable to give any depth to relations beyond the flux and instability of communication. Conscious that he is restricting precisely that quality that he set out to recapture – agency – Wendt strikes out in a number of directions to try to halt the slide into indeterminacy. So, for example, if agency is not able to exist in some sense outside of intersubjectivity, then what is to prevent a destructive process from continuing spontaneously to accumulate momentum? If there is no moment at which agency can tear itself away from this process, then eventually an 'atmosphere of distrust' becomes so entrenched that there is 'little room for...cooperation and its transformative consequences'.[33] By this logic, Wendt is no more able to explain the end of the Cold War than a neo-realist. So Wendt argues that agency must involve a moment of critical self-reflection independent of other actors' expectations. Such a moment is dependent on the development of new situations that challenge pre-given expectations. But how do these new situations arise, if not through the determinate effect of structure, or the prior exercise of another's agency? To stabilize the flux of communication, Wendt further stipulates that actors develop an interest in maintaining stable identities – but this only reverses Wendt's original proposition, by suggesting that interests are prior to identities.

Two consequences flow from grounding agency in the indeterminacy and flexibility of legal and moral discourse at the international level. First, we get a reified, juridical conception of sovereignty that is external to domestic politics. This husk of a state has no self-organizing dynamic of its own, drawn from mobilizing the collective power of its citizens, as in the example of revolutionary France. Thus in Wendt's hands, constructivism can only see mass politics as a bothersome contingency that threatens to undermine the high-level agreements of diplomats and statesmen. In answer to the question 'how much and what kind of a role [does]...domestic politics play in world politics', Wendt responds, 'The greater and more destructive the role, the more significant predation [between states] will be, and the less amenable anarchy will be to formation of collective identities.'[34] The second consequence is that international relations are reified as something beyond human agency. Instead of peoples and their governments shaping the ebb and flow of international politics, high-level agreements and conventions become the prime driver of international relations (IR).

Constructivism begins from the insight that to see sovereignty and international relations as properly social products entails the possibility of change. Yet constructivism ends by reifying sovereignty, and by transforming it into a legal arrangement extended to states on the basis of international agreement rather than something that is actively won.

Post-structuralism: denying history, denying agency

While sharing with constructivism a focus on theorizing change over stasis, post-structural theories of international relations are more scathing and extensive in their criticisms of orthodox IR. They see themselves as extending the post-modern philosophical interrogation of modernity, already carried out in the social sciences, through to IR. In the words of Erik Ringmar:

> a first thing to notice is how the debate regarding the future of the state is directly linked to a debate on the future of man...man and state were born at the same time, they grew up together, and hence it is not unreasonable to expect them to die a simultaneous death. Or more distinctly put: what we are discussing here is not only the future of the state or the future of man, but rather the future of subjectivity tout court.[35]

The wide-ranging character of the post-structural critique is evident in Richard K. Ashley's influential 1988 article 'Untying the Sovereign State'. This article begins by repudiating precisely those liberal approaches that constructivism set out to revive. Ashley does this by pointing to the paradox that, the greater the importance the scholar attaches to questions of international order, the greater the need to pay attention to the decentralized, anarchic structure of the states system. The more you want to boost international cooperation, the more you find yourself respecting the egotism of the sovereign state. In other words, liberal theories of international order are more insidious. For while the liberal scholar prefers internationalism to nationalism, elevates order and cooperation over expansionism and militarism,[36] the questions that he sets out to answer only reinforce the underlying presuppositions of realism: 'How can there be governance in the absence of government? How can order be constructed in the absence of an orderer? How can cooperation be facilitated under a condition of anarchy?'[37]

Here, Ashley is pointing to the anarchy/sovereignty paradox. That is to say, the very notion of supreme authority *within* the state logically necessitates the denial of any authority *above* the state. Ashley's point is that the deterministic element in this equation is not the structure of anarchy but sovereignty itself. In the words of R.B.J. Walker, 'State sovereignty works because it has come to seem to be simply there, out in the world, demarcating the natural orders of here and there.'[38] Talking about the deterministic structures of anarchy leaves the prior question of sovereignty unexamined. To theorize the possibility of real change in the international order, Ashley suggests, it is necessary to tackle sovereignty itself. 'Heroic practices invoke the sovereignty of reasoning man whose voice would displace the Word of God as the source of truth and meaning in the world.'[39]

In other words, the problem with the conventional focus on anarchy in IR is that it deflects the scope of inquiry away from sovereign states, whose interactions produce this anarchy in the first place. Therefore, any attempt to transform international politics is restricted if it refuses to interrogate the foundations of the system, namely, state sovereignty. Other post-structuralists have gone further, to claim that sovereignty is not external to the workings of power, but is in itself a form of domination through which political alternatives are restricted, and through which the grid of inside/outside, 'international' versus 'domestic' politics is reproduced.[40] That is why, echoing Foucault, Bartelson argues we should 'avoid the direct question of what sovereignty is, and instead ask *how* it has been spoken of and known throughout a period of time'.[41] Only when we reject the idea that sovereignty can be known can we understand how it is constituted. To begin from sovereignty as the key form of political subjectivity in international relations is to be nothing more than one of the 'irresponsible camp followers of power'.[42]

As with constructivism, however, what begins as a theoretical critique of the limits on our understanding ends by dissolving the very possibility of agency. In post-structuralist literature, sovereignty is paradoxically recognized as a product of modernity without, however, being able to endow its existence with any necessity. Rather, sovereignty is seen as the contingent product of 'a more or less random succession of discursive and epistemic events'.[43] The appeal to randomness and accident appears as the infusion of history with human agency. Contingency and contextualization is emphasized in opposition to mechanical causality and transcendental hypotheses. But the problem is that the description of pure flux entails that we are unable to specify historically any given moment.

When everything is a 'random succession of events' we are unable to isolate any key moment, and to delineate the form that human agency takes in a particular time and place. Why, for example, is sovereignty a definitive form of collective subjectivity in modernity? Because, as we discuss in the Introduction, it is the form politics takes under the specific historical conditions of capitalism. Human subjectivity assumes various forms, but it cannot just take any form at any given moment – it is socially determined. Illuminating these social determinations should open up the ways in which agency exists, is limited by existing forms, and can potentially transcend these constraints through politics. For Ashley, however, recognizing that something is socially produced entails recognizing that it is arbitrary, that is, the opposite of subjective activity, in the sense of human action that is conscious, transformative and meaningful. The slide from contextualization to vagueness, and the consequent inability to endow human agency with any concrete causality, is taken to its logical end-point by Edkins *et al.* '[Sovereignty] is an impostor, in a sense: any signifier... would do – divine providence, the invisible hand of the market, the objective logic of history, or the Jewish conspiracy, for example.'[44]

Post-structuralist theories cannot, therefore, grasp subjectivity, because subjectivity emerges consciously, and not randomly, in response to concrete historical circumstances. The theory of sovereignty as the basis for international politics is grounded in real historical experience: the modern state system developed as political communities actively pressed their own claims, from revolutionary France right through to the struggle of colonized peoples for national liberation, who forcibly proved to their colonial overlords what they had been insistently denied, namely, a political existence as collective subjects. In this sense, the right of self-determination and the sovereign rights of independence are therefore the legal registration of a political fact – what Hegel called the 'strength of existence'. This 'fact' of sovereignty exists not in the sense of a timeless given, but as a historical product, emerging through specific struggles. But it is no less real for being historical.[45] We need to look no further than the transformation of the states system through decolonization to see that sovereignty really is a constitutive factor in international politics.

The post-structural critique of sovereignty results in an ambivalent stance. If post-structuralists aggressively reject sovereignty, they are cautious about replacing it. Ashley's analysis does 'not seek to undertake an emancipatory critique',[46] and Bartelson's deconstruction 'does not tell us where to go from here, neither as political scientists nor as citizens. It proclaims modernity an absurd dream from which we are about to escape'.[47] Their claims that they seek merely to show that sovereignty 'is not necessary or essential'[48] exhibit a false modesty concealing a deep uneasiness. Walker notes

> just how fragile modern accounts of the location and character of the political have become. They are certainly much too fragile to permit much confidence in the capacity of modern theories of international relations to tell us where or what the political can now be.[49]

Here there is only a sense of what politics cannot be. It cannot 'reproduce the codes of inclusion and exclusion that have made theories of international relations what they have become'.[50] Bartelson argues that deconstructing sovereignty means showing it 'involves the political responsibility of deciding upon sovereignty'. Yet his final words are that this is 'a decision which we for the moment seem unfit to make'.[51] Given the intensity of the focus on subjection and exclusion, it is awkward, though not accidental, for post-structuralists to be unable to establish politics on a new basis. Though they draw attention to the need to understand sovereignty contextually, they are unable to translate these insights into a distinct, post-sovereign theory of politics. That is because they are victims of their own methodology. For all the talk of contingency, their reading of sovereignty is not historically specific enough.

The previous two sections argued that neither constructivism nor post-structuralism are successful in their attempts to theorize political agency without sovereignty. Here we seek to gather the two theoretical approaches together and address criticisms to them jointly. We begin with their attempt to recast agency beyond the sovereign state.

Drift as mastery

Having rejected the self-determining sovereign state pursuing its interests as their favoured model, constructivists and post-structuralists are logically forced to rediscover some measure of open ended agency elsewhere. They rediscover this sense of possibility in the way in which identities are seen as indeterminate and fluid. Wendt speaks of sovereignty as an 'ongoing accomplishment of practice';[52] Ashley speaks of how the international order 'must be daily and everywhere fabricated anew', and how 'efforts [are] concerted', 'orchestrated' in a 'global process'.[53] This emphasis on fluidity seems liberating, in contrast to the image of a self-regulating balance of power that disciplines sovereign states regardless of their will. Yet instead of emerging with the full force of logic from the structure of reflectivist arguments themselves, the suggestion of dynamism in the new theories emanates more from their earnest and effusive rhetoric ('accomplishment', 'fabrication', 'orchestration').

But the emphasis on fluidity comes across more as accommodation than emancipation. For if so much energy is absorbed simply in maintaining the international status quo as an 'ongoing accomplishment', it is difficult to see where we would have any agency left over that could be harnessed for radical transformation of the system of states. The moment of abstractness, of standing above relations rather than being fully absorbed in them, is lost, and thus one dimension of agency simply falls away. In truth, fluidity means states are buffeted here and there by the vagaries of international conventions and institutions, more than they actively shape them. There is no conceptual means provided by which to distinguish drift from mastery; all change dissolves into the ether of globalized social relations. Thus while these reflectivist theories are sensitive to the attenuation of sovereign power, they are oddly unreflective about their rediscovery of freedom in fluidity.

Rebels without a cause: losing grasp of historical change

The stress on contingency indicates a deeper lack of reflexivity on the part of the new reflectivist theories. For though they are spurred by a sensitivity to change in the post-Cold War era, as reflectivist theories lose grasp of the relationship between historical processes and historically specific forms of subjectivity, they quickly forget their own origins, with disastrous consequences for their ability to grasp what is new. The sharpness of reflectivists' analytical tools is consequently blunted, as we have a less precise sense of what it is about the post-Cold War era that is historically specific. As Hedley Bull once observed, 'An understanding of the historical conditions out of which a theory grows, or to which it is a response, provides vital materials for the criticism of that theory and, for the theorist himself, provides the correction of self-knowledge.'[54] Reflectivists tend to ignore this injunction, instead taking the contingency of the post-Cold War period from which they draw their inspiration and reading it back into international history.

To be sure, some reflectivists try to pre-empt this criticism by rejecting the argument for a historically specific approach. Ashley, for example, admits that his own work is modern in so far as modernity is defined by the use of reason to demystify arbitrary ideological limits. Nonetheless, Ashley still argues that we should not accept that our criteria of validity be bound by historically specific 'interpretative attitudes and procedures'. Such dispositions are in fact authoritarian, part of the 'disciplining' by which modernity restricts our range of thought.[55] It is here that Ashley most clearly rejects the need for reflexivity, in effect arguing that theorizing need not reflect on how it is socially embedded in a particular time and place. Ashley's revolt has ended by taking him back to the orthodoxy against which he rebelled – the conceit of an independent, social scientific enterprise that could detachedly analyse international politics as if it were entirely removed from it.[56] Hedley Bull, again, reminds us of the need for historical specificity: 'theory itself has a history, and theorists themselves elaborate their idea with the preoccupations and within the confines of a particular historical situation.'[57] When not rooted in historically specific analysis, the idea that the world is socially constructed can quite easily shade into the idea that society is constructed from the knowledge we have of it – the logical conclusion being, of course, that new types of societies can spring fully-formed from the heads of IR theorists. This is what is meant by Ruggie's vague reference to change coming about from discourse and 'collective representations'[58] and Ashley's intimations of power in 'the wave of the theorist's hand'.[59]

In effect, by casting aside the 'disciplining' of modern 'interpretative attitudes', Ashley is removing the final logical barrier to unmitigated flights of mental fancy. For all his mockery of the 'heroic discourse', Ashley is forced to marvel at a process by which

> *the orchestration of the inscription of man and domestic society in ways that make possible the co-ordinated displacement of anarchic dangers, not from one 'domestic society' onto others, but beyond the places and times of 'man' in every 'domestic society' of a multistate system* (original emphasis).[60]

The prose reflects Ashley's confusion: unable to locate human agency or identify historical specificity, the coordinated effort needed to keep modernity in motion – 'arbitrary', 'contingent', 'constructed', 'deferred' as it is – unsurprisingly begins to appear as an inscrutable effort of cosmic complexity. The invocation of a mysterious, Herculean process of coordinated 'displacement' needed to reproduce the inside/outside distinctions of modern politics is more akin to the 'hidden hand' than a historically grounded discussion of state sovereignty.

As they are unable to capitalize on their own insights about contingency, many reflectivist theories collapse back onto under-theorized 'objective developments', notably globalization, which is brought in as an intellectual *deus ex machina* to prop up the argument. John J. Mearsheimer astutely describes this limitation:

> [Reflectivists]…emphasize that the world is socially constructed, and not shaped in fundamental ways by objective factors. Anarchy, after all, is what we make of it. Yet when critical theorists attempt to explain why realism may be losing its hegemonic position, they too point to objective factors as the ultimate cause of change. Discourse, so it appears, turns out to be determinate, but mainly a reflection of developments in the objective world. In short, it seems that when [reflectivists] who study international politics offer glimpses of their thinking about the causes of change in the real world, they make arguments that directly contradict their own theory, but which appear to be compatible with the [realist] theory they are challenging.[61]

Mearsheimer uses the example of critical theorist Robert Cox. R.B.J. Walker provides another example of the reliance on globalization as the flipside of contingency: 'The most trenchant reminder that ours is an age of speed and temporal accelerations has been the simultaneous dissolution of Cold War geopolitics and the rapid entrenchment of a globally organised capitalism';[62] and 'the experience of temporality, of speed, velocity and acceleration, is more and more bewildering'.[63] The first joint criticism we advanced now folds into the second. We pointed out the reflectivist theory replaces agency with contingency. Now we see that reflectivist theory has left us without the means to distinguish fluidity from the economic networks of 'globally organised capitalism' and other transnational processes that escape our control.

A final turn: sovereignty against subjectivity

Our criticisms have accepted the reflectivist premise that agency is not limited to sovereignty. As we suggest in the Introduction, subjectivity in its political form even pushes beyond the state, insofar as it seeks a universal basis for collective action, though this often means pitting one nation against another. Here, we have instead shown that the particular way in which reflectivist theory criticizes the sovereign state leaves us with an impoverished conception of political subjectivity. If reflectivist theories have failed to introduce a superior grasp of the role and possibilities of human agency in international politics than traditional theories, their diminished conception of political possibility does not always take the form of a straightforward attack on sovereignty. As a brief examination of a proponent of a third reflectivist school – Andrew Linklater's critical theory – demonstrates, a retreat from collective subjectivity is achieved through a back-handed defence of the sovereign state.

Linklater has added his voice to those criticizing sovereignty. In particular, he argues that national citizenship is only one arbitrary exclusion among many: 'the nation-state is one of the few bastions of exclusion which has not had its rights and claims against the rest of the world seriously questioned'.[64] Yet Linklater also frequently reaffirms the stable requirements of order as a precondition for moral progress. In *The Transformation of Political Community* (1998), Linklater argues that expanding the boundaries of the political community beyond the nation-state means that it is citizens that must adapt to the challenge of globalization. In Linklater's words 'communities will not survive unless their members are prepared to define their interests in the light of a more general good'.[65] But shifting the burden of change onto the behaviour of citizens means that the states system is left the same. Human agency is exhausted by the achievement of the ethical duty of broadening community, rather than the greater project of systemic transformation. Therefore, of necessity, Linklater's project forces him to fallback onto the existing system of sovereign states:

> A pluralist international society strikes a balance between the principle of state sovereignty and universal principles of order and peaceful co-existence. A solidarist international society endorses the principle of state sovereignty but strives to balance it with a commitment to universal moral principles.[66]

It is the latter, 'solidarist', international society that wins Linklater's sympathy. Linklater further argues that 'post-Westphalian' political arrangements can be pioneered by 'the majority' *or* 'the most powerful' of nation-states – with the caveat, of course, that these states are 'committed to constitutional rule, deliberative politics, social welfare and universalistic moral beliefs which value radical cultural differences'.[67] In Linklater's innocuous, back-handed reaffirmation of state sovereignty there lurks a conservative scepticism towards the exercise of human agency. Arguing for 'inclusion' within the existing international order downplays criticizing the nature of the order in which we are to be included. Thus we can see that when state sovereignty is reaffirmed even by one of its reflectivist critics, this reaffirmation expresses the same impulse that leads to the attack on state sovereignty in the first place – namely, scepticism towards the exercise of human agency.

The new camp followers

As a consequence of this scepticism towards agency, existing power relations are tacitly reaffirmed, by being recast as the domain within which agents act. But the problem is not exclusive to Linklater. It plagues all reflectivist theories because of their inability to grasp adequately the specific forms in which power is exercised in contemporary politics. Indeed, one of the most remarkable aspects of reflectivist theories is the way they present themselves as radical critiques of existing orthodoxies when they have, in fact, substantially replaced realism as the intellectual accomplices of the present. For example, writing in 1992, Wendt bitterly polemicized:

> Sovereignty norms are now so taken for granted, so natural, that it is easy to overlook the extent to which they are both presupposed by and an ongoing artifact of practice. When states... kill thousands of Iraqis in one kind of war and then refuse to 'intervene' and to kill even one person in another kind, a 'civil' war... they are acting against the background of, and thereby repro-ducing, shared norms about what it means to be a sovereign state. If states stopped acting on those norms, their identity as 'sovereigns' (if not necessar-ily as 'states') would disappear.[68]

It is clear in retrospect that Wendt was kicking against an open door. Since he wrote these words over a decade ago, Western states have repeatedly violated state sovereignty by intervening in civil conflicts throughout the world, including the civil war that Wendt is referring to (in former Yugoslavia). Britain and the United States have even found their way back to Iraq. This 'new interventionism' indicates the extent to which 'sovereignty' is far from 'taken for granted'. As Philip Cunliffe's chapter in this volume suggests, those who have set about redefining sovereignty as 'responsibility', through international conventions and inter-elite consultation, are demonstrating that sovereignty is seen as an artefact that can be rewritten following the latest international report. But it is an elite artefact, not a social artefact, as it is arbitrarily redefined apart from mass politics. The Report of the International Commission on Intervention and State Sovereignty clearly draws upon new IR theories when it makes a thinly veiled attack on realist ideas about structure:

> The notion of responsibility itself entails fundamental moral reasoning and challenges determinist theories of human behaviour and international relations theory. The behaviour of states is not predetermined by systemic or structural factors, and moral considerations are not merely after-the-fact justifications or simply irrelevant.[69]

Ashley too is unaware of how much his ideas accommodate contemporary politics. In 1988, Ashley placed his hopes for a deconstruction of traditional international politics in non-state actors such as non-governmental organizations (NGOs):

> once nonstate actors are introduced into [the] discourse and taken seriously, every attempt to represent such a [sovereign] is immediately undone. It is no longer possible *even ideologically* to represent a coherent sovereign presence, an identical source of meaning and power.[70]

Today, we have NGOs directly involved in governing countries in the developing world, sitting on committees alongside major international organizations like the World Bank, as John Pender's discussion of governance in Tanzania, and David Chandler's discussion of global civil society in this volume make clear. James Heartfield's chapter on the European Union in this volume makes clear how another non-state actor has pushed ahead not by expanding political horizons, but by systematically lowering and restricting them.

Jenny Edkins was cited earlier as condemning the realists for being 'camp followers of power', but as the examples from Linklater, Wendt and Ashley suggest, reflectivist theories have somewhat unreflectively become the new camp followers. In their haste to attack sovereignty as an exclusive, tyrannical political form, they have overlooked the reorganization of power on non-sovereign terms. They have repeated the same mistakes as realism by intellectually formalizing the contemporary period. And with their underlying suspicion of decisive, unifying political acts such as struggles for self-determination and state-based mass politics, they even ditch the conceptual apparatus by which these power relations can be called into question as a whole.

Conclusion

We have argued in this chapter that critical new theories of IR, principally constructivism and post-structuralism, have difficulty grasping the dynamics of international relations. While they are alive to the way in which state sovereignty can no longer be taken for granted in international politics, they overreach themselves in their attacks, leaving them unable to theorize the efficacy and meaning of human agency. As a result, their radical claims to rethinking politics outside states in fact serves to limit political possibilities. In their critiques of sovereignty, they lose what the concept has historically expressed, however imperfectly, which is the exercise of political subjectivity. A fuller grasp of agency should identify the significance of sovereignty, both historically and conceptually, and point beyond it. Constructivists and post-structuralists help us achieve neither.

Notes

1 There is no ideal way of bracketing the theoretical developments that emerged in response to the neo-realist and neo-liberal schools. Keohane's label 'reflectivism' has been chosen here in preference to 'post-positivism' because the latter falsely suggests that positivism is a spent force in the academy, which is far from being the case.
2 K. Waltz, *Theory of International Politics*, Columbus: McGraw Hill, 1979.
3 Ibid., p.90.
4 Waltz, cited in J. Lewis Gaddis, 'International Relations Theory and the End of the Cold War', *International Security* 17:3, 1992/93, p.9.
5 Gaddis, 'International Relations Theory', pp.5–6.
6 T.C. Walker and J.S. Morton, 'Re-Assessing the "Power of Power Politics" Thesis: Is Realism Still Dominant?', *International Studies Review* 7:2, 2005, p.353.

7 O. Waever, 2002, 'The Rise and Fall of the Inter-paradigm Debate', in S. Smith, K. Booth and M. Zalewski (eds), *International Theory: Positivism and Beyond*, Cambridge: Cambridge University Press, 2002, pp.149–185.

8 R. Keohane, 1988, 'International Institutions: Two Approaches', in J. Der Derian (ed.), *International Theory: Critical Investigations*, Basingstoke: Macmillan, 1995, p.284.

9 J. Ruggie, 'What Makes the World Hang Together? Neo-utilitarianism and the Social Constructivist Challenge', *International Organization* 52:4, 1998, p.856.

10 A. Wendt, *Social Theory of International Politics*, Cambridge: Cambridge University Press, 1999, p.374.

11 A. Wendt, 1992, 'Anarchy is What States Make of It: The Social Construction of Power Politics', in Der Derian, *International Theory*, pp.130–131.

12 J. Fearon and A. Wendt, 2002, 'Rationalism versus Constructivism: A Skeptical View', in W. Carlsnaes, T. Risse and B. Simmons (eds), *Handbook of International Relations*, London: Sage, 2002, p.57.

13 J. Bartelson, 'Second Natures: Is the State Identical with Itself?', *European Journal of International Relations* 4, 1998, pp.295–296.

14 R.B.J. Walker, 1989, 'History and Structure in International Relations', in Der Derian, *International Theory*, pp.313–314.

15 Ibid., p.316.

16 A.J.P. Taylor, *The Struggle for Mastery in Europe: 1848–1918*, Oxford: Oxford University Press, 1992, pp.xxi–xxii.

17 R. Gilpin, 'The Richness of the Tradition of Political Realism', in R.O. Keohane (ed.), *Neorealism and Its Critics*, New York: Columbia University Press, 1986, p.318.

18 Ruggie, 'What Makes the World Hang Together', p.875.

19 Wendt is of course not the only significant constructivist, others of which include John Ruggie, Friedrich Kratochwil, Christian Reus-Smit and Kathryn Sikkink. We focus on Wendt because, in this particular case, he best expresses their common presuppositions. Wendt's later work like *Social Theory of International Politics* (Cambridge: Cambridge University Press, 1999) is less important for our argument in this chapter, than his earlier articles, which focus more directly on sovereignty. Also, see Michael Savage's chapter in this volume, where he extends the critique of constructivists, including Kratochwil.

20 Wendt, 'Anarchy is What States Make of It', pp.130–131.

21 Wendt, *Social Theory of International Politics*, p.374.

22 Wendt, 'Anarchy is What States Make of It', p.161.

23 Ibid., p.139.

24 Ibid., p.136.

25 Ibid., p.139.

26 Ibid., p.135.

27 Ibid., pp.151–153.

28 Ibid., p.150.

29 Ibid., p.139.

30 Ibid., p.150.

31 G.W.F. Hegel, in Allen W. Wood (ed.), trans. H.B. Nisbet, *Elements of Philosophy of Right*, Cambridge: Cambridge University Press, 2000, p.367.

32 A. Boyd, *United Nations: Piety, Myth, and Truth*, New York, Penguin Books, 1966, p.110.

33 Wendt, 'Anarchy is What States Make of It', pp.156–157.

34 Ibid., p.144.

35 E. Ringmar, 'On the Ontological Status of the State', *European Journal of International Relations* 2:4, 1996, pp.458–459.

36 R.K. Ashley, 'Untying the Sovereign State: A Double Reading of the Anarchy Problématique', *Millennium: Journal of International Studies* 17:2, 1988, pp.237–238.

37 Ibid., p.227.

38 R.B.J. Walker, 1995, 'International Relations and the Concept of the Political', in K. Booth and S. Smith (eds), *International Relations Theory Today*, Cambridge: Polity Press, 1995, p.322.
39 R.K. Ashley, 1988, 'The Powers of Anarchy: Theory, Sovereignty, and the Domestication of Global Life', in Der Derian, *International Theory*, p.107.
40 R.B.J. Walker, *Inside/Outside: International Relations as Political Theory*, Cambridge: Cambridge University Press, 1993.
41 J. Bartelson, *A Genealogy of Sovereignty*, Cambridge: Cambridge University Press, 1995, p.4.
42 J. Edkins, N. Persram and V. Pin-Fat (eds), *Sovereignty and Subjectivity*, Boulder: Lynne Rienner, 1999, p.7.
43 Bartelson, 'Second Natures', p.246.
44 Edkins, Persram and Pin-Fat, *Sovereignty and Subjectivity*, pp.6–7.
45 The same could be said for the individual, legal subject or the 'man' that Engmar sees as the flipside of the modern state. See J. Heartfield, 'Rights and the Legal Subject', unpublished, 1996.
46 Ashley, 'Untying the Sovereign State', p.228.
47 Bartelson, 'Second Natures', p.248.
48 Ibid., p.239.
49 Walker, 'International Relations and the Concept of the Political', p.324.
50 Ibid.
51 Bartelson, 'Second Natures', p.248.
52 Wendt, 'Anarchy is What States Make of It', p.151.
53 Ashley, 'Powers of Anarchy', p.117.
54 H. Bull, 1972, 'The Theory of International Politics, 1919–1969', in Der Derian, *International Theory*, p.183.
55 Ashley, 'Untying the Sovereign State', p.231.
56 R.K. Ashley, 'The Poverty of Neorealism', in Keohane, *Neorealism and Its Critics*.
57 Bull, 'Theory of International Politics', p.183.
58 Ruggie, 'What Makes the World Hang Together?', p.884.
59 Ashley, 'Untying the Sovereign State', p.250.
60 Ibid., p.259.
61 J.J. Mearsheimer, 'The False Promise of International Institutions', *International Security* 19:3, 1994/95, p.43.
62 Walker, 'International Relations and the Concept of the Political,' p.322.
63 Ibid., p.5.
64 A. Linklater, 'The Question of the Next Stage in International Relations Theory: A Critical–Theoretical Point of View', *Millennium: Journal of International Studies* 21:1, 1991, p.93.
65 A. Linklater, *The Transformation of Political Community: Ethical Foundations of the Post-Westphalian Era*, Cambridge: Polity Press, 1998, p.1.
66 Ibid., p.176
67 Ibid., p.169
68 Wendt, 'Anarchy is What States Make of It', pp.150–151.
69 International Commission on Intervention and State Sovereignty, *The Responsibility to Protect: Research, Bibliography, Background*, Ottawa: International Development Research Centre, 2001, p.129.
70 Ashley, 'Untying the Sovereign State', p.235.

2 Sovereignty and the politics of responsibility

Philip Cunliffe

Introduction

The traditional idea of sovereignty as autonomy, or freedom from external interference, faces a serious challenge in the idea of 'sovereignty as responsibility'. This new doctrine holds that state sovereignty cannot be restricted to inviolable legal authority. Rather, sovereignty must be extended to embrace not only authority, but also a two-fold 'responsibility to protect', as it is called in the official literature.[1] The first responsibility of the state is to protect the welfare of the citizens that fall within its jurisdiction. The second responsibility is to the wider society of states. The state is also responsible for preventing human suffering within its borders from spilling over into threatening 'international peace and security', in the words of the United Nations (UN) Charter. This framework of overlapping obligations is held to derive from the UN Charter itself. David Chandler summarizes the new doctrine thus: 'In brief, the three traditional characteristics of a state . . . (territory, authority, and population) have been supplemented by a fourth, respect for human rights.'[2] If a sovereign state is unwilling to uphold these obligations to either its internal or external constituency, or even if a state is merely unable to do so, then its authority is forfeit. In such a scenario, the doctrine of sovereignty as responsibility holds that the UN, and even states acting outside the UN's authority, have the duty to alleviate human suffering however they can.

The purpose of this chapter is to advance some criticisms of this new doctrine of sovereignty, which has won such widespread support throughout the world. The key criticism that I want to make is that the new doctrine is incompatible with a proper politics of responsibility. For power to be truly responsible, it needs to be at least potentially accountable. Sovereignty as responsibility, however, makes the exercise of power unaccountable, and therefore ultimately irresponsible. One of the virtues of the traditional understanding of sovereignty is that, through its claim to supremacy, it clarifies the exercise of power. Obviously, no state ever possesses 'total' power over every event that occurs under its jurisdiction. But the fundamental point is that by *claiming* supremacy, the sovereign cannot defer responsibility for its actions elsewhere. Mohammed Ayoob writes that sovereignty 'acts as a "no trespassing" sign protecting the exclusive territorial domain of states'.[3] This is true (or should be true) from the external perspective of all other states. But from the *internal* perspective, the supreme power of sovereignty also means 'the buck stops here'. Regardless of whether its government is liberal or authoritarian, almost every state in the world today is based on the *idea* of popular sovereignty, the idea that the state exists to enforce the will of the people.[4] As the people are formally sovereign, this means that everyone within a state is ultimately responsible for what happens in their own societies. The state thus gives societies a stable, recognized source of power that makes it possible to hold to account someone, an individual or group of individuals, as responsible for particular political decisions. As we shall see, these two facets of sovereignty are integrally related. The demarcation of authority between sovereigns is crucial to understand how far power extends, and thus how far it can be held accountable.

I emphasize the aspect of supremacy inherent in sovereignty because that is what the 'responsibility to protect' denies. It claims that the power of the sovereign state can be legitimately revoked if the international community decides that the state is not protecting its citizens. I would like to focus on two problems with this idea. First, the supremacy and inviolability of the state is necessary to guarantee the sovereignty of the people. That means that violating the autonomy of the state violates popular sovereignty. Second, if popular sovereignty seems like a remote ideal in the context of atrocity and tyranny, the international community is even more remote and abstract. While it is not asking too much to admit the existence of an international community of some description, it would nonetheless be 'a dangerous illusion', as E.H. Carr puts it, 'to suppose that this hypothetical world community possesses the unity and coherence of communities of more limited size up to and including the state'.[5] In short, the international community is not an entity sufficiently stable or coherent that it can replace the sovereign state. The international community cannot provide a standing institution through which a polity can exercise its collective agency. It is the abstraction of the international community, I argue, that makes the exercise of power remote and unaccountable to a much greater degree than the sovereign state.

My argument proceeds as follows. First, I demonstrate how widely and rapidly this new doctrine of sovereignty of responsibility has been absorbed into international politics. I trace the origins of this doctrine to the failures of the 'new interventionism' of the 1990s.[6] While many suggest that the 'responsibility to protect' emerged in response to Southern resistance to the new interventionism, I examine and reject this thesis. I argue instead that the 'responsibility to protect' arose out of the incoherence of humanitarian intervention itself. I then discuss how the new doctrine sought to compensate for the weakness of humanitarian intervention by consolidating the newly elevated status of human rights. It did this by shifting the definition of sovereignty from autonomy to responsibility. Here, my argument shifts gears, moving from a historical argument about the doctrine's evolution to a logical examination of its implications. I conclude by explaining how subordinating the supremacy of state sovereignty to the higher authority of the international community undermines the project of making power more accountable, and restrains the exercise of political agency in international politics.

The responsibility to protect

Though it was not the first document to suggest the concept of 'sovereignty as responsibility', the Report of the International Commission on Intervention and State Sovereignty (ICISS), *The Responsibility to Protect* (2001), is most closely associated with this new doctrine. The Commission itself was the initiative of Canadian Foreign Minister Lloyd Axworthy, and included such luminaries as Michael Ignatieff, Ramesh Thakur (Senior Vice Rector of the UN University) and the former Australian Foreign Minister Gareth Evans.[7] Given the composition of the Commission, it is no surprise that the ICISS Report is an eloquent and nuanced document. The document has gained quick acceptance as a promising solution to the bitter 'clash of rights' of the 1990s. This clash pitted the rights of sovereign states against those claiming a 'right of intervention' to defend the human rights of individuals within states. The dust has settled on this battle, and the doctrine of sovereignty of responsibility securely holds the terrain. For example, its tenets have been seamlessly integrated into the report on UN reform by former UN Secretary-General Kofi Annan's High-level Panel on Threats, Challenges and Change.[8] It has also been welcomed by leading International Relations (IR) scholars, who were glad to have moved beyond what they saw as an increasingly sterile debate between the 'pluralists' who championed the rights of states, and 'solidarists' who elevated the human rights of individuals. [9]

On one level, the speed with which the doctrine has been accepted reflects its plain, commonsensical appeal. 'It is acknowledged', states the Report, 'that sovereignty implies a dual responsibility: externally – to respect the sovereignty of other states, and internally, to respect the dignity and basic rights of all the people within the state.'[10] Of course, states should be responsible to their people. Why else are they there, if not to serve their people? It is on this incontrovertible proposition that the remaining structure of the doctrine is built up. But if the reasonableness and innocuousness of the doctrine is its strength, it also begs the question of why the doctrine needs articulating with all the pomp of an international commission in the first place. Indeed, if the idea of responsible sovereigns was merely commonplace, the findings of the ICISS Report would belie the ambitions of the Commission, who have explicitly modelled their aims on the 1987 Brundtland Report. Published by the World Commission on Environment and Development in 1983, the Brundtland Report is renowned for the way in which it reconciled the previously opposed ideas of development and conservation. But if a conceptual tectonic shift on the scale of the Brundtland Report is needed, then it is reasonable to suppose that sovereignty and responsibility are not so compatible after all.[11] We shall return later in the chapter to this ambivalence towards the idea of sovereignty within the ICISS Report. But first let us examine how the Report emerged from the experiences of the post-Cold War era.

The failure of humanitarian intervention

The idea of 'sovereignty as responsibility' was first put forward by the Sudanese scholar and Special Representative of the UN Secretary-General for Internally

Displaced Persons, Francis M. Deng, principally in a publication by the Brookings Institute, *Sovereignty as Responsibility: Conflict Management in Africa* (1996). This document came after the exhaustion of the first burst of humanitarian intervention and peacekeeping that inaugurated the post-Cold War era.[12] Africa in particular was the site of two major 'defeats' for the new interventionism, following the ignominious withdrawal of UN forces from Somalia in 1993, and the failure to halt atrocities in Rwanda in 1994. Almost as rapidly as it had expanded, the new interventionism began to retreat. Whereas in 1993 over this number 70,000 UN peacekeepers were deployed globally, dropped precipitously to 20,000 in 1996.[13] The idea of 'sovereignty as responsibility' was thus explicitly designed as an antidote to what Deng and his co-authors identified as 'the isolationist tendency emerging within the major powers'.[14] The idea that the sovereign state had a key role to play in upholding human rights could be seen as a way of asking African states to pull themselves up by their own bootstraps, as it were, to compensate for the retrenchment of the major powers. Indeed, Deng *et al.* linked their new idea of sovereignty to the failure of the United States' Operation Restore Hope in Somalia:

> If militia leaders claim to be … custodians [of sovereignty], as happened in Somalia, then the responsibilities of state sovereignty logically fall upon them. The withdrawal of the international community from Somalia was a way of telling the people and their militia leaders that they were responsible for the sovereignty that they were so sensitive about.[15]

Deng envisioned the sovereign state as the primary guarantor of human rights and human security, whose authority and responsibilities were embedded within overlapping support structures composed of regional and continental organizations, which were then further interlinked with wider international structures.[16]

The doctrine got its second, more successful outing, with the publication of the ICISS Report in 2001. Superficially, the context seemed very different. The intervention preceding the Report was widely perceived to have been a dramatic success. The North Atlantic Treaty Organization's (NATO) 1999 bombing of Yugoslavia was seen as having halted an avalanche of atrocities in Kosovo. For the first time since the founding of the UN, a group of states had explicitly justified war in the name of protecting a minority within another state. But even this apparently successful humanitarian intervention was more ambivalent than initially appeared. It was controversial because NATO had acted without the authorization of the UN Security Council under Chapter VII of the UN Charter, required by international law for all use of force beyond self-defence.

Whatever moral legitimacy the NATO powers could claim, the war was significantly undermined by its illegality, which the then UN Secretary-General and the Independent International Commission on Kosovo both openly acknowledged. The latter especially focused on the need to close the gap between legality and legitimacy by clarifying the 'grey zone' of moral consensus.[17] More than this, there was a widespread discomfort about the potentially destabilizing consequences of eroding legal barriers to the use of force. The world's most powerful military alliance had launched a devastating campaign against a Third World state outside the framework of the UN Charter. This could not fail to stir unease among developing countries, who already felt constrained in a post-Cold War environment in which Western power was no longer balanced by Soviet power.[18] The Permanent Representative of India to the UN, Nirupam Sen, captured this pervasive sense of powerlessness when he said

> in recent years ... the developmental activities of the UN have diminished while the regulatory and punitive aspects have acquired prominence. The developing countries are the target of many of these actions which has led to a sense of alienation among the majority of UN Member States [. . .] The Security Council's legislative decisions and those on the use of force ... appear as an arbitrary and alien power: this is an alienation not of the individual or class but of countries.[19]

Indian diplomacy still bears the imprint of Third Worldist politics, with a principled attention to issues of self-determination, development and non-intervention – a politics that does not resonate as widely today as it once did. But the basic sentiment was affirmed shortly after the NATO war, when the foreign ministers of the Non-Aligned countries reaffirmed their long-standing opposition to humanitarian intervention at their April 2000 meeting, proclaiming: 'We reject this so-called "right" of humanitarian intervention, which has no legal basis in the UN Charter or in the general principles of international law.'[20]

This opposition did not go unnoticed. The ICISS Report identified the clash of rights thus: 'For some, the new interventions herald a new world in which human rights trumps state sovereignty; for others it ushers in a world in which big powers ride roughshod over the smaller ones, manipulating the rhetoric of ... human rights.'[21] Deng's solution, to 'contract out' responsibility for human rights beyond the major powers, seemed to square the circle. If all states were acknowledged to be the primary guarantors of human rights, this would allay fears of humanitarian imperialism. The grounds for this extension of responsibility could already be found in the provisions of the UN Charter and subsequent UN covenants. It could not be denied, after all, that since the end of empire, it was sovereign states that bore the responsibility to serve their peoples. The ICISS Report worked hard to meet Southern concerns, organizing roundtable discussions in Beijing, Cairo, Maputo, New Delhi, St Petersburg and Santiago. The Report appeared to provide a resounding affirmation of state sovereignty. First, states were explicitly charged with being 'the frontline defence of the rule of law'.[22] Second, the Report recognized that it is the citizens of a particular state who have the greatest interest in building peace, and who provide the best, ready-made means of ensuring state accountability.[23] Third, the Report affirmed a liberal defence of 'non-interference' because it guarantees diversity and autonomy, 'enabling societies to maintain the religious, ethnic, and civilizational differences that they cherish'.[24] Finally, the Report acknowledged that elevating interventionism in world politics can be gravely destabilizing, by encouraging oppositional forces within states deliberately to stoke conflict and goad the international community into intervening in their favour.[25]

Beyond a putative reaffirmation of state sovereignty, the Report also provided criticisms of humanitarian intervention. It noted that speaking about 'rights of intervention' elevates the stature of intervening states in inverse proportion to the true beneficiaries of intervention, namely, the victims of human rights abuses. The Report also observed that the focus on humanitarian intervention collapses the idea of 'human protection' into a single moment, ignoring preventive efforts before a military intervention, and the crucial tasks of post-conflict reconstruction. The Report conceded that even to speak of military intervention as humanitarian is problematic, because 'it loads the dice in favour of intervention before the argument has even begun, by tending to label and delegitimize dissent as anti-humanitarian'.[26] Thakur took this latter argument further, when he drew attention to the ethical repugnance of claiming that the NATO intervention was humanitarian, as this would mean that 'it must necessarily also have been humanitarian bombing'.[27] The Report also warned of the dangers of creating political dependence in post-conflict zones, eloquently arguing that 'international authorities must take care not to confiscate or monopolize political responsibility on the ground', and that 'local political competence' must be preserved and cultivated (for a critique of this 'bottom up approach' to conflict resolution, see Christopher Bickerton's chapter in this volume).[28]

It is incontrovertible, then, that the ICISS Report was alive to criticisms of humanitarian intervention. As Thakur, one of the Report's prime authors, notes, the language of altruism in humanitarianism simply cannot be taken at face value:

> 'Humanitarian intervention' conveys to most Western minds the idea that the principle underlying the intervention is not self-interested power politics but the disinterested one of protecting human life. It conjures up in many non-Western minds historical memories of the strong imposing their will on the weak in the name of spreading Christianity to the cultivation and promotion of human rights.[29]

Third World resistance?

On the face of it, the Report is trying to integrate Southern concerns in order to ensure that the consent of the majority of states can be harnessed to the project of 'human protection'. Jennifer Welsh argues that humanitarian intervention remained 'a controversial norm largely because of continued opposition from certain members of international society'.[30] The implication then, is that the Southern resistance halted the forward march of human rights. But how realistic is this assumption of Southern resistance to a new imperialism?

However vociferous the Southern opposition to so-called rights of intervention, the fact remains that Southern states' political strength is severely diminished in the post-Cold War era. The end of rivalry between the Soviet and capitalist blocs undermines much of the rationale for Southern political solidarity in a 'Third World' bloc. Nicholas Wheeler points out this lack of solidarity when seven non-NATO developing countries – Argentina, Brazil, Bahrain, Malaysia, Gabon and Gambia – voted down a Russian-sponsored UN resolution on 26 March 1999 that condemned NATO's illegal bombing of Yugoslavia.[31] The South's limited power is exemplified by the case of Yemen during the 1990–91 Gulf War. During the UN debates over how to respond to the Iraqi invasion of Kuwait, Yemen was the only country to voice concern about the 'extraordinary breadth' of Resolution 678, which authorized the US-led coalition to unleash its might against Iraq in the name of restoring 'international peace and security *in the area*' (emphasis added).[32] For daring to vote against this highly permissive resolution, the US punished Yemen by cutting $70 million in annual aid. A senior US diplomat reportedly told the Yemeni representative at the time, 'that was the most expensive no vote you ever cast'.[33] The only other country to vote against the resolution, Cuba, had already been besieged by US sanctions for many years.

If Yemen and Cuba are unrepresentative of the global South given their exceptional isolation, consider the global South's contribution to peacekeeping.[34] The common view in academia and among the Western public is that the majority of peacekeeping and intervention is carried out by Western powers. But the critical role that developing countries have played in trendsetting interventions of the post-Cold War era, which pushed against traditional understandings of sovereignty, is often overlooked (e.g. the roles played by Pakistani peacekeepers in the UN operation Somalia, and the role of Indian forces in Sierra Leone).[35] With a vast expansion of peacekeeping since the turn of the twenty-first century, it is largely Southern troops that have met the UN's appetite for manpower.[36] At the time of writing, South Asian peacekeepers are fighting a counter-insurgency campaign in the eastern Democratic Republic of Congo, armed with Chapter VII powers.[37] All of this suggests that developing countries' response to the 'new interventionism' is far more ambivalent and complex than the common misperception of 'resistance', as suggested in the ICISS Report.

The tug of war over the UN Charter

However ambivalent the Southern response to the 'new interventionism', some critical scholars have championed the sovereign rights of states by arguing that humanitarian intervention and 'sovereignty as responsibility' undermines both the spirit and the letter of the UN Charter.[38] Article 2 of the Charter defends the 'principle of the sovereign equality of all its Members', discourages 'the threat or use of force' against 'the territorial integrity or political independence of any state', and solidly affirms that 'Nothing contained in the present Charter shall authorize the UN to intervene in matters which are essentially within the domestic jurisdiction of any state' (the 'peace enforcement provisions' of Chapter VII notwithstanding). Simon Chesterman, for example, has argued that the increasingly flexible invocation of Chapter VII powers to meet ever-expanding 'threats to international peace and security' has substantially reduced the barriers to the use of force, thereby eroding the normative framework of the UN's collective security system.[39]

This is not a debate that I will rehearse here, partly for reasons of space, but more importantly because I believe this line of argument is ultimately futile. However well-intentioned the scholars are who defend the sovereign equality of states on the basis of the UN Charter, they cripple themselves by arguing through the Charter framework. Nicholas Wheeler, a key proponent of humanitarian intervention, argues that the

> [Security] Council's extension of its enforcement role to encompass the protection of human rights, far from subverting... 'The very purpose for which the Charter was written', is a long-awaited development that integrates the security and human rights dimensions of the UN Charter.[40]

Whereas waging war was once considered the prerogative of any sovereign, the Charter's limitation of the use of force did not eliminate the right to wage war as much as restrict it to the permanent members of the Security Council, the victors of the Second World War. Bardo Fassbender has argued that the restriction of the use of force does not impinge sovereignty, but in fact *constitutes* it. It is the restricted use of force, argues Fassbender, that allows so many sovereign states to survive as formal equals, despite substantive inequalities of power. What the sovereign equality of the UN Charter really means then, according to Fassbender, is equality before the law; that is, equality of law-*taking* rather than law-*making*.[41] In Fassbender's view, the Charter is effectively an international constitution that already established the parameters of sovereignty long before the era of the 'new interventionism'. Thus it is reasonable to shift the parameters of sovereignty to accommodate greater respect for human rights. The international community also has sufficient legal personality and purpose that 'it can set against the opinion and action of a recalcitrant state'.[42] The ICISS Report seems to affirm Fassbender's, not Chesterman's, view: 'the state *itself*, in signing the Charter, *accepts* the responsibilities of membership flowing from that signature' (emphasis added).[43]

Instead of playing this tug of war over the UN Charter, a more powerful line of attack is to analyse the internal incoherence of humanitarian intervention, and to take sovereignty as responsibility on its terms. This means interrogating its claims to be strengthening sovereignty and promulgating humanistic political responsibilities. Indeed, if sovereignty, self-determination and equality are of any value, they should be able to stand alone without the scaffolding provided by the victors of the Second World War.

The incoherence of humanitarian intervention

If we cannot explain the ICISS as a response to Third World power, then how are we to do so? The ICISS grows, I argue, out of the internal incoherence of the principles of humanitarian intervention, more than the strength of any external forces pushing back against it. This incoherence becomes apparent in those suggestions that try to give a substantive institutional form to humanitarian intervention. Ayoob, for example, has suggested that the clashes over humanitarian intervention could be ironed out by establishing a 'Humanitarian Council':

> A new more broadly based body...with adequate representation from all regions with rotating membership reflecting the diverse composition of the United Nations...Decisions to intervene...must require at least a three-quarters majority of the membership of the proposed Council.[44]

Sympathetically analyzing Ayoob's work, Welsh argues that the problems raised by human rights include questions such as who 'is it that decides when a state has not fulfilled its responsibilities and determines that only force can bring about its compliance...[W]ho should play the role of judge and enforcer in international society?'[45] The real problem is that, if your standard is a moral one, this question answers itself. In the context of gross and massive human rights violations, the question of *who* is authorized to act rapidly becomes secondary to the moral imperative to act. In practice, of course, this means that the powerful have the final word on whether intervention will occur or not because, by definition, they are the best placed to act. Indeed, it is this that troubles Chesterman about the new interventionism. Its logic, if not its explicit purpose, is to ratify war-making by the powerful.

The imperative of action during moral emergencies constantly strives to liberate itself from the letter of the law and the time-consuming fetters of forging a diplomatic consensus. As Wheeler points out in criticizing Ayoob's 'Humanitarian Council': 'changing the decision-making mechanism will not eliminate the challenge of balancing the moral imperative to use force to rescue imperilled humanity against the pragmatic question of whether force will succeed and do more good than harm'.[46] There is an urgency, a sharpened sense of immediacy, involved in responding to moral outrages that is lacking in the more prudential calculations of national interest and *realpolitik*. The national interest by definition requires a detached, long-term perspective (for a discussion of the national interest, see Alexander Gourevitch's chapter). As Zaki Laïdi says in relation to the conflict in former Yugoslavia, '[Western] societies claim that the urgency of problems forbids them from reflecting on a project, while in fact it is their total absence of perspective that makes them slaves of emergencies.'[47] The ICISS Report is cognizant of this, noting that 'human protection' requires the anticipation of human suffering if it is to be morally justifiable. If it did not include this anticipatory element, then moral action would be illegitimate by default, as it could only ever occur *post hoc*, after the crimes had already been committed.[48] But this element of anticipation introduces a further element of subjectivism and uncertainty to the entire apparatus of intervention – how are we to judge at which point humanitarian crisis should precipitate military intervention?

There is no source of objective, independent authority in international affairs that could allow us to know when a conflict has reached proportions that would render null and void the authority of the incumbent sovereign state (the International Committee of the Red Cross adamantly refused such a role when solicited by the ICISS).[49] But this leaves us with the same uncertain array of authorities (international organizations, non-governmental organizations, UN officials, etc.)[50] whose eclectic judgements were relied upon to justify humanitarian intervention throughout the 1990s – authorities whose claims often proved partial and unfounded, to say the least.[51] For these reasons, it is intrinsically difficult to construct an institution like the Humanitarian Council, or some other form of long-term alliance united around the principle of humanitarian intervention. This difficulty has little to do with Third World solidarity. Rather, it is this internal incoherence of humanitarian intervention that has made it so difficult to sustain its momentum. While humanitarian intervention can gnaw away at state sovereignty by claiming a higher ethical legitimacy, it cannot aspire to the role of political creation. The 'rights of intervention' cannot create viable institutions that draw their legitimacy from the universal consent of international society. The internal weakness of this fissiparous doctrine of intervention is given an external form in the 'resistance' of the South.

The suppression of sovereign supremacy

Faced with the difficulties of cementing humanitarian intervention in a positive, stabilized institutional form, the ICISS Report effectively sought to square the circle by borrowing Deng's idea of diffusing responsibility to sovereign states themselves. However, this still leaves the problem of how to ensure that there is no question of illegitimacy or illegality when an external agent pierces the sovereign state in defence of human rights. The only way to do this is to revoke the sovereign's claim to freedom from external interference. Humanitarian intervention is clearly not problematic if freedom from external interference is no longer considered a foundational right. As they cannot exist in the form of a Humanitarian Council, the rights of intervention can only sink roots by becoming legal. The legal barrier is removed by denying supremacy to the sovereign state. This denial means that there is no longer any clash of the rights of autonomy against the rights of intervention.

The ICISS Report claims that avoiding talk of the rights of intervention places the focus on the victim and not the intervener. But as David Chandler has argued, moving away from a clash of rights, in the interests of elevating the rights of the victim, is far more insidious than it looks. A clash of rights at least makes it clear that there is a political confrontation. When there are competing principles of legitimacy and political order at stake it is easier to clarify the coercion and resistance involved. Claiming a right to intervention places the onus of justification on the intervener to defend his violation of state sovereignty. But, under the cover of elevating the victim, the ICISS Report effectively shifts the onus of justification away from the intervening state to the state being intervened in. This is analogous to shifting from the presumption of innocence to the presumption of guilt. Any potential target of an intervention has to substantiate why it should remain free from external interference.[52] For all its talk of not extending the rights of war, the ICISS Report shifts the presumption in favour of military intervention.

Peter Gowan denounces the 'oleaginous jargon' of global governance, claiming that a new framework of global disciplinary regimes has recast sovereignty 'as a partial and conditional licence, granted by the "international community," which can be withdrawn should any state fail to meet the... standards laid down... by liberal governance'.[53] Gowan's polemic is stirring, but the supporters of 'liberal governance' are not embarrassed about using the same language. Paul Taylor for example, demands that sovereignty be viewed 'as a license from the international community to practice as an independent government in a particular territory'.[54] As Ignatieff makes clear, this is how things really are at the moment: 'in practice the exercise of state sovereignty is conditional, to some degree, on observance of proper human rights behaviour.'[55]

So what then does sovereignty as responsibility really mean? As I observed earlier in the chapter, the ICISS Report ricochets between two conceptions of sovereignty. Recall the words of the Report: 'state authorities are responsible for the functions of protecting the safety and lives of citizens and promotion of their welfare [and] the national political authorities are responsible to the citizens internally and to the international community through the UN'.[56] Does this mean that under sovereignty as autonomy, state authorities are *not* responsible for protecting their citizens' welfare? Not according to the Report:

> The defence of state sovereignty, by even its strongest supporters, does not include any claim of the unlimited power of a state to do what it wants to its own people. The Commission heard no such claim at any stage during our worldwide consultations.[57]

But if sovereignty as autonomy does not mean totalitarianism, then what is it precisely that the doctrine of 'sovereignty as responsibility' is counterposing itself to? The research essay on state sovereignty in the supplementary volume to the Report invokes a widely cited article that former UN Secretary-General Kofi Annan wrote for the *Economist*. In this article, Annan articulated 'two concepts of sovereignty'. For Annan, sovereignty remained the ordering principle of international affairs, but he stressed that it was 'the peoples' sovereignty rather than the sovereign's sovereignty'.[58]

Here Annan was promulgating a widely held misconception of sovereignty – that the claim to supremacy, the 'sovereign's sovereignty', is totalitarian. The problem with Annan's idea is that even with popular sovereignty the state has to take the form of an institution that is over and above society. Collective political interests can only be pursued among modern individuals if these individuals abstract themselves from their differing circumstances to become citizens in a common political process. It is the state that enshrines this common political process as a distinct, institutionalized sphere external to everyday life. The separation of the state from society provides the sovereign people with a barometer by which to observe whether their collective, general will is being carried out. Though the state is necessary to make possible the exercise of the general will, it is still the people, not the state, that is sovereign, *regardless of how despotic any individual state might be.* Popular sovereignty, therefore, is a mediated relationship between people and state; it *cannot* belong to the body of the people separate from the state. Without a state, modern society cannot conceive of itself as a polity.[59]

The idea of supremacy means that the sovereign is subject to no higher law, not because it is arbitrary and despotic, but because it has final authority. In popular sovereignty, this means that the people are supreme. The idea that finality lies with all members of society implies agency and responsibility for everyone in society even if the people's supremacy is indirect, by virtue of being mediated through the state. The institutionalization of public power over and above society means, of course, that the apparatus of the state can be used to tyrannize the society from which it springs. But, as Martin Loughlin notes, 'general will, although absolute, has nothing in common with the exercise of an arbitrary power'.[60] A *sovereign* state can *never* rule by pure coercion alone. For if a state cannot engage the subjectivity of its citizens, it will find it impossible to mobilize their collective power to meet internal and external challenges. James Heartfield, alluding to the USSR, writes:

> Those...regimes that have sought to crush freedom and supplant the democratic will have been marked not just by violent repression, but, perhaps more appallingly, by a slow degeneration, as the population withdraws consent, turns inward, refuses to engage and ceases to produce.[61]

In other words, pure tyranny is not sovereignty because, by definition, tyranny cannot draw upon the willed consent of its members. When consent dries up entirely, the result is not an impregnable, monolithic state sovereignty, as Kofi Annan and the ICISS seem to imagine. Rather, what you get is the USSR: a rotting state that eventually folds in on itself. The element of rationality in sovereignty has been stressed, quite consistently and coherently, by all social contract theorists. Rousseau, for instance, argues that the sovereign cannot act against the public interest 'because it is impossible for a body to wish to hurt all of its members'.[62] This also means that if the state acts irrationally, if it tyrannizes its own people, then it no longer expresses the general will. This does not mean, however, that the international community can legitimately sever the relationship between the state and the people. It must be up to the people to restore their own supremacy by recapturing the state. A despotic state does not completely nullify popular sovereignty. The moment that popular sovereignty truly becomes null and void is when the people do not assert their sovereignty by disciplining their state. This is what Michael Walzer means when he writes that:

> Self-determination and political freedom are not equivalent terms. The first is the more inclusive idea; it describes not only a particular institutional arrangement but also the process by which a community arrives at that

arrangement... A state is self-determining even if its citizens struggle and fail to establish free institutions, but it has been deprived of self-determination if such institutions are established by an intrusive neighbour.[63]

It is important not to confuse the external and the internal perspective here, as Kofi Annan does. From the external perspective of all other states, it is the state that embodies sovereignty, that sets up the 'no trespassing' sign around its jurisdiction. But it is the people behind the state who are substantively sovereign. The ICISS Report accepts that the state should be the instrument of the people; it certainly pays lip service to 'popular sovereignty'. But the deeper point is that a people without a state are not sovereign. There is no 'people's sovereignty', as Annan puts it, without a state, because then the people have no way of gauging and instantiating their collective will. The sovereign people cannot measure the extent of their rule if the 'no trespassing' sign is uprooted. It is in this sense that sovereignty not only implies but *guarantees* responsibility. That the sovereign is supreme, by virtue of drawing on the consent of all of society, is what ensures responsibility; the responsibility of every member of society, for society.

So where does all this leave us with regards to the 'responsibility to protect'? The fact that military intervention in the South meets with less resistance reflects the ebb of Third World nationalism, and the expansion of Western power in the absence of any countervailing Soviet power. The fact that the claim to supremacy embodied in sovereignty is mistaken for totalitarianism reflects less a simple logical error, so much as a disenchantment with the mass politics of the twentieth century. (These historical developments are covered in greater detail in James Heartfield's, Alexander Gourevitch's and Christopher Bickerton's chapters.) The fact that panels of eminent persons can set about redefining sovereignty in the space of under 100 pages, on the back of a series of elite consultations, indicates just how far sovereignty has been taken beyond the mass politics that once inspired it. The problem today, however, is that what is on offer in the 'responsibility to protect' is much less than the doctrine of sovereignty as autonomy that I have sketched out here.

In so far as sovereignty is the exercise of the general will, the idea of sovereigns being responsible to their citizens is merely tautologous. Insofar as sovereignty is accountable to external power, it means that the sovereign is evidently not supreme, and therefore, logically speaking, not sovereign. As David Chandler points out, the idea of a qualified or limited sovereignty is sophistry: 'a power which is "accountable" to another, external body clearly lacks sovereign authority'.[64] In the doctrine of sovereignty as autonomy, responsibility can only be grounded on the prior assumption of supremacy. It is obvious that if a person or agent does not hold supreme power, then they cannot be held ultimately responsible. Let us illustrate what we mean by this. It is considered perfectly legitimate if a group of citizens holds an elected minister to account for an error committed by his ministry, even if it is not the minister but a civil servant that is directly responsible for the mistake. It is in this sense that supremacy means not omniscient power, but responsibility. If it happens under the minister's watch, the minister is politically responsible. What is more, with the citizens treating him *as if* he were ultimately responsible, the minister is pressured to modify his behaviour to act more responsibly, in the expectation that his constituents will hold him to account once again in future.[65] People in a dictatorship obviously have little chance of holding ministers or civil servants to account. But the point I am making here is that the assumption of supremacy clarifies the exercise of political power. It means that people can be held responsible. As we have seen, the doctrine of sovereignty as responsibility believes itself to be suppressing totalitarian sovereignty in favour of popular sovereignty. But this is because it mistakes the claim to supremacy as totalitarian. In fact, the suppression of supremacy is the suppression of sovereignty itself. The idea of sovereignty being qualified by accountability to an external power means that it is not supreme, and therefore, *not accountable.*

If we pursue the example of the responsible minister further, what happens when the minister is not accountable just to the citizens, but to the international community as well? How is the minister to resolve such a clash of responsibilities? What happens when the democratic will of the people demands that the state oppose the international community? Ostensibly, the 'responsibility to protect' wins out, because its human rights content is presented as a set of absolute moral standards, rising above politics, and that no state can justifiably violate. Indeed, this is the only way the ICISS Report really deals with the possibility of conflicting priorities – by transforming a political conflict into a question of morality versus politics. For a state to side decisively with its domestic responsibilities would require it to make reference to a conception of sovereignty as autonomy, demanding independence from external interference. Yet on the terms of the ICISS, this can only be seen as a move towards tyranny rather than greater accountability. In the name of human rights, the doctrine of 'sovereignty as responsibility' pulls the state into orbit around the international community, away from its own populace. Perversely, the 'responsibility to protect' permits the state to regard its relationship with its own people as less central to its political legitimacy. Under the terms of 'sovereignty as responsibility', a state can downplay domestic demands in the interests of living up to its international duties. In other words, the 'responsibility to protect' easily translates into states becoming less responsible to their citizens.

But does this mean that the international community, or its representatives, are supreme in place of the sovereign? Hobbes famously characterized the sovereign as an 'artificial man', by which he meant the sovereign had to be a clearly identifiable agent to whom power was delegated, in order that society could clearly observe the exercise of its own will. The institutionalization of the general will in the form of public power means that it is recognizable, and therefore (potentially) accountable. Can this be said of the international community? The various military interventions since the end of the Cold War have been carried out by a plethora of agencies: UN peacekeeping forces cobbled together from disparate national armies, various regional organizations (NATO, the Economic Community of West African States, the Commonwealth of Independent States), and most notoriously of all, coalitions of the willing. Coalitions of the willing are the most extreme example of this instability of international agency, for coalitions of the willing are not stable organizations, but rather exhaust themselves in the process of acting.

None of these organizations, not even the UN, can establish itself as the stable representative of the international community, as a clear source of relatively autonomous power that could claim to represent the general will of humanity. Even the ICISS Report admits that human suffering might necessitate that 'concerned states' act outside the remit of the UN, as the NATO powers did over Kosovo.[66] Speculating in 1984 on the prospect of an era concerned with human rights, Hedley Bull reasoned, 'If unilateralism could be avoided and intervention was seen as expressing the collective will of the society of states, the harmony and stability of international society could be maintained.'[67] Clearly, by this measure, the military defence of human rights has failed to instantiate the collective will of international society. It has spectacularly failed to bind the society of states together. We need look no farther than the schism between France and the US over the invasion of Iraq in 2003 for evidence of this. If anything, 'sovereignty as responsibility' enables a more temperamental and arbitrary exercise of power, that is less easily identified as political, and less accountable.

For all these reasons, it is difficult to discern in the new interventionism the 'transition' that the ICISS Report hopes for, 'from a culture of sovereign impunity to a culture of national and international accountability'.[68] We have diffuse and overlapping moral duties, but little sense of clear political responsibility. Sovereign states are no longer supreme, but then neither is there an evident power that can claim to embody or represent the international community in the way the sovereign can claim to represent the general will. Welsh speculates that, '[p]erhaps, by taking on the viewpoint of the victim, those with the power and capability to intervene can finally balance the desire to resist evil against the dangers of succumbing to righteousness.'[69] But what is particularly appealing about victims is that they are weak and powerless by their very nature. Victims offer moral appeal to the righteous, as well as the bonus that, by definition, they cannot hold the righteous to account. Victims are, in short, a perfect license for the exercise of power.

Thus the question of agency is critical to this elevation of victim-centred foreign policy 'because', as Ayoob argues, 'those who define human rights and decree that they have been violated also decide when and where intervention to protect such rights should and must take place'.[70] In other words, since the *content* of human rights is decided independently of the *capacity* of the subjects of rights, this contradiction is resolved by yoking in the agency of external power. In Chandler's words, 'because the human subject is defined as being without autonomy [i.e., a victim], some external source has, of necessity, to be looked to.'[71] The inner logic of human rights tends to prise apart the subject and agent of rights. Power is exercised in the name of the victims of human rights abuses, but that power itself is so immeasurably distant and arbitrary that it cannot be held to account. It is here that the politics of 'sovereignty as responsibility' finally come out in the open. It is less an attempt to prise open weak states to imperialist influence as much a diffuse and halting attempt to limit open conflict between rights and interests. It takes the incomplete and incoherent exercise of power by shifting coalitions of states, and recasts it as a new international principle of ethical action. In all, it presents us with a constrained form of international politics in which the unaccountable exercise of power is coupled with the suppression of political conflict in the name of ethical responsibility.

Conclusion

In many ways, the doctrine of 'sovereignty as responsibility' exemplifies the state of affairs identified in the Introduction of this volume; namely, a world where we endure all the worst aspects of sovereignty and yet are denied most of its benefits. On the one hand, the doctrine reaffirms a world of (nominally) sovereign states, with all the political parochialism and uneven development that accompanies it. Yet on the other hand, the autonomy of these states is denied, as they are ultimately behest to a shimmering, remote international community. When a supreme power cannot be identified, political responsibility is diluted; the claims of the doctrine of responsibility are itself belied. In this, the doctrine of 'sovereignty as responsibility' is a mockery of a properly responsible politics. Of course, the autonomy of politics enshrined in state sovereignty is always buffeted by other forces – the wills of other powers, and not least the international economy. The content of sovereign supremacy shifts over time. But this does not make it meaningless. Nor can it be defined out of existence with no political or legal consequences. As Chris Brown argues, it is less 'the *fact* of autonomy which makes a difference' as much as 'the *claim* to autonomy symbolized by the terms "sovereign" and "sovereignty" ', because 'a world in which such claims are made has a different politics from a world in which such claims are not made'.[72]

In place of a proper ethics of responsibility, the 'responsibility to protect' offers odious ethical compromises. The ICISS notes that *realpolitik* would dictate that the permanent five members of the Security Council and other major powers are safe from intervention, as any attempt to coerce them may backfire into a wider conflagration.[73] But what all this means is that the strong have no responsibilities, except to police the weak. Both supporters and opponents of humanitarian intervention are quick to point to the hypocrisy of intervention happening in weak states, when there is not even a slender chance of intervention in Chechnya and Tibet, despite the gravity of human rights abuses there. On this 'question of double standards', the ICISS Report offers a lacklustre compromise: 'the reality that interventions may not be able to be mounted in every case... is no reason for them not to be mounted in any case'.[74]

No such ethical contortions would afflict a politics based on self-determination. Any oppressed group that organized itself sufficiently to fight for its own ends would be able to force recognition of its demands. In other words, political movements that successfully claim supreme power over a particular territory and population are, by definition, not dependent on the moral gaze of an outside power to decide who is fit to be rescued and who has to be consigned to oblivion. True responsibility involves claiming authorship for one's own position and status. The principle of the 'responsibility to protect' nullifies the political responsibility of individuals for their own societies, and masks power in the garb of morality. Arbitrary power cannot be held to account; and power that cannot be held to account is ultimately irresponsible power. In the words of J.S. Mill:

> Politics cannot be learned once and for all, from a textbook, or the instructions of a master. What we require to be taught . . . is to be our own teachers. It is a subject on which we have no masters; each must explore for himself, and exercise an independent judgement.[75]

It is precisely this responsibility for our own autonomy that the ICISS would deny us.

Notes

1 International Commission on Intervention and State Sovereignty (ICISS), *The Responsibility to Protect*, Ottawa: International Development Research Centre, 2001.
2 D. Chandler, '*The Responsibility to Protect?* Imposing the "Liberal Peace" ', *International Peacekeeping* 11:1, 2004, p.65.
3 M. Ayoob, 'Humanitarian Intervention and State Sovereignty', *The International Journal of Human Rights* 6:1, 2002, p.83.
4 Contrast this with the 'Constitutional Framework for Provisional Self-Government in Kosovo', discussed in Christopher Bickerton's chapter in this volume.
5 E.H. Carr, *The Twenty Years' Crisis 1919–1939: An Introduction to the Study of International Relations*, Basingstoke: Palgrave, 2001, p.147.
6 See chapter 4 of S. Chesterman, *Just War or Just Peace? Humanitarian Intervention and International Law*, New York: Oxford University Press, 2003.
7 For a full list of participants see ICISS, *Responsibility to Protect*, p.iii.
8 United Nations, *A More Secure World: Our Shared Responsibility*, New York: UN, 2004, pp.66–67.
9 See D. Chandler, *Constructing Global Civil Society: Morality and Power in International Relations*, Basingstoke: Palgrave, 2004, p.91.
10 ICISS, *Responsibility to Protect*, p.8.
11 R. Thakur, *The United Nations, Peace and Security*, Cambridge: Cambridge University Press, 2006, p.249.
12 Humanitarian intervention is generally defined as coercive interference within states in defence of human rights. But this is too restrictive, as it ignores a wide range of post-1988 peacekeeping operations that pushed against traditional ideas of sovereignty, even though they may have had the consent of the host state, for example, the UNTAC mission in Cambodia. For my purposes here I will define 'humanitarian intervention' as intervention with a humanitarian justification, with or without host state consent, in what would have previously been considered the internal affairs of a state. By the 'new interventionism', I mean the wider proclivity to intervene within states, including, but not restricted to, humanitarian interventions. While the debates around these definitional issues are not unimportant, we can bracket them for the sake of the analysis in this chapter. See further Chesterman, *Just War or Just Peace?*

13 A.J. Bellamy, P. Williams and S. Griffin, *Understanding Peacekeeping*, Cambridge: Polity Press, 2004, p.84.
14 F.M. Deng et al., *Sovereignty as Responsibility: Conflict Management in Africa*, Washington, DC: the Brookings Institution, p.xv.
15 Ibid., p.xvi.
16 See Chapters 5 and 6 in ibid.
17 D. Chandler, *Constructing*, p.103.
18 See further T. Weiss, D.P. Forsythe and R.A. Coate, *The United Nations and Changing World Politics*, Boulder, CO: Westview Press, 2004, pp.337–339.
19 N. Sen, 'Statement by Mr Nirupam Sen on the Report of IGH Level Panel on Threats, Challenges and Change at the Informal Meeting of the Plenary of the 59 session of the General Assembly', 27 January 2005. Online. Available at HTTP: <www.un.int/india/2005/ind1059.pdf> (accessed 30 May 2006).
20 Cited in N. Wheeler, 2004, 'The Humanitarian Responsibilities of Sovereignty: Explaining the Development of a New Norm of Military Intervention for Humanitarian Purposes in International Society', in J. Welsh (ed.), *Humanitarian Intervention and International Relations*, New York: Oxford University Press, 2004, p.46.
21 ICISS, *Responsibility to Protect*, p.2.
22 Ibid., p.14.
23 Ibid., p.17.
24 Ibid., p.31.
25 Ibid.
26 Ibid., p.16.
27 Thakur, *United Nations*, p.250.
28 ICISS, *Responsibility to Protect*, pp.44–45.
29 Thakur, *United Nations*, pp.250–251.
30 J. Welsh, 2004, 'Introduction', in Welsh, *Humanitarian Intervention*, p.2.
31 Wheeler, 'Humanitarian Responsibilities', p.44.
32 Chesterman, *Just War or Just Peace?*, p.164.
33 Cited in Chesterman, *Just War or Just Peace?*, p.181
34 See P. Cunliffe, 'Understanding Peacekeeping Contribution from the Developing World', paper presented at British International Studies Association annual convention, December 2006.
35 These operations were UNOSOM I and II (1992–95) and UNAMSIL (1999–2005), respectively.
36 M. Berdal, 'The UN After Iraq', *Survival* 46:3, 2004, pp.83–102.
37 See M. Lacey, 'U.N. Forces Using Tougher Tactics to Secure Peace', *New York Times*, 23 May 2005.
38 For example, Ayoob, 'Humanitarian Intervention' and Chesterman, *Just War or Just Peace?*
39 Chesterman, *Just War or Just Peace?*, p.128.
40 N. Wheeler, 'Decision Making and Procedures for Humanitarian Intervention', *The International Journal of Human Rights* 6:1, 2002, p.130.
41 B. Fassbender, 2003, 'Sovereignty and Constitutionalism in International Law', in N. Hart (ed.), *Sovereignty in Transition*, Hart Publishing, 2003, pp.124–131.
42 Ibid., p.130.
43 ICISS, *Responsibility to Protect*, p.13.
44 Ayoob, 'Humanitarian Intervention', pp.95–96.
45 J. Welsh, 2004, 'Taking Consequences Seriously: Objections to Humanitarian Intervention', in Welsh, *Humanitarian Intervention*, pp.66–67.
46 Wheeler, 'Decision Making', p.134.
47 Z. Laïdi, *A World Without Meaning: The Crisis of Meaning in International Politics*, trans. June Burnham and Jenny Coulon, London, New York: Routledge, 1998, p.11.
48 ICISS, *Responsibility to Protect*, p.33.

49 Ibid., pp.34–35.
50 Ibid., p.33.
51 See for example, J. Pilger, 'John Pilger Doesn't Buy the Sales Pitch of War Lovers', *New Statesman*, 27 March 2006.
52 D. Chandler, *Constructing*, p.90.
53 P. Gowan, 2003, 'The New Liberal Cosmopolitanism', in D. Archibugi (ed.), *Debating Cosmopolitics*, London: Verso, 2003, p.52.
54 P.G. Taylor, *International Organization in the Age of Globalization*, New York: Continuum, 2003, p.33.
55 M. Ignatieff, 2001, 'Human Rights as Politics and Idolatry', in A. Gutmann (ed.), *Human Rights as Politics and Idolatry*, Princeton, NJ: Princeton University Press, 2001, p.17.
56 ICISS, *Responsibility to Protect*, p.8.
57 Ibid.
58 K. Annan, 'Two Concepts of Sovereignty', *Economist*, 18 September 1999.
59 I. Hont, 'The Permanent Crisis of a Divided Mankind: "Contemporary Crisis of the Nation State" in Historical Perspective', *Political Studies* 42:SI, 1994, pp.185–186.
60 M. Loughlin, 'Ten Tenets of Sovereignty', in Hart, *Sovereignty in Transition*, p.73.
61 J. Heartfield, *The 'Death of the Subject' Explained*, Sheffield: Sheffield Hallam University Press, 2002, p.7.
62 J.J. Rousseau, *The Social Contract*, London: Penguin, 1968[1762], p.63.
63 M. Walzer, *Just and Unjust Wars: A Moral Argument with Historical Illustrations*, New York: Basic Books, 2000, p.87.
64 D. Chandler, *Constructing*, p.65.
65 I owe this example to Michael Savage.
66 ICISS, *Responsibility to Protect*, p.xiii.
67 Cited in A. Roberts, 2004, 'The United Nations and Humanitarian Intervention', in Welsh, *Humanitarian Intervention*, p.80.
68 ICISS, *Responsibility to Protect*, p.14.
69 Welsh, 'Consequences', p.183.
70 Ayoob, 'Humanitarian Intervention', p.81.
71 D. Chandler, *From Kosovo to Kabul: Human Rights and International Intervention*, London: Pluto Press, 2002, p.109.
72 C. Brown, *Sovereignty, Rights and Justice: International Political Theory Today*, Cambridge: Polity, 2003, p.5.
73 ICISS, *Responsibility to Protect*, p.37.
74 Ibid.
75 Cited in R. Jackson, *Classical and Modern Thought on International Relations: From Anarchy to Cosmopolis*, New York: Palgrave, 2005, p.157.

3 National insecurities

The new politics of the American national interest

Alexander Gourevitch

The national interest is the conceptual foundation of international relations. Its relation to sovereignty is at once intimate and straightforward. If the state's purpose is to protect its own society from external threats, then it must be sovereign. No higher authority can legitimately constrain the sovereign in its quest for self-preservation. Indeed, a state acts irresponsibly if it sacrifices its own interests to the obligations of international law, or to the temptations of universal morality.[1] To do so would be to place these goals above the obligations to the nation that it represents, thereby violating its contract with its people. The national interest is therefore a concept that justifies both the constitutional independence of the sovereign state, and implies a political relation binding the general will to the autonomy of the state. To pursue the national interest, the state must be independent not only from external obligations, but, in the words of George Kennan, also 'from the demands emanating from the "rough and tumble" of [its own] society'.[2]

The purpose of this chapter is to reassess this concept of the national interest through an analysis of American foreign policy. In contrast to Europe's 'postnational constellation',[3] in which nation-states hand their sovereignty over to the European Union (see James Heartfield's chapter in this volume), the USA seems to continue to act in more narrow, national terms. The popular conception that the US is the last remaining sovereign state with national interests makes it an ideal case study for the concept of the national interest in general. Recent thinkers have produced penetrating critiques of the national interest, amply demonstrating that it is a non-neutral, subjective concept tightly linked to a narrow vision of politics.[4] However, as criticisms of the concept in general, or American foreign policy in particular, these authors have taken aim at a straw-man. I want to suggest here that post-Cold War American diplomacy reveals less the perils of a rapacious, egotistical national interest, and more the problems with post-national interest diplomacy, for which we still lack adequate conceptual categories. Beginning the task of forging these categories is part of the purpose of this chapter.

To substantiate this claim, I begin with two predominant debates about post-Cold War American foreign policy. The first is whether the US is or should be 'unilateral' or 'multilateral' in its diplomacy. The second is how and why the end of the Cold War has made American national interests difficult to identify. An examination of these arguments produces a provisional claim that US foreign policy has an *ad hoc*, short-term character, in which longer term strategic concerns play little or no part. The chapter then proceeds to pick apart the inner logic of the national interest. I look particularly at the constitutive function of foreign policy and its relation to domestic politics. I then move on to sketch out the historical process by which internal dynamics propelled the American state into the international sphere, the effect of which was to make the US exceptionally dependent upon foreign policy for its domestic political system. Over time, the political conflicts that drove US foreign policy, and gave it a strategic function, have fallen away, resulting in a tumultuous, post-national interest foreign policy through which the US has tried to renegotiate the boundaries between national and international politics. The dangers of this foreign policy lie less in the insidiousness of its long-term objectives, than in the way it closes off the very possibility of debating and politicizing these broader aims.

Unilateralist turn?

It is commonly argued that America has become unilateralist, concerned only with its own interests.[5] This trend has been most visible under President George W. Bush, who rejected the need for UN Security Council authorization to invade Iraq, undermined the International Criminal Court, withdrew from the Kyoto Protocol, violated the Geneva Conventions, and has appeared to shirk the need for international cooperation generally.[6] This vigorous 'unilateral' turn compels some to consider Bush a radical departure from the norm: 'the prime author of the huge growth in international law since 1945 has, in effect, suddenly chosen to opt out'.[7] His policies have even earned the name 'the new sovereigntism'.[8] Yet the trend predates Bush. President Bill Clinton controversially bypassed the UN Security Council in 1999, when he bombed Yugoslavia. This illegal war capped a decade of minor and major US decisions that undermined international legal norms and institutions,[9] leading two prominent international lawyers to ask in 1999, 'Has US Power Destroyed the UN?'.[10]

The US has also developed permissive foreign policy doctrines. Clinton embraced humanitarian intervention, which constantly pushes back the boundaries of international legality in the name of the higher, moral legitimacy of human rights.[11] In contrast to conventional self-defence doctrines, the Bush doctrine of 'pre-emptive war' does not even require an immediate, visible threat to American security, substituting perceptions of threat for recognized international standards.[12] Beyond these formal changes, the US has also actively undermined its broader, informal system of alliances. The overthrow of Saddam Hussein is only the most recent example of the betrayal of an authoritarian ally, who once would have been seen as instrumental in cementing US power in the international order. Other examples of such pro-US strongmen, whom the US turned on, include: Manuel Noriega (Panama–1989), Samuel Doe (Liberia–1990), Raoul Cedras (Haiti–1994), Mobutu Sese-Seko (Congo–1997) and Haji Mohammad Suharto (Indonesia–1999).[13] The US has also frequently alienated its fellow industrialized powers. Japan and Germany financed the first Gulf War, but refused to finance the second; France had already withdrawn from policing no-fly zones over Iraq in 1997, before openly challenging the American war drive against Iraq in the Security Council in 2003.

Yet this unilateralist turn is only one side of the story. The fact is, America no longer fights its wars alone. The last military intervention the US launched alone was its 1989 invasion of Panama. Though the US is the only military power in the world capable of independently launching operations in any theatre, and formally maintains the ability to fight two major theatre wars simultaneously,[14] every military campaign following the invasion of Panama has been launched in a multilateral context, either under an established organization (the UN or NATO) or via informal coalitions. This applies even to military interventions in 'America's backyard', the Caribbean – historically, a region in which America has not brooked the exercise of any other state's military power. Yet both the 1994 and the 2003 interventions in Haiti were launched via coalitions of the willing with the backing of the UN, and were transformed into UN peacekeeping operations.[15] Even as the US 'unilaterally' invaded Iraq, it spearheaded a multilateral approach to negotiations over North Korea's nuclear weapons programme. North Korea initially demanded bilateral negotiations, and other regional powers were reluctant to get involved in region-wide diplomacy, but the US *insisted* upon and achieved six-way negotiations that included China, Japan, South Korea and Russia along with North Korea and the US.[16] Even with regard to Iraq, the US sought out approval from the UN, rather than simply invading at will.[17] The point I am making is a general one. Although the US did establish virtually all the formal institutions of the post-1945 international order, it has never consistently followed the letter of international norms and procedures. 'The special prerogatives enjoyed by the US ... within the post-war institutional order were many' including waivers, extra-legal interventions, weighted voting rights, as well as an informal deference by other powers towards American leadership.[18] Such were the benefits of the *Pax Americana*. In short, the US has always pursued a combination of 'unilateral' and 'multilateral' policies in the international sphere, both in the past and in the present.

Thus, counter-posing unilateralism and multilateralism emphasizes a formal distinction between different kinds of cooperation, or attitudes towards international law, and fails to capture what is distinctive about US foreign policy today. The change in the exercise of American power lies at a deeper level. A closer look at recent foreign policy reveals that American decisions reflect a fore-shortened time horizon, in which immediate concerns crowd out the kind of long-term, prudential considerations normally associated with national interest politics. For example, Franklin D. Roosevelt began planning the reconstruction of Germany as early as 1941, and created the Bretton Woods institutions in July 1944, a full year before the war was over.[19] George W. Bush appears not to have planned reconstruction at all. At the same time, the North Korea negotiations, while cooperative in character, also have no enduring quality. The six-country coalition is cobbled together under no institutional auspices, for the single purpose of dealing with a specific problem, but not for the purpose of developing any broader strategic alliance. While one policy (Iraq) is considered unilateral, and the other (North Korea) multilateral, each is discrete and exceptional, determined almost entirely by the contingencies of the issue itself, rather than mediating any broader concerns.

Moment to moment decisions are a recurring pattern in post-Cold War foreign policy. Each 'coalition of the willing' of the 1990s was brought together for that event only, sometimes nominally under the auspices of an international organization, like the UN (Somalia) or NATO (Kosovo), but not always (Haiti). None indicated the development of a new, stable form of cooperation, nor institutionalized a new norm or interest, tying together disparate decisions. In fact, in each of its major foreign policy initiatives of the 1990s, the US actively avoided establishing a new precedent for international intervention and organization, preferring instead to emphasize their exceptional character.[20] Rather than a self-confident master of the international environment, the US is unclear about what its foreign-policy aims are. As the primary constituent power of the post-1945 world order, US hegemony was mediated during the Cold War through international institutions and alliance systems, balanced against unilateral prerogatives, which were justified in the interests of the stability of the overall system. This was a sign of strength, not just in the sense of brute power, but also of relative clarity about the general interests that could ground lasting institutions. The mark of a sovereign pursuing its interests is not just reflected in breaking the law, but also in making it in concert with others.

Today, US political power leans more toward exceptionalism, but in a form that is not counterbalanced or justified by reference to maintaining a wider multilateral order. There is, to be sure a certain élan and freedom in being able to respond to events on a more *ad hoc*, case-by-case basis without reference to any wider framework or global order. Zaki Laïdi describes the new dynamic of political power, shorn of the need to uphold a wider framework or ideological vision:

> Power – understood in its widest sense – is conceived and experienced less and less as a process of taking over responsibilities, and more as a *game of avoidance*: avoidance of collective engagement by individuals, ... avoidance of planetary responsibilities by states.[21]

The 'game of avoidance' is superficially liberating. One is unbound by commitments to specific programmes or accountability to a concrete people; the US is free to pick and choose its engagements. However, as Laïdi further observes, this freedom comes at a cost. It is offset by a politics of crisis, which imprisons politics in the present: 'the nature of immediacy and urgency is to asphyxiate every day a little more of [politicians'] political imagination, their ability to set out a path, a way, a project.'[22] A quasi-permanent state of exception[23] is maintained not because it is the best way of pursuing US interests, but because it is the only way to act in the absence of any orienting, long-term interests. For all the gravitas with which US administrations have tried to endow their post-Cold War foreign policies, the result has been not a 'high politics', but the attenuation of politics in favour of the crisis-oriented criteria of efficacy, and a fluid diplomacy whose actions are judged according to their immediate effects or intentions.

Beyond the Cold War: after the national interest?

It is a widely expressed concern that post-Cold War American diplomacy is not guided by a consistent strategic orientation. In 1992, a Clinton advisor said, 'We have a foreign policy today in the shape of a doughnut – lots of peripheral interests but nothing at the centre.'[24] Stephen Del Rosso Jr, a liberal foreign policy insider, observed that Clinton's foreign policy was 'largely devoid of any coherent, overarching framework'.[25] More recently, realist Andrew Bacevich has argued that President Bush 'acts apart from calculations of power and self-interest',[26] while liberal John Ikenberry notes that Bush's foreign policy has been curiously 'silent on the full range of global challenges and opportunities that America faces', such as the rise of China, which would, one would think, be considered strategically important.[27] Yet only a few decades earlier, the national interest seemed self-evident, to the point that the problem was not finding it so much as straying from it, leading George Kennan to say '[we should] have the modesty to admit that our own national interest is all that we are capable of knowing and understanding'.[28]

On all accounts, the end of the Cold War is to blame for this disorientation. But the significance of the Cold War is differently interpreted. For some, the disappearance of a common enemy has undermined the state's ability to discipline partial interests, pulling the US in a number of disparate and disorganized directions.[29] On this account, the US possesses national interests, but has consistently been tempted away from them by moral ideals, narrow interests (the oil lobby the Israel lobby or neoconservatives), or the promise of globalization.[30] A different possibility is that the end of the Cold War has produced not a distraction from but the withering away of national interests. Consider the following statements:

> one's enemies...help define one's 'national interest'... Without such enemies, one flounders amidst a plenitude of rather trivial, or at least marginal, options.
>
> (Irving Kristol 1990)[31]

> while during the Cold War 'there was little disagreement about what was ultimately meant by security' within the establishment, post-Cold War policymakers were caught between 'scores of competing paradigms or quasi-paradigms'.
>
> (Stephen Del Rosso Jr 1995)[32]

> From the start, Americans have constructed their creedal identity in contrast to an undesirable 'other.'.... If there is no evil empire out there threatening those principles, what indeed does it mean to be an American, and what becomes of American national interests?
>
> (Samuel Huntington 1997)[33]

The United States has found it exceedingly difficult to define its 'national interests' in the absence of Soviet power.

(Condoleezza Rice 2000)[34]

On these accounts, the collapse of the USSR removes the fundamental object of national security, undermining the very possibility of identifying national interests. One progressive response is to embrace the new flexibility: ' "making history" in the new era is a matter not merely of defending the national interest but of defining it'.[35] It allows for infusing the concept of national interest with a new, more moral content. As Jessica Mathews argues, national security should now include the 'competing notion of human security' (see Tara McCormack's chapter in this volume).[36] The neoconservative response is, similarly, to sideline power-political considerations in favour of using foreign policy for the sake of moral and civic renewal. William Kristol and Robert Kagan argue that 'the remoralization of America at home ultimately requires the remoralization of American foreign policy'.[37] A new enemy must be found to replace the old, and reconstitute a sense of national purpose.

Yet whether they interpret the end of the Cold War as a distraction or as an opportunity, these various arguments cannot fully account for the significance of the collapse of the USSR. It is not the removal of an external enemy alone that throws into confusion American national interests. After all, as I will show presently, the US pursued national interests well before the Soviet Union came into existence, so its collapse alone cannot serve as an explanation. Rather, the end of the Cold War is a moment in a historical process in which political contestation itself declines. What is lost in the assessments of the Cold War is this deeper historical change, in part because most understandings of the national interest fail to appreciate the centrality of domestic political conflict in defining the national interest. The logical priority of the domestic sphere is, in turn, often overlooked due to a historical change: the increasingly constitutive role of foreign policy in American politics during the twentieth century. The following two sections seek to address the logical and the historical point.

The conservatism of national interests: the logical priority of domestic politics

The conventional understanding of national interest is that it flows from the survival imperative that is intrinsic in the anarchical structure of international relations. Recent scholarship has drawn attention to the contingent character of these 'pre-given' interests, and the way the national interest functions as a political concept, policing the boundaries between the domestic and international spheres. At the most abstract level, it is only with the historically specific separation of social power into economic and political spheres (property and sovereignty), that general interests take an abstract form, suspended above all particular interests. That is to say, the security and stability of social arrangements based on the free competition of private interests can only be ensured by an autonomous state enforcing rules and managing conflicts, and separated from the realm of private interaction. This boundary between the state and society is not given in the nature of things but emerged historically, and must be constantly managed and reproduced.[38]

The idea of the national interest logically presents foreign policy as a matter of sheer survival, and therefore beyond political dispute. The only possible debates are over prudential calculations of power, and these require specialized knowledge of state experts, insulated from social disagreement and political demands. While presented in the language of objectivity or 'realism', this is an ideological position. The national interest can only be seen as neutral and objective if we presuppose that there is a given consensus on fundamentals. But this is not a valid assumption. For example, in 1812, while Britain was burning its way to the capitol in Washington DC, the American states did not band together to defend their national-state against a common enemy. Rather, the northern states formed a separate faction, welcoming the British in, and calling for secession from the Union.[39] It is more accurate to say that the pursuit of a national interest has a constitutive function. 'By telling us what to fear', the state attempts to define 'who "we" are'.[40] The act of identifying a threat logically presupposes agreement, but in practice takes sides in conflicts over what the general interest is. As Barry Buzan notes, this contest over the national interest revolves not just around immediate material questions of physical and institutional survival, but also around the more abstract matter of a 'distinctive idea of some sort which lies at the heart of the state's political identity', such as nationalism or socialism. Buzan's 'idea of the state' points to the way the national interest refers conceptually to a political project, and that the pursuit of the national interest engages with basic questions of the political order.[41] Therefore, despite (indeed because of) its claim to objectivity and generality, the national interest is an inherently political, partisan concept.

Moreover, in giving priority to international politics, the idea of the national interest imposes limits on domestic politics. Most obviously, the national interest raises the stakes, as dissidents can be recast as allies of foreign enemies. That is to say, the choice of foreign policy objectives in the name of national interest always mediates a broader, political conflict over what it is that must be preserved. In other words, the national interests does not simply protect a given domestic order from external threats – it also help to produce and maintain this domestic order. It does so symbolically, through the creation of a national identity and a defence of a particular set of ideas, and materially, in the decision to seek out certain economic opportunities and not others, or to support some political movements and not others.

It should not be said that because foreign policy plays this constitutive role, the choice of enemies is therefore arbitrary. Rather, the idea of the national interest is dependent upon domestic conflict. For it is only when the fundamental organizing institutions of society are challenged that the question of the national interest poses itself in a consistent way. It is only in the face of such a challenge that the preservation of existing political and social institutions requires the coercive power of the state to separate itself from particular interests, and guarantee the wider interests of the social order as a whole. Therefore, if foreign policy is constitutive of the domestic order, domestic politics is nonetheless logically prior. There *are* conditions in which the state really does pursue a national interest, but this interest is not necessarily a neutral, common objective. It always has a conservative cast and purpose. The American understanding of national security expresses this political dimension clearly: national security is '*preserving* the United States as a free nation, with its fundamental institutions and values intact' (emphasis added).[42]

That national interests constitute the domestic order but are in turn constituted by it appears at first sight as a tautology. But this would be mistaken; rather the reciprocal relation between national interests and domestic order allows us to conceptually approach the fact that international and domestic politics are internally related. The precise boundary between the two spheres shifts over time according to the changing dynamics of domestic conflict and international relations. Keeping a view of the logical priority of domestic politics helps us answer the earlier question: why do American national interests seem to be so difficult to specify? Why did this difficulty emerge with the end of the Cold War, and produce a new, crisis-oriented foreign policy? If the national interest is in preserving existing institutions, what this requires at any given moment, at the domestic and international level, can only be answered historically.

Passages within the national interest: from conflicts of interest to ideological conflict

In 1951, Hans Morgenthau wrote a polemic entitled *In Defense of the National Interest* in which he objected to the shift away from the narrow conception of national interests in favour of a more overtly ideological one. Morgenthau argued 'a generation of Americans must shed the illusions of its fathers and grandfathers and relearn the great principles of statecraft which guided the republic in the first decade and – in moralistic disguise – in the first century of its existence.'[43] Morgenthau mistakenly took the development of ideological appeals of anti-communism to be the sign of an un-strategic reorientation in American foreign policy. In fact, it was a highly strategic response to the rise of democratic movements in the late nineteenth and early twentieth centuries, which forced a renegotiation of state power.

After the Civil War (1861–65) established decisively the sovereignty of the national state against the secessionist claims of the South, the US experienced a period of internal development during which 'both political parties were agreed' that the national interest was equivalent to commercial expansion.[44] This foreign policy consensus was 'asserted as axioms, apparently regarded as so obvious as to call for no demonstration'.[45] However, the intense industrialization which this commercial expansion facilitated produced its own contradictions. Working class movements and agrarian populists began making democratic demands, even as burgeoning financial, industrial and agricultural interests made competing claims for state favours. To preserve domestic institutions the state now had to take on a more activist role than merely securing domestic law and order. As Charles Beard observes, to maintain itself in this new era, the state 'must be active, must take the initiative, must encourage industrialists to seek foreign markets, must lend official support to every kind of . . . business abroad'.[46]

The emergence of American imperialism saw a renegotiation of the relationship between the state and society. The US state was forced to play an increasingly direct role in managing the conflict of social interests. But this more intimate involvement in society in turn forced the state to flag up its autonomy from society and its need to plan actively for the future of society as a whole. As Beard notes, in this period

> political institutions and practices become inextricably involved in private institutions and practices until it is impossible to tell where one begins and another ends, whether economic forces outside the Government are driving it or political forces within the Government are stirring up and enlisting business support for foreign policies.[47]

In foreign affairs, this meant the national economy became more dependent upon political involvement in the world economy. The voracious demands of American capitalism pushed America outwards into the world. For this reason, by the early decades of the twentieth century, parts of the government were already employing a 'broad conception of defense as *the protection and promotion of world-wide American interests*'.[48] National self-preservation was no longer limited to the territorial boundaries of the United States of America.[49] As a consequence, foreign policy became an increasingly political issue, in the sense that American diplomacy played a more significant role in determining the outcome of domestic conflicts of interest.

The rise of class conflict in the US gradually called into question the imperialist consensus, first with the anti-imperial candidacy of William Jennings Bryan in 1896, and coming to a head with the First World War. The common misperception that Wilson was a naïve, starry-eyed idealist overlooks that Wilson's 'idealism' was a hard-headed response to new political realities after the First World War. Europe's descent into barbarism and the rise of revolutionary movements alerted Wilson to the dangers of the competitive struggle between nations. According to Wilson, as domestic class conflict intensified, and foreign affairs were more openly criticized by popular movements, a pure and openly 'interest-based' diplomacy was untenable and quite possibly dangerous. As society began to polarize politically, the state had to maintain its integrity by avoiding becoming 'abject servants of capital and labour' and transcending the 'lurching from one political extreme to another'.[50] Wilson 'drafted the Fourteen Points in full awareness of the Allied crisis' and therefore 'combined his war message with a summons to a crusade for democracy'.[51] In the face of democratic movements at home and revolution abroad, the US had to recast itself as a democratic power, and it did so through its foreign policy.[52]

The foray into idealism was in this sense a strategic, calculated response to far more radical demands emanating from within American society, and which required a reinterpretation of American interests.[53] That Wilson's 'idealism' was motivated by security fears is most clearly seen in the fact that, at the very moment when he was drawing up plans for exporting democracy to Europe, his administration was engaged in landmark pieces of domestic repression, including anti-union violence, suppressing freedom of speech and the famous detention and expulsion of immigrants during the Palmer Raids, prefiguring subsequent 'Red Scares' throughout the twentieth century.[54] Bringing idealism to the national interest through calls to spread democracy abroad facilitated the vigorous pursuit of domestic repression. Wilson's innovation, then, was to defuse class conflict by sublimating it through foreign policy, all the while strengthening state power. This displacement meant that foreign policy gradually moved to the centre of political debate. Theories of the national interest now came into being to defend the autonomy of statesmen. As E.H. Carr notes, 'the popularization of international politics...heralded the birth of a new science' of the national interest.[55] The theoretical attempt to defend the objectivity of the national interest was, in this context, a reaction against the democratization of foreign policy, which called into question those diplomatic orientations that once had been simply given in practice. The new science of national interest was an effort to recast the autonomy of the state as something given by necessity, and therefore not amenable to popular demands.

Throughout the Second World War, 'the major source of insecurity [was] the possibility of domestic class conflict'.[56] Every policy decision was forced to confront how it related to this broad political struggle, impelling American statesmen to take a longer term view. As the US faced a prostrate post-war Europe, it therefore decided to erect a series of institutions that cemented American economic and political domination: the United Nations, International Monetary Fund, World Bank, North Atlantic Treaty Organization, among others. Hegemonic stability theorists such as Robert Gilpin and Stephen Krasner, have suggested that the US bore the costs of providing the 'public goods' of international institutions because it received greater private economic benefits.[57] But this is too simplistic. It was not just that domestic stability rested on international economic expansion, but that the international arena was the terrain on which sublimated political battles were fought. The international institutional architecture existed to manage and prove the vitality of liberal capitalism against communism. It was at this moment that the American state dramatically reorganized itself around international affairs. Under the auspices of the Cold War, liberal President Harry Truman used initiatives such as the Executive Order 9835 and the Communist Control Act, each purging leftists from government offices, to create a lasting national security state.

The war in Vietnam was traumatic precisely because the management of domestic affairs had come to depend so heavily on the projection of American power abroad. The stagnation of the world economy by the late 1960s had already undermined the politics of growth and the vitality of capitalism, while defeat in Vietnam called into question the moral and political authority of capitalism's global defender. However, the revival of political contestation at home produced a number of contradictory tendencies. On the one hand, there was a revival of challenges to the status quo – labour militancy, anti-imperial and civil rights movements. These potential threats to liberal capitalism remained active through the Reagan years. The move away from détente to the second Cold War of the 1980s, marked a domestic counter-offensive against the social movements of the 1960s, as much as an international counter-offensive against Third World revolution. Reagan's use of anti-communist rhetoric to justify firing nearly 13,000 striking air traffic controllers and jailing their leaders in 1981, is a landmark moment in the disciplining of the organized labour movement in the US, which Reagan understood even then. In one report from the time, the strikers 'thought they were involved in a labour-management dispute, the President saw their strike as an affront to law and order and as something more'.[58]

But the momentum of the anti-Vietnam war movement dissipated, particularly as the anti-war activists failed to mobilize popular working class discontent with the war.[59] The gap between organized labour and the new social movements continued, the latter especially liable to fragmentation due to their eclectic, decentralized agenda (see David Chandler's chapter in this volume). Others concluded that 'politics itself was an empty charade'.[60] By the early 1970s, 'even as protest against the "establishment" seemed to reach new heights, the foundation of collective action on the left was crumbling'.[61] The failure of the new social movements and counter-culture signalled the beginning of an epochal retreat from politics. This transformation of domestic politics is the key to understanding the post-Cold War reorientation of American foreign policy. While the dominant trend through the 1980s remained one of a dialectic between right and left, this political axis weakened, and the impact of public withdrawal from politics became increasingly evident. Despite the formal inclusion of broader swaths of the population in the electoral process off the back of the 1960s civil rights movement, voting still declined,[62] and parties found it difficult to organize disenchanted and single-issue voters into a set of coherent interests amenable to clear representation:

> Those aroused by the new issues found the existing major parties to be indecisive and unresponsive on these matters, even to a large extent irrelevant. Public opinion polls showed that more and more voters were rejecting both parties, calling themselves independents. Split-ticket voting increased, and single-issue groups rose and flourished as the parties declined.[63]

As the fabric of political parties unravelled, the President found his foreign policy autonomy increasingly compromised. On foreign policy 'congressional bipartisanship eroded significantly from pre-Vietnam levels'.[64] Congress rapidly expanded its involvement in foreign affairs:

> Whereas it was a rare Senator before Vietnam who had a foreign policy specialist, now almost all did, as did a growing number of House members...[and] the Senate Foreign Relations staff went from twenty-five in 1960, to thirty-one in 1970, to sixty-two in 1975, and the House Foreign Affairs Committee staff jumped from fourteen to twenty-one and then to fifty-four over the same period.[65]

At the time, this extension of Congress into international affairs was understood as increased democratic control, via Congressional oversight. Yet it was also a product of the stagnation of domestic party politics. With the weakening of party ties, Congressional representatives began to style themselves as little presidents. While at the height of the Cold War 'many members of Congress seemed to relish their ignorance of foreign policy as reflection of their trust in presidential judgment', the post-Vietnam era produced a 'new type of legislator – the bona fide foreign policy expert – who, by total immersion in a necessarily narrow range of issues...could often mount damaging challenges to executive positions...'.[66] In other words, if the increasing interest of Congress in foreign affairs signalled a democratic interest in checking executive power on the one hand, on the other it also signalled a reorientation away from local constituent concerns, and a corresponding attenuation of the relation between the people and their representatives. In elevating their own authority in relation to that of the president in world affairs, the new chieftains of foreign policy in Congress took advantage of the fact that America's global leadership had suffused the entire vocabulary of American politics by the late twentieth century. Even as the waning of the left removed part of the original rationale for this emphasis on international affairs, foreign policy came to acquire a new valence.

The weakening of political parties has also lead to a more highly personalized and isolated presidency. As Theodore Lowi noted in his classic *The Personal Presidency* (1986), 'the vacuum left by the parties has been filled by what have come to be called the "special-issue groups" and by the masses'.[67] The weakening of parties places greater burden on presidents to rule. Yet they find themselves unable to act decisively because parties only weakly play the mediating, constituent function necessary for building support for significant political projects. By contrast, foreign affairs therefore provide greater room to exercise the qualities of leadership. According to Lowi, this leads presidents to escalate even the most trivial threats so they acquire greater significance:

> Even where a low-key definition of our national interest might justify a direct involvement with a country or its internal conflicts, that ordinary interest does not seem to be sufficient for maintaining the president's popular support. It has to be pushed up at least one step on the ladder of escalation.[68]

Lowi was speaking about Carter and Reagan, for whom the national interest still had some meaning – a general threat to America's fundamental institutions could still be perceived, even if it had already receded. What is important in Lowi's observation, however, is the identification of a trend. The use of foreign policy to establish the moral authority of the presidency, in the absence of a cohering national interest, has elevated the ever-present symbolic and rhetorical dimensions of foreign policy. The invocation of interest has become increasingly metaphorical. Instead of sublimating a protracted political conflict between opposing social forces, the invocation of interest struggles to resolve a different kind of crisis of political legitimacy.

The end of the Cold War revisited

The collapse of the USSR was a world-historical event because it removed the practical force in world affairs that at least claimed to represent a challenge to capitalist society's basic institutions. The end of the USSR removed the animating rationale not only of US foreign policy, but also of American politics, which had come to be built on the idea of American global leadership. The collapse of the USSR further helped to open up major markets in the developing world, with very little direct political pressure from the American state, thereby helping to attenuate the fluctuations of the boom-and-bust economic cycle that had haunted the twentieth century.[69] At the same time, the exhaustion of traditional party politics became especially pronounced. In the first post-Cold War presidential election, an independent candidate, Ross Perot, achieved 19 per cent of the popular vote, even as voting hit historic lows (a 10 per cent drop from the 1970s).[70] Party membership decreased, and apathy became a pronounced political issue.[71] In an essay with the subheading 'Cynicism and Withdrawal from Public Life', two influential foreign policy intellectuals wrote about a 'breakdown in trust in our public institutions'.[72]

Among the most vivid expression of this 'breakdown in trust' has been a greater preoccupation with scandal, which, as James Heartfield observes in this volume, also became a political issue in Europe. By the end of his second year, President Clinton was faced with five scandals, even before the affair with Monica Lewinsky that ended in impeachment. President George W. Bush has also faced scandals, such as forged intelligence documents, torture of prisoners in American custody and the indictment of a vice-presidential aide. The effect of these scandals, and the broader exhaustion with politics, is to produce a 'crisis of governability' in which 'citizens do not so much confront their states with demands as they back away in disillusion'. This condition is one of 'historical dislocation...disaffection with political leadership...and recurring scepticism about doctrines of social progress'.[73] What has produced this crisis of governability is, as the political theorist Bernard Manin suggests, 'the persistence, possibly even the aggravation, of the gap between the governed and the governing elite'.[74] The problem facing the state is not organized challenges, but a more diffuse and entrenched distrust of politics itself. As the representative system of liberal democracy is founded on consent and public participation, the result of this historic mass withdrawal is that mobilizing and sustaining support for the exercise of political power has become that much more difficult.

In addition to this, contemporary American policy-makers have inherited a specific political legacy, in which foreign policy is the principal means by which domestic affairs are managed politically. It is therefore no surprise to find that statesmen have been especially concerned with the impact that public withdrawal from politics has had on the conduct of foreign policy. In so far as the national interest has traditionally embodied the highest political good – self-sacrifice for one's state – the public withdrawal has often been interpreted as a sign of public decadence. Opinion-makers blame the loss of 'our "sense of platoon" ' on the 'unbridled quest for consumption'.[75] Clinton's national security advisor, Anthony Lake's greatest concern was 'the capacity of the American people to see the project through'.[76] Neoconservative commentator William Kristol criticized Clinton's 'liberal internationalist side' because in it 'commerce replaces politics'.[77] General Wesley Clark, who directed the NATO bombing of Yugoslavia in 1999, recounts General Colin Powell counselling him 'the American people never got involved in the Kosovo campaign; it wasn't their war'[78] – which was reflected in polls at the time.[79] Indeed, it was during the debates about intervention in Rwanda and Bosnia that liberals began to accuse the public of a lack of virtue and of moral indifference. For example, the *New Republic* published articles speaking about the need to exercise 'the noble virtues' and asking questions such as 'how can we respect ourselves' if we do not intervene abroad.[80] More recently, conservative thinkers have worried that Americans are unwilling to make sacrifices for 'wars waged in their names'.[81] According to Francis Fukuyama, 'American willingness to maintain the force levels to stay the course is limited'.[82]

However, the reason American statesmen are unable to sustain support for their initiatives is not because of moral decadence on the part of the public. It is that the actions of statesmen do not possess the character of necessity. In the absence of political contestation, all wars have become wars of choice. Foreign policy has become a more fluid, punctuated sequence of 'varied attempts to replace one enemy with (an)other'.[83] As I have already noted earlier in the chapter, there is a freewheeling character that comes about with the absence of any political basis on which to assess competing demands. Zaiki Laïdi suggests contemporary states have

> lost what one might call the 'language of priorities'... They behave rather like actors involved in a succession of plots who are asked to use their skills, as different scenes take place, to provide the appropriate reaction to any given situation.[84]

In the absence of clear political and strategic priorities, the problem of 'chaos' has thus become a central concern of foreign policy, and it is for this reason that crisis management has become the dominant way of relating to the international sphere.[85] Everything presses with equal urgency, yet cannot be assessed in relation to a higher standard of national interests, transcending the particularities of the matter at hand.

Presidents have attempted to make a virtue out of (the lack of) necessity. They highlight the exceptional character of major international initiatives as a sign of personal resolution and moral conviction – qualities more difficult to display in domestic politics. Through this they try to restore a degree of lost political legitimacy. This was a major attraction of the First Gulf War for the first President Bush:

> [The President] said that some people asked why he could not bring the same kind of purpose and success to domestic policy as he did to the war in Iraq. His answer: 'I didn't have to get permission from some old goat in the United States Congress to kick Saddam Hussein out of Kuwait. That's the reason.'[86]

Clinton carried forward the tradition. A memo regarding the 1994 Haiti invasion stated that Clinton's advisers believed the invasion would be politically desirable because it would highlight for the American public 'the President's decision making capability and the firmness of leadership in international political matters'.[87] Clinton was aware that bypassing congressional authorization was of dubious democratic legitimacy. But he wore this as a badge of honour: 'I realize it is unpopular. I know it is unpopular. I know the timing is unpopular. I know the whole thing is unpopular. But I believe it is the right thing.'[88]

So too for the second President Bush. As Robert Jervis notes, Bush bucked international public opinion as a way of signalling his moral resolution:

> When Kofi Annan declared that an American attack without Security Council endorsement 'would not be in conformity with the [UN] Charter,' he may not have realized that for some members of the Bush administration this would be part of the point of the action.[89]

This kind of foreign policy is deeply undemocratic. Through the invocation of moral conviction, or of national emergency, or both, it forestalls political criticism. Fabricating policy in a permanent state of exception refuses to recognize any common standard or norm by which to assess political action, let alone allow discussions about those standards to take place. More insidiously, the fluidity with which this kind of policy is conducted means that the standards of assessment offered by the actors themselves constantly change. This makes even the informal accountability of public criticism extremely difficult. By elevating the imperative to act over the need to articulate objectives, this new way of exercising power substitutes a criterion of immediate efficacy over long-term political necessity. Power is always immediately efficacious, and so this crisis-politics does indeed sustain and justify the exercise of American power abroad. But this adventurist drift is *not* the same as imperial mastery. For the immediate efficacy comes at the expense of considering the long-term objectives and consequences of the exercise of power. Therefore, even on their own terms, these various efforts to restore the authority of the state via the personality of the president cannot succeed. The underlying crisis of legitimacy which they mediate is the product of political exhaustion. Yet such a crisis-driven foreign policy closes off debate about political projects or the 'idea of the state'. The 'remoralization of America at home'[90] cannot be achieved through dramatic, risky acts unconnected to institutions and political processes that mediate and express popular will. They can only be the lonely acts of isolated statesmen.

Conclusion

The national interest has justifiably come under a great deal of theoretical criticism over the past decade. It was never a particularly democratic or progressive idea. It has justified political repression and aggressive imperialism, and falsely cast foreign policy as something beyond political disagreement. However, amidst all the criticism, what is generally missed is that the age of national interests has been largely surpassed. While one might take this as a sign of political progress, the American case suggests otherwise. What has replaced the national interest is a new anti-political, evasive foreign policy. The traditional national interest sought to defuse struggles within domestic politics by subsuming it within the existential struggle between nations. Contemporary crisis politics, however, arises out of and reproduces political exhaustion. It seeks not to drown out domestic politics by waging war against enemies abroad, but perpetuates depoliticization through a skittering series of symbolic moments, aimed at bolstering legitimacy while evading responsibility for formulating a coherent political vision. American statesmen act in a permanent state of emergency, flitting from one crisis to the next, forestalling any attempt to mount a wider discussion about the goals and political projects that we should collectively aspire to.

Notes

1 For a contemporary statement of this familiar view see A. Bacevich, 'The Realist Persuasion', *Boston Globe Ideas Section*, 6 November 2005.
2 G. Kennan, 'Morality and Foreign Policy', *Foreign Affairs* 64:2, 1985/6, p.210.
3 J. Habermas, *The Postnational Constellation*, London: Polity Press, 2001.
4 J. Rosenberg, *The Empire of Civil Society: A Critique of the Realist Theory of International Relations*, London: Verso, 1994, ch.1; and D. Campbell, *Writing Security: United States Foreign Policy and the Politics of Identity*, Minneapolis: University of Minnesota Press, 1992.
5 I. Daalder and J.M. Lindsay, 'America Unbound: The Bush Revolution in Foreign Policy', *Brookings Review* 21:4, 2003, pp.2–8; A. Schlesinger, *War and the American Presidency*, New York: W.W. Norton, 2004, ch.1.
6 N. Krisch, 2003, 'More Equal Than the Rest? Hierarchy, Equality, and U.S. Predominance in International Law', in M. Byers and G. Nolte (eds), *United States Hegemony and the Foundations of International Law*, Cambridge: Cambridge University Press, 2003, pp.135–175.
7 M. Jacques, 'Above the Law', *Guardian*, 26 March 2005.
8 P. Spiro, 'What Happened to the "New Sovereigntism"?', *Foreign Affairs*, 28 June 2004. Online. Available at HTTP: <http://www.foreignaffairs.org/20040728faupdate83476/peter-j-spiro/what-happened-to-the-new-sovereigntism.html> (accessed 30 May 2006).
9 S. Chesterman and M. Byers, 2003, 'Changing the Rules about Rules? Unilateral Humanitarian Intervention and the Future of International Law', in J.L. Holzgrefe and R.O. Keohane (eds), *Humanitarian Intervention: Ethical, Legal and Political Dilemmas*, Cambridge: Cambridge University Press, 2003, pp.177–203; A. Branch, 'The United States and UN-Authorized Military Intervention 1991–1995: The Fall of the International Rule of Law', unpublished paper, Columbia University, 2004.
10 S. Chesterman and M. Byers, 'Has US Power Destroyed the UN?', *London Review of Books* 21:9, 29 April 1999.
11 A. Rubinstein, A. Shayevich and B. Zlotnikov (eds), *The Clinton Foreign Policy Reader*, New York: M.E. Sharpe, 2000, pp.165–173.
12 R. Jervis, 2005, 'Understanding the Bush Doctrine', in G.J. Ikenberry (ed.), *American Foreign Policy: Theoretical Essays*, New York: Pearson Longman, 2005, p.588.
13 See also J. Heartfield, 'Friends, Allies and Enemies', *Spiked-Online*, 16 November 2001. Online. Available at HTTP: <www.spiked-online.com/articles/00000002D2D4.htm> (accessed 30 May 2006).

14 Global Security, 'Major Theater War', 2006. Online. Available at HTTP: <http://www.globalsecurity.org/military/ops/mtw.htm> (accessed 30 May 2006).

15 P. Halward, 'Option Zero in Haiti', *New Left Review* 27, 2004, pp.23–47.

16 BBC News, 'Timeline: N Korea nuclear standoff', 2005. Online. Available at HTTP: <http://news.bbc.co.uk/1/hi/world/asia-pacific/2604437.stm> (accessed 30 May 2006); P. Pan, 'China Treads Carefully Around North Korea', *Washington Post*, 10 January 2003.

17 B. Cronin, 'The Paradox of Hegemony: America's Ambiguous Relationship with the United Nations', *European Journal of International Relations* 7:1, 2001, pp.103–130; M. Dunne, 'The United States, the United Nations and Iraq: "Multilateralism of a Kind"', *International Affairs* 79:2, 2003, pp. 257–277.

18 D. Skidmore, 'Understanding the Unilateralist Turn in U.S. Foreign Policy', *Foreign Policy Analysis* 2, 2005, p.210.

19 A. Brinkley, 'Roosevelt, Franklin Delano', 2000. Online. Available at HTTP: <www.fdrheritage.org/fdrbio.htm> (accessed 30 May 2006).

21 Z. Laïdi, *A World Without Meaning: The Crisis of Meaning in International Politics*, trans. J. Burnham and J. Coulon, London: Routledge, 1998, p.13 (original emphasis).

22 Ibid., p.107.

23 US foreign policy is frequently interpreted in light of categories drawn from Carl Schmitt. See, for example, N. Bhuta, 'A Global State of Exception? The United States and World Order', *Constellations* 10:3, 2003, pp.1–27. While the formal analysis is generally accurate, these arguments tend to miss the underlying political weakness and disorientation behind the contemporary politics of emergency.

24 R. Kaplan, 'The Coming Anarchy', *The Atlantic Monthly* 273:2, 1994, pp.44–76.

25 S.J. Del Rosso Jr, 'The Insecure State: Reflections on "the State" and "Security" in a Changing World', *Daedalus* 124:2, 1995, p.190.

26 Bacevich, 'Realist Persuasion'.

27 G.J. Ikenberry, 'The End of the Neo-Conservative Moment', *Survival* 46:1, 2004, p.18.

28 G.F. Kennan, cited in M. Wight, *International Theory: The Three Traditions*, London: Leicester University Press, 1994, p.113.

29 P.G. Peterson and J.K. Sebenius, 1992, 'The Primacy of the Domestic Agenda', in G. Allison and G.F. Treverton (eds), *Rethinking America's Security*, New York: W.W. Norton & Company, 1992, pp.57–93.

30 Bacevich, 'Realist Persuasion'; R.S. Boynton, 'The Neocon Who Isn't', *The American Prospect Online*. Online. Available at HTTP: <http://www.prospect.org/web/page.ww?section=root&name=ViewWeb&articleId=11352> (accessed 30 May 2006); A. Bacevich, 2005, 'The Strategy of Openness', in G.J. Ikenberry (ed.), *American Foreign Policy: Theoretical Essays*, New York: Longman and Pearson, 2005, pp.167–199; Coalition for a Realistic Foreign Policy, 'The Perils of Empire', 2004. Online. Available at HTTP: <http://www.realisticforeignpolicy.org> (accessed 30 May 2006); J. Mearsheimer and S. Walt, 'The Israel Lobby and US Foreign Policy', *London Review of Books*, 28:6, 23 March 2006; M. Peretz, 'Oil and Vinegar', *New Republic*, 10 March 2006; Ikenberry, 'End of the Neo-Conservative Moment'.

31 I. Kristol, 'Defining Our National Interest', *The National Interest*, Fall 1990, pp.16–25.

32 Del Rosso Jr, 'Insecure State', p.192.

33 S. Huntington, 'The Erosion of American National Interests', *Foreign Affairs* 76:5, 1997, p.30.

34 C. Rice, 'Campaign 2000: Promoting the National Interest', *Foreign Affairs* 79:1, 2000, p.45.

35 J. Ruggie, 'What Makes the World Hang Together? Neo-Utilitarianism and the Social Constructivist Challenge', *International Organization* 52:4, 1998, p.875.

36 J. Matthews, 'Power Shift', *Foreign Affairs* 76:1, 1997, p. 51.

37 R. Kagan and W. Kristol, 'Toward a Neo-Reaganite Foreign Policy', *Foreign Affairs* 75:4, 1996, p.31.

38 Rosenberg, *Empire of Civil Society*, ch.1/conclusion.

39 A. Martin Simons, *Social Forces in American History*, Lawrence: Carrie Books, 2003, p.216.

40 Campbell, *Writing Security*, p.195.

41 B. Buzan, *People, States and Fear*, Hempel Hempstead: Harvester Wheatsheaf, 1991, p.70.

42 E.R. May, 'National Security in American History', in Allison and Treverton *Rethinking America's Security*, p.94.

43 H. Morgenthau, *In Defense of the National Interest*, New York: Knopf, 1951, p.3.

44 C. Beard, *The Idea of the National Interest*, Chicago: Quadrangle Books, 1934, p.166.

45 Ibid., p.167.

46 Ibid., p.119.

47 Ibid., p.119.

48 Ibid., p.228.

49 May, 'National Security', p.97.

50 L.C. Gardner, *Safe For Democracy: The Anglo-American Response to Revolution, 1912–1923*, Oxford: Oxford University Press, 1984, p.44.

51 A. Mayer, *Wilson v. Lenin: Political Origins of the New Diplomacy*, Princeton: Princeton University Press, 1967, pp.344, 353.

52 I. Oren, 1996, 'The Subjectivity of the "Democratic" Peace: Changing U.S. Perceptions of Imperial Germany', in S. Lynn-Jones, M. Brown and S. Miller (eds), *Debating the Democratic Peace*, Princeton: Princeton University Press, 1996, pp.263–300. Also Gardner, *Safe for Democracy* and Mayer, *Wilson V. Lenin*.

53 Charles Beard notes that Wilson was in a sense forced by domestic disenchantment not to seize the opportunity to dominate Europe entirely: 'when Germany was prostrate and Great Britain staggering under debts, when the United States Navy was just on the point of wresting supremacy from the British at sea, on account of the fever of national solidarity raised during the war, the opportunity to grasp the trident of commerce was allowed to pass ... With mankind still reeking in the blood of the World War and torn by a revolutionary sentiment which had upset Tsarism, with the old conflict of American domestic politics renewed, with the American people disillusioned by the impact of "secret treaties" and by the unreality of such slogans as "making the world safe for democracy" and "the war to end war," compromise seemed necessary; and it was reached in a series of agreements at the Washington and London conferences which made dangerous the ruthless pursuit of *Machtpolitik* by any of the participating powers'. Beard, *Idea of the National Interest*, pp.143–144.

54 On American imperialism and labour militancy see D. Jenkins, 'Justice and Imperialism', *Alternatives* 30, 2005, pp.223–248.

55 E.H. Carr, *The Twenty Years' Crisis, 1919–1939*, New York: Harper & Row, 1939, p.2.

56 May, 'National Secutity', p.97.

57 S. Krasner, 'State Power and the Structure of International Trade', *World Politics* 28:3, 1976, pp. 317–347; R. Gilpin, *War and Change in World Politics*, Cambridge: Cambridge University Press, 1981.

58 H. Raines, 'Tower Power; Controllers Discover the Ceiling After Reagan Hits It', *New York Times*, 9 August 1981.

59 G. Kolko, *Anatomy of a War: Vietnam, the United States, and the Modern Historical Experience*, New York: Free Press, 1994, pp.172–173.

60 W. Chafe, *The Unfinished Journey: America Since World War II*, Oxford: Oxford University Press, 2003, p.394.

61 Ibid., p.394.

62 T. Patterson, 'Where Have All The Voters Gone', *History News Network*, 2002. Online. Available at HTTP: <http://hnn.us/articles/1104.html> (accessed 30 May 2006).

63 J. Sundquist, *Dynamics of the Party System: Alignment and Realignment of Political Parties in the United States*, Washington, DC: Brookings Institution Press, 1983, p.vii.

64 R. Melanson, *American Foreign Policy Since the Vietnam War: The Search for Consensus from Richard Nixon to George W. Bush*, 4th Ed., Armonk: M.E. Sharpe, 2005, p.22.
65 Ibid., p.20
66 Ibid., p.21.
67 T. Lowi, *The Personal President: Power Invested, Promise Unfulfilled*, Ithaca: Cornell University Press, 1986, pp.99–100.
68 Ibid., p.171.
69 J. Rosenberg, 'Globalization Theory: A Post Mortem', *International Politics* 42:1, 2005, pp.48–49.
70 Bacevich, 'Strategy of Openness', p.194.
71 N. Eliasoph, *Avoiding Politics: How Americans Produce Apathy In Everyday Life*, Cambridge: Cambridge University Press, 1998.
72 Peterson and Sebenius, 'Primacy of the Domestic Agenda', p.84.
73 C. Maier, 'Democracy And Its Discontents', *Foreign Affairs* 73:4, 1994, pp.48–64.
74 B. Manin, *The Principles of Representative Government*, Cambridge: Cambridge University Press, 1997, p.233.
75 Peterson and Sebenius, 'Primacy of the Domestic Agenda', p.84.
76 Bacevich, 'Strategy of Openness', p.182.
77 Boynton, 'Neocon Who Isn't'.
78 W. Clark, *Waging Modern War: Bosnia, Kosovo, and the Future of Combat*, New York: Public Affairs, 2001, p.xx.
79 D. Chandler, *From Kosovo to Kabul: Human Rights and International Intervention*, London: Pluto Press, 2002, p.300.
80 P. Berkowitz, 'The Good Fight', *The New Republic*, 10 May 1999, p.220.
81 V. Davis Hanson, 2005, 'Iraq's Future - and Ours', in G. Rosen (ed.), *The Right War? The Conservative Debate on Iraq*, Cambridge: Cambridge University Press, 2005, p.13.
82 F. Fukuyama, 'Symposium: The Sources of American Conduct', *The American Interest* 1:1, 2005, p.9.
83 Campbell, *Writing Security*, p.8.
84 Laïdi, *World Without Meaning*, p.107.
85 Thomas Friedman, for example, has suggested the new polarity is 'the World of Order versus the World of Disorder'. 'Nato's New Front', *New York Times*, 30 March 2003.
86 L. Fisher, 'Sidestepping Congress: Presidents Acting Under the UN and NATO', *Case Western Reserve Law Review* 47, 1997, p.1268.
87 Ibid., p.1270.
88 Ibid., p.1270.
89 Jervis, 'Understand the Bush Doctrine', p.583.
90 Kagan and Kristol, 'Toward a Neo-Reaganite Foreign Policy', p.31.

4 From state of war to state of nature

Human security and sovereignty

Tara McCormack

Introduction

Of the many developments in international relations since the end of the Cold War, perhaps none has received so much official attention, energy and rhetorical appreciation as the idea of human security. The foreign ministries of countries as diverse as Japan, Norway and South Africa have all adopted the concept as a guiding principle of foreign policy. It is the defining concept of some of the most significant United Nations (UN) documents, including the recent UN reform proposal, *A More Secure World: Our Shared Responsibility* (2004), and the 1994 *Human Development Report*. Leading non-governmental organizations (NGOs), such as the International Red Cross and Oxfam, have sought to promote the idea that 'achieving human security – focused on the protection of the lives and livelihoods of people – is a key to achieving global security'.[1] Many International Relations (IR) scholars have also promoted the idea that security needs to be transformed from a 'state-centred' to a 'human-centred' concept. In short, human security has been heralded as nothing less than a 'tool for solving the problems confronting the majority of humanity'.[2]

This chapter seeks to evaluate human security on its own terms, in its claims to represent an advance over state-centred security policies. The proponents of human security claim they not only provide more thoroughgoing security for individuals, but that they also open up pressing issues, such as poverty and environmental degradation, that traditional security ignores. In their eyes, human security is quite simply more humanistic, and expands the possibilities for addressing major global problems. In contrast, I will suggest that by securitizing social problems, the human security framework is depoliticizing. That is to say, human security closes down, rather than opens up new possibilities, and it strips individuals and the issues that confront them of their social and political context. Far from emancipating us through security, the human security framework causes security problems to proliferate, pushing humanity into something like a neo-Hobbesian state of nature.

From national security to human security

The definition of security did not always seem to be in urgent need of redefinition. Indeed, since 1945, the object of security appeared to be perfectly evident – it was the state. During the Cold War, security studies, as a subdiscipline of IR, was relatively narrowly defined in terms of the 'high politics' of military-security issues, and was heavily policy oriented. The odd exception notwithstanding, the seemingly immutable Cold War framework of geopolitical rivalry and balance of power was reflected in the absence of any analysis of the concept of security itself.[3] In the words of Barry Buzan, throughout this period there was a 'persistent underdevelopment of thinking about security'.[4] Instead, security studies concerned itself with questions such as how 'to secure the state against those objective threats that could undermine its stability and threaten its survival'.[5] The imperative of national security was reflected in analyses of the causes of war, developments in military technology, nuclear weapons, first strikes, defensive deterrence, the capability and the intentions of the USSR and so on.[6]

To be sure, Cold War security studies, let alone actual security policy, was not without its critics. A few argued that the focus on military force and interstate war blinded states to more pressing security threats. The influential 1972 report of the Club of Rome, *The Limits to Growth*, made the Malthusian case that the greatest security threat facing mankind was not war but population growth and diminishing energy supplies. Lester R. Brown's 1977 paper 'Redefining National Security' made the same argument, and explicitly aimed it at the scholarly consensus on national security. In a different vein, Barry Buzan's *People, States and Fear*, first published in 1981, argued that military security was only a part of state security, which needed to be broadened to include political, economic, societal and environmental security.[7] Spurred on by the anti-nuclear and peace movements, ideas of 'Common Defence' and 'Alternative Defence' also gained ground in the 1980s, arguing that the threat of nuclear war transcended the geopolitical rivalry of the superpowers, whose concerns were parochial when compared to the threat to humanity at large posed by nuclear weapons.[8] They questioned whether policies of national security based on nuclear weapons were rational.

If in their own time these ideas made relatively little headway in the scholarly literature, with the collapse of the USSR they quickly became mainstream. In Gwyn Prins' evocative phrase, for security studies the end of the Cold War signalled a 'bonfire of the certainties'.[9] Within a few years, questioning national security grew from being the preserve of radicals, peace campaigners and environmentalists into a 'mature and booming industry'.[10] Great effort was poured into uncovering a variety of new threats that made old political and conceptual categories redundant.[11] Newly discovered dangers included disease, drug trafficking, over-population, environmental degradation, the proliferation of weapons of mass destruction and resource scarcity. 'The assumptions and institutions that have governed international relations in the post-war era are a poor fit with these new realities,'[12] argued Jessica Tuchman Mathews in 1989.

The idea that new security concepts were needed was rapidly absorbed by political leaders. In his 1993 inaugural address, President Clinton stated that although the post-Cold War world was freer, it was also less stable, threatened by new security problems such as HIV/AIDS and environmental collapse.[13] Clinton was not alone: 'former Central Intelligence Agency (CIA) Director James Woolsey has remarked: "We have slain a large dragon, but now we find ourselves living in a jungle with a bewildering number of poisonous snakes. And in many ways, the dragon was easier to keep track of." '[14] These new security threats prompted the world's most powerful military alliance, the North Atlantic Treaty Organization (NATO), to shift gears, with the announcement of a New Strategic Concept based around uncertainty, instability and risks that are 'multi-faceted in nature and multi-directional, which makes them hard to predict and assess'.[15] By the time critical security theorists Keith Krause and Michael C. Williams argued in 1997 that 'both the object of security (what is to be secured) and the means for studying it are treated as largely given and self-evident'[16] they were well out of date. It was abundantly clear to academics and policy-makers alike that old ideas could no longer be taken for granted.

These changes in security doctrine fed into the policy responses to post-Cold War crises. The UN Charter defines international peace and security as the absence of inter-state war. But in 1991, UN Security Council Resolution 688 tacitly broke with this conception, when it held that Iraqi treatment of Kurdish minorities constituted 'a threat to international peace and security'. This key resolution helped to establish in diplomatic practice a link between human suffering and security. In January 1992, the Security Council met at the level of Heads of State and Government for the first time, to symbolize the importance of the redefinition of international peace and security. It formalized this redefinition in a joint proclamation arguing for an expansion of security to encompass issues previously reserved for domestic concern, such as poverty and related economic and social problems.[17] Changing diplomatic practice and security policy crystallized in the 1994 *United Nations Human Development Report* (UNHDR). This document spelt out the morally charged nature of the new security concept. Human security is 'not a concern with weapons – it is a concern with human life and dignity ... Human security is people centred'.[18]

Human security as real security

As we can see, human security has a powerful appeal, in so far as it moves away from states and armies, tanks and missiles, in favour of placing the 'individual at the centre of debate, analysis and policy'.[19] By making the individual the referent object of security, the advocates of human security claim to be providing real security. In their view, state security is problematic for two reasons. First and most straightforward, the state has historically been one of the greatest sources of insecurity. Liberal political theory has it that individuals trade the radical uncertainty of the state of nature for the stability of social relations that are guaranteed by a rule of law, enforced by the supreme authority of the sovereign state. Karl Marx described this liberal vision of society thus: 'Security is the highest social concept of civil society, the concept of the police. The whole of society is merely there to guarantee to each of its members the preservation of his person, rights and property.'[20] Marx's criticism in this passage hinges on the word 'merely'. Marx is not debating whether or not elevating the 'concept of the police' to the 'highest social concept' succeeds in providing security. Rather, he is saying that the elevation of security itself reduces all the abundance and potential of human relations into an instrumental means by which the individual preserves his property rights.

Rather than seeing traditional security as insufficiently social, the doctrine of human security assesses the state and civil society in their provision of security, and finds both wanting. As one major report puts it, 'too often in the past... preserving the security of the state has been used as an excuse for policies that undermined the security of people'.[21] These ideas have been honed in the school of Critical Security Studies, whose proponents argue that focusing on the state simply fails to understand that for most people the greatest security threats come from one's own state, in the form of censorship, torture, ethnic cleansing and so on,[22] and not from the cross-border aggression of other states. In addition, the wars that have blighted the system of states over the last century have also perpetrated insecurity throughout the world. Either way you look at it, the state seems to have reneged on the promise of security offered in the social contract. In this regard, human security has the powerful evidence of an entire century of devastating conflict with which to attack the traditional view of state security, and to justify the new focus upon the security of the individual.

Second, human security has the benefit of a lively, up-to-date understanding of the new type of threats putatively emerging from globalization. As the former UN Secretary-General Boutros Boutros-Ghali's 1992 *Agenda for Peace* noted, the 'integrated approach to human security' recognizes a broad spectrum of security threats, ranging from 'ethnic, religious, social, cultural or linguistic strife' to racial tensions, ecological damage, population growth, debt, barriers to trade, drugs, poverty, the gap between rich and poor.[23] Whereas only military threats and severe economic crises count as threats to the state, 'there are many threats that are common to all people – such as unemployment, drugs, crime, pollution and human rights violations'.[24]

The sweep of human security constitutes one of its greatest attractions. The expansiveness of human security means that many progressive impulses (such as alleviating poverty and tackling environmental damage) can be endowed with greater social significance and urgency, once they are associated with security. In Andrew Mack's words

> to be concerned about human security is to be concerned about the threats to peoples posed by human rights abuses, poverty, hunger... From this perspective, human security's importance lies less in its explanatory power than as a signifier of shared political and moral values.[25]

In other words, what may be sacrificed in conceptual precision is compensated for by greater moral meaning. For Ken Booth, this shared morality of security encourages concerned individuals to think in universal terms about the protection and promotion of human life and human dignity.[26]

The emphasis on the individual necessitates rethinking the role of the state in security. Yet however much the doctrine of human security derives its force from questioning national security, the doctrine certainly does not set out to supersede the state. The *Agenda for Peace* explains the role of the state in the following terms:

> The foundation-stone of this work is and must remain the State. Respect for its fundamental sovereignty and integrity are crucial to any common international progress. The time of absolute and exclusive sovereignty, however, has passed; its theory was never matched by reality. It is the task of leaders of States today to understand this and to find a balance between the need for good internal governance and the requirements of an ever more interdependent world.[27]

Human security seeks to harness other institutions alongside the state, to the pursuit of 'an integrated approach to human security', including NGOs, the UN system and the UN Security Council.[28]

But the traditional understanding of sovereignty poses a problem here. For those attracted to the progressive promise of human security, sovereignty is too closely tied to a narrow conception of individual security. Sovereignty denotes public power, whose purpose is to preserve the rule of law, and protect the individual from the most immediate, violent threats to person and property. The only insecurity that sovereignty recognizes is the one created by general disorder and the absence of known, general laws by which we can predict each other's actions. This means that sovereignty is unable to accommodate those other threats to individuals, such as globalization, poverty and environmental degradation, that cannot be addressed simply by enforcing the rule of law.

From the human security perspective, the individual is embedded in a number of relationships that can be a potential source of insecurity. As J. Ann Tickner puts it, a central aspect of the human security framework is a 'focus on social relations as sources of insecurity'.[29] In this sense, the problem with sovereignty is not just that the state may very well be the source of, rather than remedy for, insecurity. It is also that sovereignty arbitrarily gives priority to one kind of relationship, and one kind of insecurity, over others. There is no logical reason to do so from the human security standpoint. The polemical intent here cannot be over-stated. Whereas security was once the 'highest concept' in Marx's words, by which state sovereignty was politically defended and established, it has now become the chief weapon for attacking and transforming it.

Criticisms: securitization and operationalization

The powerful appeal of human security cannot be denied. It taps into our moral intuitions as well as the historical experience of the twentieth century, which saw so many sacrificed on the altar of national security. If the promise of the social contract was that the sovereign state would emancipate the individual from the radical insecurity of the state of nature, the reality seems to have been to create even greater and more dangerous sources of insecurity. Moreover, the historical experience of welfare states and of economic crises has also illuminated the way in which the market is just as significant a source of insecurity as the threat of physical violence. Why not, then, add job security, food security, health security, social security and even cultural security to our conception of security? Surely the sovereign state, by separating the question of physical security from the economic issues of the global market, has failed adequately to address such immediate and pressing sources of insecurity raised by globalization?

Yet the virtues of human security cannot be judged by the vices of the sovereign state. Human security must be assessed on its own terms, as a claim to be a progressive step forward both politically and morally. The literature is now well-developed enough that human security has gone through a period of external as well as self-assessment, and two characteristic problems emerge.

The first problem is the stretching of the concept of security to the point where it means everything and nothing. According to the UNHDR, 'human security is a child who did not die, a disease that did not spread, a job that was not cut, an ethnic tension that did not explode in violence, a dissident who was not silenced'.[30] As Roland Paris notes, this is not so much a concept as a banal 'laundry list'[31] of things the UN would like to prevent. Keith Krause, a sympathetic critic, similarly worries that human security has become a synonym for 'bad things that can happen'.[32] In official circles, different governments have argued over just how far the concept can be expanded. Japan and Canada, two founders of the 13-state Human Security Centre, have adopted different visions of human security. Canada has defended a 'narrow' vision that aims to protect individuals and communities from violence.[33] Japan has adopted a more expansive definition, as exemplified by the 2003 report *Human Security Now*, which stresses the need to both protect and empower people: '[human security] means creating political, social, environmental, economic, military and cultural systems that together give people the building blocks of survival, livelihood and dignity'.[34] It appears that the only constraint on the concept of human security is the individual preferences of its proponent. This conceptual slipperiness has made human security the object not just of academic contention but of political disagreement among foreign ministries. Even its proponents worry about the potential of the concept to swallow up and 'securitize' all issues facing leaders and policy-makers.

The second, related problem is the implication for coherent policy development.[35] As King and Murray argue, 'With no consensus or theoretical definition, the goal of measuring and enhancing human security is beyond reach.'[36] Without any clear standards of measurement, it is not clear what specific policies are best to further the aims of human security. Extensive research has gone into trying to define the exact institutional means by which individuals might be made secure, and which kinds of policies are implied by human security.[37] Few disagree that safeguarding human security does imply a commitment to the use of military force[38] to stop grave human rights abuses, but few think human security is restricted to fighting wars. For many, human security can only have meaning if it also entails commitment to preventative action[39] and extensive social, economic and political intervention in post-conflict countries.[40] For all the problems of definition, as we have seen, human security can only justify itself by embracing the kinds of social problems and human rights issues that its forebears ignored.[41]

Therefore, upholding human security can encompass military intervention, peacekeeping, democratization assistance, poverty-reduction programmes, environmental protection and much more. This in turn raises the question of identifying the agent responsible for acting in any given situation. To some, embracing a flexible framework bypasses this problem: 'each human security crisis calls for a different set of instruments calibrated to local circumstances'.[42] While state security required the creation of mediating institutions to facilitate compromises between states, human security 'brings together states, international organizations, ... NGOs, and individuals in radically new combinations'.[43] As an example of the many issues and means to security that a people-centred approach takes, the Canadian government lists (to name a few): the Ottawa Convention on the prohibition of the use of land mines; the Kosovo war; the establishment of the International Criminal Court; intervention and peace-building in Haiti and Sierra Leone; international agreement on terrorism.[44] In each situation, it was not an existing, formalized set of relations that determined the agents and instruments responsible for providing security, but rather the situation itself. In other words, the de facto way in which human security has answered the problem of 'operationalization' is to let circumstances decide.

If securitization and operationalization are the main acknowledged problems facing human security, they are generally seen as technical issues that can be resolved through greater investigation, more conceptual clarity or improved practical experience. Yet what even some external critics seem to have missed is the way that securitization of social phenomena emerges from the internal logic of human security itself. I want to argue that the problems of human security cannot be resolved through clarification of normative ideals, or technical improvement in the way in which human security programmes are administered. The remainder of this chapter aims to show how the very premises of human security are self-defeating. It is these flawed premises that throw up the recurring problems of securitization and operationalization. To understand this, we must address the political nature of human security.

The politics of human security

As we have already seen, one telling criticism levelled against human security is the way that it tends to expand indefinitely, transforming all sorts of social issues and relations into security threats. So one obvious problem with this is that it may be self-defeating in policy terms, when, say, an environmental problem is understood as a security problem, with the result that the wrong policy instruments are adopted to resolve the issue.[45] The point is not that human security theorists are simply oblivious to the deep-seated, structural sources of 'security threats'. As one important contributor to the debate points out, 'much human insecurity surely results from structural factors and the distribution of power, which are essentially beyond the reach of individuals'.[46] The real problem is that human security simply does not provide us with a conceptual means of grasping problems whose origins and dynamics are not reducible to being immediate threats.

The inclusion of a broad range of concerns under the rubric of security is achieved only by abstracting them from their social and historical context, and positing them as external, reified objects in relation to the individual. By shifting the evaluative standpoint of security from the collective viewpoint of the state, issues such as women's rights, crime, drug use and food scarcity are evaluated through their impact on the individual, rather than as sites of broader social and political conflict. Thus, the redefinition of security at once entails the expansion of the concept, *and* the transformation of political problems into security questions. This is how security thinking 'depoliticizes' society. On one level, this depoliticization is self-evident. Giving an issue, such as global poverty, the stamp of urgency and necessity by talking about it in security terms may well help to push poverty to the forefront of public opinion. But talking of a social issue purely in terms of security also places it outside of politics. The urgency and necessity that is always implied in talking about security, means that the issue in question is no longer seen as open to reflection, discussion and debate about first principles.

This depoliticization implied in new security thinking is not a semantic problem. Rather it expresses the intrinsic limits of human security. Although human security derives its polemical strength from claiming to shift away from the traditional idea of state-centred security, human security does not totally break with that tradition. What it takes from the traditional liberal definition of security is a pre-political conception of the individual. What do I mean by this? In liberal political theory, every individual participates in society on the basis of trading away certain freedoms in return for the collective security provided by the state, both in terms of physical protection and the stability in social relations that results from the ultimate guarantee of physical security (civil society). The rule of law and the state thus derive their legitimacy from the people, who have consented to follow these rules in return for the provision of security. In the intellectual division of labour that developed between IR and political theory during the Cold War, IR took the validity of this social contract for granted. By presupposing the legitimacy of the sovereign state, IR generally, but especially the security studies subdiscipline, could concern itself exclusively with how the state guaranteed its own security, and by extension the security of its citizens in external confrontations with other states.

Human security theory mobilizes the historical insight about the predatory and oppressive nature of the state, to imply that the state does not embody the individual's needs and interests. In other words, there is no longer anything *distinctive* about the relationship of the individual to the state; it is merely one potentially threatening power relationship among many. Severing the relationship between the individual and the state also severs the relationship between the individual and civil society, whose stability can no longer be taken for granted, given that this stability is meant to be provided by the state. Without the guarantee of security provided in liberal theory by the sovereign state, social relations are consequently more fluid, unstable and risky. Without the state acting on the individual's behalf to organize society, all social relations remain anonymous forces that are entirely external to the person. All we are left with is the isolated, vulnerable individual, shorn of any political and social context.

The logical consequence of reasoning from the isolated individual outwards, then, is to view *all* relations as pathological or imbued with potential conflict. Conflict becomes a catchall term to refer to any kind of relationship, at any level of society, in which a threat to some human need has become imminent. The things that place populations ' "at risk"... [of] the effects of chronic threats as hunger, disease and repression... [are] sudden and hurtful disruptions in the patterns of daily life – whether in homes, in jobs or in communities'.[47] In the bloodless and managerial language of risk assessment, conflict is generalized to all social relations. Once conflict is no longer seen as something with a distinctively political meaning, it rapidly becomes a metaphor for society as a whole.

It is this downplaying of the centrality of the sovereign state as the guarantor of security that, perversely, leads to the expansion of security threats. By treating the state as a potential security threat, human security implies that the state reneged on the bargain to provide security for the individual. Unsurprisingly, this condition of generalized insecurity looks very similar to the radical uncertainty portrayed in the classical liberal conception of the state of nature. The only logical conclusion that we can draw from this is that we never really escaped the state of nature after all. For all the problems associated with the idealized depiction of society as emerging from the state of nature, it nonetheless provided a powerful way of representing the problem of managing spontaneous, uncontrolled social relations among individuals. The liberal solution to security came from the exercise of political agency on the part of individuals, who consent to create a sovereign authority that can impose collectively binding rules, and impose their common interest in security on each of its members. As Emma Rothschild notes, in the liberal view of individual security:

> The essential characteristic of security is a political relation, which is not voluntary, between the individual and the political community... Security... is the condition of political freedom. But it is the political choice to live under the rule of law that is in turn the condition for security.[48]

Within this vision of security as a political relation, what the concept of sovereignty does is make clear the identity of the agent responsible for security, and carves out a sphere of activity in which individuals meet not as self-interested, antagonistic atoms, but as equal beings seeking a common solution to problems of general concern. Security is therefore never merely a physical condition, in which a particular threat is removed, but also always a political relation between 'the secured' and those agents responsible for security.

Sovereignty is therefore not just a theory of power, but the form that collective political agency takes among individuals separated and alienated from each other. This abstract general will, standing over and above society can, of course, always be a means by which the state tyrannizes its populace. This possibility reflects the fact that the sovereign is Janus-faced. The political representative who acts on behalf of the sovereign people appeals to his constituents on the basis of their particular interests, while also claiming to represent a broader, general will. This contradiction is revealed in the fact that, though authorized by particular interests, representatives are also free to act against those interests. But they do so at the risk of eventually being held to account by their constituents: they must simultaneously concern themselves with the general and the particular. Thus the concept of sovereignty articulates a view of the distinctiveness of politics, as a special sphere of human activity in which individuals attempt to impose order upon the spontaneous, unpredictable relations that emerge among atomized individuals making private choices. But it does more than this – sovereignty also offers the means by which the actions of the state can be assessed. When the state produces insecurity for its citizens, it is the sovereign people themselves who must act to check the state, to ensure that it is acting in their interests.

As Rothschild discusses, the conception of security that emerges from a human-centred perspective is a considerable retreat from the political view:

> the 'human security' of the new international principles seems to impose relations that are only tenuously political. The security of an individual in one country is to be achieved through the agency of a state (or a substate group, or a suprastate organisation) in another country. The individual is thereby very much less than a co-lawmaker, in Kant's sense, in the political procedure that ensures security. She is less, even, than a co-beneficiary … she is not even a partner in being protected.[49]

Let us unpack some of the implications of the way in which human security depoliticizes society. As we have seen, the idealism of the sovereign state lies in the fact that it can emancipate individuals from radical insecurity. By contrast, the human security framework reminds us of the reality of the state, in that it is a key source of insecurity. Human security is also (overly) sensitive to the many ways in which atomized individuals can experience insecurity. But there are several problems with this drive to provide a more thoroughgoing vision of security than that supposedly provided by the state. The first is that, by treating the individual rather than the state as the referent of security, human security has constructed a new state of nature, where everything social is potentially a threat. Perversely, the drive to provide 'real' security can only sustain itself by constantly discovering, even manufacturing, new sources of insecurity. Hence the notorious problem of conceptual over-stretch, which we have already discussed. On this front, in the drive to provide real security, 'human security' fails by its own standards.

Second, by taking the individual as the referent of security, all social, institutional and political relations are seen as external to the individual. The result of this is that unlike the theory of sovereignty, the human security framework offers no theory of the institutions through which individuals may organize themselves into a collective force for addressing that vast array of social problems that human security identifies. The difficulty in 'operationalizing' human security, therefore, emerges from the fact that human security is a theory hostile to politics. From the human security framework, institutions gain their justification not from whether they are accountable to, or representative of, the individuals they exercise power over, but whether they meet the abstracted criteria of security as defined by the powerful.

Worse, not only does human security lack any coherent theory of legitimate agency, human security actually calls into question agency, that force that is necessary to push through social change. In the liberal conception of the state of nature, human beings transcend their condition of insecurity through the exercise of their own agency. Their consent is the foundation of the social contract. It is precisely this exercise of agency that human security deems as problematic, as it produces the sovereign state and all its attendant insecurity. But progressive social and political change is often preceded by struggle, strife and even war. In short, the collective action needed to address deep-seated social problems may result in human insecurity, at least in the short term. Such a conclusion may seem brutal and insensitive to, say, an official caught up in administering aid, or drafting laws to address people's fears. But in this regard, human security reveals just how far removed it is from a properly humanistic conception of society. For people have demonstrated time and again throughout history that they are prepared to experience privation and even risk death in the pursuit of higher goals. From the human security standpoint, such risk acceptance is morally suspect, because the physical, biological existence of the individual is given priority over any exercise of politics that might risk the individual's life. After all, it would be meaningless to give up one's own life to spread human security around the world.

In the neo-Hobbesian vision of human security, the drive to provide 'real' rather than merely national security perversely means that the condition of insecurity is made quasi-permanent. This insecurity calls forth an endless series of interventions and administrations from third parties whose political responsibility and formal accountability is never made a question. This takes us to the third, and final, problem with the anti-political nature of human security. For all its seeming hostility to state sovereignty, the demands of human security seem constantly to demand the power of the state. To call something a security problem is to suggest that it must be tackled immediately and forcefully – and a response on such a scale often requires the intrusion of organized power that only the state is able to provide.

In this way, human security further undermines itself, in that it tends to sanctify inequalities of power that are themselves sources of insecurity. Judging social problems from the urgent viewpoint of security means that political criteria of legitimate responsibility are set aside, in favour of the criteria of effectiveness. In other words, responsibility for upholding human security is determined by who is *able* to act, not who is *authorized* to act. The achievement of human security then provides *ex post* legitimation for the exercise of power, regardless of whether this power could claim any valid consent. But those most able to act are those with the most power. Power becomes its own justification. The extent to which the agency of the powerful has been relegitimized by human security is abundantly evident in the way in which weak states have been reinterpreted as posing the greatest threat to world order (see further Christopher Bickerton's chapter in this volume). As Tony Blair argued in his Chicago speech during the 1999 NATO attack on Yugoslavia, 'We are all internationalists now, whether we like it or not... We cannot turn our backs on conflicts and the violation of human rights within other countries if we want still to be secure.'[50]

Assessing power solely by its provision of security means that it knows no boundaries, whether these be international borders, or realms of privacy within the domestic sphere. For example, the defining context for security policy in the European Union is one in which internal and external aspects of security are indissolubly linked.[51] As we saw earlier in the chapter, the UN Security Council has formalized this new vision of security in a series of resolutions expanding the definition of threats to international peace and security. It is difficult to find the progressive aspect in this vision of security. Not only does it provide normative justification for existing inequalities of power, it also severs individuals from any necessary, privileged connection with the politics of their own state, in favour of more tenuous and distant relations with international organizations, military alliances and powerful states, none of which they have any means of holding to account.

Conclusion

It has been said that the anti-US terror attacks of September 2001 have undermined the human security framework and ushered in a 'new Cold War'.[52] On this reading, human security smacks too much of politically correct social work to survive for long in a world where decisive confrontation with terrorists is needed. But in fact, the human security framework has if anything only gained in stature. The focus on the vulnerable, impoverished individual being drawn into terrorism, and the potential insecurities arising from 'failed states' as the well-springs of terror, is more clearly emphasized than ever before. US President George W. Bush's *National Security Strategy 2002* reflects the standard human security concerns: 'poverty, weak institutions, and corruption can make weak states vulnerable to terrorist networks and drug cartels within their borders'[53] and stresses the need to engage in development to overcome poverty.[54] The resilience of the human security paradigm is exemplified in this interpretation of terrorist violence as a result of deprivation – a paradigm that exists in spite of all the evidence that Al Qaeda terrorists in particular are, on the whole, educated and middle class.[55]

Given the conceptual vacuity of the human security framework, it is hardly surprising that it has simply absorbed terrorism as yet another threat to the individual. The UN Secretary-General's 2004 High-level Panel on Threats,

Challenges and Change paints a dramatic picture of the way in which social, political and economic problems are all bundled together under the heading of insecurity:

> International terrorist groups prey on weak States for sanctuary. Their recruitment is aided by grievances nurtured by poverty, foreign occupation and the absence of human rights and democracy; by religious and other intolerance; and by civil violence – a witch's brew common to those areas where civil war and regional conflict intersect... Poverty, infectious disease, environmental degradation and war feed one another in a deadly cycle.[56]

These themes are echoed in the *European Security Strategy*[57] and countless foreign policy papers issued by national governments throughout the world.

If human security is offered as a step forward from traditional ideas of national security, then it must be evaluated on its own terms. It has wide support among governments, policy-makers and scholars who believe that it can be used to open up international relations to a more progressive vision of security. It cannot be denied that, from the standpoint of human security, the horrors of the sovereign state become especially vivid, and that the many other problems facing individuals, such as hunger, disease and unemployment, acquire a greater sense of urgency and importance. But, as I have argued throughout this chapter, this new-found emphasis comes at too high a price. What seems an initially progressive new emphasis rapidly degenerates into an attack on politics itself. Human security offers to emancipate us from the insecurity of the state, only to leave us in a twenty-first century state of nature, with new security threats multiplying before our eyes. Hobbes' famous depiction of the state of nature provides a stark warning of the impoverished existence that is the result of individual energy being absorbed by questions of security:

> In such condition, there is no place for Industry; because the fruit thereof is uncertain; and consequently no Culture of the Earth; no Navigation, nor use of the commodities that may be imported by Sea; no commodious Buildings; no Instruments of moving...no Knowledge of the face of the Earth; no account of Time; no Art; no Letters; no Society; and which is worst of all, continuall feare, and danger of violent death; And the life of man, solitary, poore, nasty, brutish, and short.[58]

If human security has it right, and state sovereignty does not transcend the radical insecurity of the state of nature, then the alternative that human security offers is the impossibility of transcendence itself. Instead, the logic of human security is to clamp down on all aspects of social life, reorganizing political institutions around the technical tasks of risk management. As the UNHDR has it, 'Human security is easier to ensure through early prevention than later intervention.'[59] The consequence is not to open new political possibilities but to broaden the deadening, apolitical language of necessity, wherein the injunction to act relativizes and overwhelms the possibility for disagreement and dissent, and where 'responsiveness' and 'efficacy' become the measures of political authority rather than 'accountability' and 'legitimacy'. In this light, we might say that the progressive aura of human security derives more from the borrowed authority of the wider disillusionment with state sovereignty, than from the inner logic of its own principles.

Notes

1 B. Buell, 'Words to Deeds: A New International Agenda for Peace and Security', *Oxfam Briefing Paper 14*, Washington, DC: Oxfam International, 2006.
2 C. Thomas, 'A Bridge Between the Interconnected Challenges Confronting the World', *Security Dialogue* 35:3, 2004, p.354.
3 D. Baldwin, 'The Concept of Security', *Review of International Studies* 23:1, 1997, p.8.
4 B. Buzan, *People, States and Fear*, 2nd Ed., Harlow: Pearson Longman, [1982] 1991, p.7.
5 R.D. Lipschutz (ed.), *On Security*, New York: Columbia University Press, 1995, p.5.
6 S. Dalby, 'Geopolitical Change and Contemporary Security Studies: Contextualizing the Human Security Agenda', *Working Paper No. 30*, Canada: Institute of International Relations, The University of British Columbia, 2000, p.3.
7 Buzan, *People, States and Fear*.
8 On Cold War alternative security thinking generally, see S.J. Del Rosso Jr, 'The Insecure State: Reflections on "the State" and "Security" in a Changing World', *Daedalus* 124:2, 1995, pp.175–207.
9 G. Prins, 'The Four-Stroke Cycle in Security Studies', *International Affairs* 74:4, 1998, p.794.
10 Del Rosso Jr, 'The Insecure State', p.187.
11 Dalby, 'Geopolitical Change', p.2.
12 J. Tuchman Mathews, 'Redefining Security', *Foreign Affairs* 68:2, 1989, pp.162–177.
13 W.J. Clinton, 'Inaugural Address of United States President', 20 January 1993. Online. Available at HTTP: <www.law.ou.edu/hist/clinton.html> (accessed 30 May 2006).
14 P. Chalk (ed.), *Non-Military Security and Global Order, The Impact of Extremism, Violence and Chaos on National and International Security*, London: Macmillan Press, 2000, p.2.
15 North Atlantic Treaty Organisation (NATO), 'The Alliance's New Strategic Concept', 1991. Online. Available at HTTP: <www.nato.int/docu/comm/49–95/c911107a.htm> (accessed 30 May 2006).
16 K. Krause and M.C. Williams (eds), *Critical Security Studies, Concepts and Cases*, Minneapolis: University of Minnesota Press, 1997, p.ix.
17 Statement by the President of the Security Council, UN Document ref. number S/23500, 31 January 1992.
18 United Nations Development Programme, *United Nations Human Development Report*, New York: Oxford University Press, 1994, pp.22–23.
19 R. Thakur, 'A Political Worldview', *Security Dialogue* 35:3, 2004, pp.347–348.
20 K. Marx, 1843, 'On the Jewish Question', in D. McClellan (ed.), *Karl Marx: Selected Writings*, New York: Oxford University Press, 1977, p.53.
21 The Commission on Global Governance, *Our Global Neighbourhood*, Oxford: Oxford University Press, 1995, p.81.
22 K. Booth, 'Security and Emancipation', *Review of International Studies* 17, 1991, p.318; Krause and Williams, *Critical Security Studies*, p.44.
23 B. Boutros-Ghali, *An Agenda for Peace, 1995 Second Edition, With the New Supplement and Related UN Documents*, New York: United Nations,1995, pp.41, 42, 44.
24 United Nations Development Programme, *Human Development Report*, pp.22–23.

25 A. Mack, 'A Signifier of Shared Values', *Security Dialogue* 35:3, 2004, pp.366–367.
26 United Nations Development Programme, *Human Development Report*, p.22; C. Thomas and P. Wilkin (eds), *Globalization, Human Security and the African Experience*, Boulder: Lynne Rienner Publishers, 1999, p.3.
27 Boutros-Ghali, *Agenda for Peace*, p.44.
28 Ibid., p.44.
29 J. Ann Tickner, 1999, 'Feminist Perspectives on Security in a Global Economy', in Thomas and Wilkin, *Globalization*, p.50.
30 United Nations Development Programme, *Human Development Report*, p.22.
31 R. Paris, 'Human Security: Paradigm Shift or Hot Air?', *International Security* 26:2, 2001, p.91.
32 K. Krause, 'The Key to a Powerful Agenda if Properly Delimited', *Security Dialogue* 35:3, 2004, pp.367–368.
33 For a list of Canada's position as well as that of other countries, see the Human Security Centre's homepage available at HTTP: <www.humansecuritycentre.org> (accessed 30 May 2006).
34 Commission on Human Security, *Human Security Now*, New York: Commission on Human Security, 2003, p.4.
35 S.M. Walt, 'The Renaissance of Security Studies', *International Studies Quarterly* 35:2, 1991, p.213.
36 G. King and C.J.L. Murray, 'Rethinking Human Security', *Political Science Quarterly* 116:4, 2002, p.292.
37 For example, see King and Murray, 'Rethinking Human Security'.
38 K. Bajpai, 'Human Security: Concept and Measurement', *Kroc Institute Occasional Paper #19* OP:1, 2000, p.30.
39 International Commission on Intervention and State Sovereignty (ICISS), *The Responsibility to Protect: Report of the International Commission on Intervention and State Sovereignty*, Ottawa: International Development Research Center, 2001, p.27.
40 L. Brahimi, *Report of the Panel on United Nations Peace Operations* (aka 'The Brahimi Report'), New York: United Nations, 2000, p.3.
41 L. Axworthy, 'Human Security: Safety for People in a Changing World', 1999. Online. Available at HTTP: <www.humansecurity.gc.ca/safety_changingworld-en.asp> (accessed 30 May 2006).
42 R. Mcrae, 2001, 'Human Security in a Globalized World', in R. Mcrae and D. Hubert (eds), *Human Security and the New Diplomacy*, Montreal: McGill-Queen's University Press, 2001, p.24.
43 Ibid., p.20.
44 Mcrae and Hubert (eds), *Human Security*.
45 D. Deudney, 'The Case Against Linking Environmental Degradation and National Security', *Millennium* 19:3, 1990, pp.461–476.
46 E. Newman, 'Human Security and Constructivism', *International Studies Perspectives* 2:3, 2001, pp.239–251.
47 United Nations Development Programme, *Human Development Report*, p.23.
48 E. Rothschild, 'What is Security?', *Daedalus* 124:3, 1995, p.80.
49 Ibid., pp.70–71.
50 T. Blair, 'Doctrine of the International Community', speech given to the Economic Club of Chicago, 22 April 1999. Online. Available at HTTP: <www.globalpolicy.org/globaliz/politics/blair.htm> (accessed 30 May 2006).
51 J. Solana, *A Secure Europe in a Better World. European Security Strategy*, Paris: The European Union Institute for Security Studies, 2003, p.5.
52 See interviews quoted in M. Duffield and N. Waddell, *Human Security and Global Danger, Exploring a Governmental Assemblage*, London: BOND, 2004. Online. Available at HTTP: <http://www.bond.org.uk/pubs/gsd/duffield.pdf> (accessed 30 May 2006).

53 G.W. Bush, *The National Security Strategy of the United States of America*, Washington, DC: White House, 2002, p.4.
54 Ibid., pp.21–23.
55 Marc Sageman has shown in his study of 400 Al Qaeda terrorists that three quarters come from the upper or middle classes and had gone to study abroad. M. Sageman, *Understanding Terror Networks*, Pennsylvania: University of Pennsylvania Press, 2004.
56 A. Panyarachun, *A More Secure World: Our Shared Responsibility, Report of the High Level Panel on Threats, Challenges and Change* (A/59/565), 2004, paragraphs 21–22.
57 Solana, *A Secure Europe*, pp.5–9.
58 T. Hobbes, *Leviathan*, London: Penguin Books, [1651] 1985, p.186.
59 United Nations Development Programme, *Human Development Report*, p.23.

5 State-building

Exporting state failure

Christopher J. Bickerton

Introduction

There is a consensus today that it is urgently necessary to use international support to sustain domestic institutions in the developing world, even sometimes to the extent of rescinding self-determination in favour of trusteeship. Whereas in the last century, the threat to international peace was perceived to come from strong, aggressive states with ambitions on their neighbours' territory, today it is weak and failing states that are seen as major sources of global insecurity, drawing in their neighbours and the international community against their will. Internationalized state-building is seen as necessary in order to ensure international security and to enable societies to function effectively. Initially confined to 'post-conflict reconstruction' and peacekeeping operations in war-torn societies, state-building policies are now seen as applicable to a wide spectrum of developing countries, both in war and peace. International stability, economic progress and political development are increasingly fused together under the rubric of strengthening domestic governance.

This chapter explores the contradictions in the theory and practice of this new form of internationalized state-building. After establishing state-building as a leading form of international intervention today, I shall argue that state-building cannot succeed in the goals it sets itself. As a process that draws in international institution and external forces, state-building today necessarily relegates citizens to the role of passive recipients of the institutions being built. In short, removing popular will from the process of political creation, as state-building does, produces hollow institutions with shallow roots in the societies for which they are being built. While many analysts, policy-makers and occasionally even the viceroys of state-building are at least dimly aware of this problem, they are unable to grasp its origins, magnitude and full implications. The purpose of this chapter is to make some of these flaws of state-building apparent, by demonstrating that they inhere in the enterprise itself. Since these problems arise from the political nature of the state-building project, they are not amenable to mere technocratic solutions.

After demonstrating some of the contradictions of state-building, I will provide a historical sketch of the emergence of internationalized state-building through a discussion of the concept of state failure. The theory and practice of state-building logically flows from the problematic concept of 'state failure'. This concept is based on a particular understanding of sovereignty drawn from the disastrous development of some post-colonial states. The highly influential theory of state failure led to a reworking, perhaps even an inversion, of the basic categories of International Relations (IR). Traditional IR theory was built on the assumption that state sovereignty was the precondition for social and political order within domestic society. In the absence of any ultimate political authority, the international realm, by contrast was seen as a domain of strife, where all political and legal order was undermined by the ever-present possibility of conflict. Thus one of the traditional problems for liberal theories of international politics in the last century was how to 'domesticate anarchy'; that is, how to make the world order more like the domestic order.

The theory of state failure helped to change this perspective. This theory held that state sovereignty in vast swathes of the post-colonial world was a sham, disguising societies riven with conflict, with no political life or social order to speak of. This focus on the problem of domestic disorder, against the backdrop of an increasingly harmonious international order, raised the prospect that the international order could offer a solution to the problems of war-torn domestic societies. In this new context, the 'domestication of anarchy' effectively has come to mean the 'internationalization of the state'. State-building is thus a form of political intervention that seems to uphold autonomy by seeking to create sovereign states where they appear to have failed. However, state-building actually extends and radicalizes a critique of sovereignty that, as we shall see, first emerged as a response to problems facing post-colonial states.

The new state-building agenda

State-building has emerged as the leading form of international intervention in recent years. Writing in 2004, Francis Fukuyama argued that 'the ability to shore up or create from whole cloth missing state capabilities and institutions has risen to the top of the global agenda and seems likely to be a major condition for security in important parts of the world'.[1] Writing about 'state failure in a time of terror', Robert J. Rotberg echoes Fukuyama: 'how best to strengthen weak states and prevent state failure are among the urgent questions of the twenty-first century'.[2] The Dutch Africanist Martin Doornbus notes: 'Increasingly, international agencies ... representing a new type of "staying" element in a rapidly changing global context, find themselves called upon to restore law and order and to initiate peacebuilding processes in these internal conflict situations.'[3]

These statements attest to the fact that state-building informs policy-making at the highest national and international levels. Former Canadian Prime Minister Paul Martin wrote in 2004 that one of the key foreign policy questions faced by Western governments was 'how well are we doing in helping to make weak states stronger so that they can better fulfil their responsibilities to their own people and others?' He went on to state that 'all the aid in the world will have only a fleeting effect if a country does not have functioning public institutions and a rule of law. Development depends on good governance.'[4] US President George W. Bush echoed the same sentiments in his second inaugural speech in January 2004. Commenting on the speech, the editor-in-chief of the *Washington Times* observed: 'Four years ago George W. Bush was bubbling with scepticism, if not barely concealed contempt, for the notion of "nation-building." Yesterday he promised to rebuild the world.'[5] More recently US Secretary of State Condoleezza Rice placed state-building at the heart of what she called 'transformational diplomacy'. In Rice's words, the objective of transformational diplomacy is 'to work with our many partners around the world, to build and sustain democratic, well-governed states that will respond to the needs of their people and conduct themselves responsibly in the international system'.[6]

The state-building agenda has transformed foreign policy bureaucracies and the agencies of government throughout the world. In August 2004, former US Secretary of State Colin Powell announced the creation of the Office of the Coordinator for Reconstruction and Stabilization, designed to enhance America's 'institutional capacity to respond to crises involving failing, failed, and post-conflict states and complex emergencies'.[7] In the same year, the UK government set up the interdepartmental Post-Conflict Reconstruction Unit, a body with a very similar mandate to the Office of the CRS.[8] The state-building agenda is also central to the concerns of key international organizations. The 2004 United Nations Report of the Secretary-General's High-level Panel on Threats, Challenges and Change envisaged the establishment of a new 'Peacebuilding Commission' – a body with the responsibility to advise the UN in its various 'peacebuilding missions', and to better coordinate information and funding for such operations.[9] This move was a response to both the proliferation of UN state-building activities, and the coordination problems this has thrown up between various international bodies. The Commission was duly brought into being at the sixtieth meeting of the UN General Assembly in late 2005, the text of the resolution being adopted without a vote.[10]

From the World Bank and the International Monetary Fund to the European Union (EU), other organizations have also heavily invested in the state-building agenda (see further John Pender's chapter in this volume). Fukuyama gives an indication of the diversity of actors involved in state-building when he writes that for 'weak' non-Western states today,

> 'stateness' has to be begged, borrowed, or stolen from other sources, ranging from multilateral agencies like the UN or the World Bank in such places as East Timor or Sierra Leone, to the European powers running the Office of the High Representative [in Bosnia Herzegovina], to the United States as occupying power in Iraq.[11]

The EU's recent enlargement, which extended membership to eight former Soviet bloc states in 2004, has been hailed as 'member state-building'.[12] Stanford political scientist and director of Policy Planning at the US State Department Stephen Krasner, has argued that the EU has been one of the few international actors able to design a coherent state-building policy:

> Only in Europe – where the European Union has both held out a set of policy tools and held up a beacon of principles for leaders and citizens in the fledgling post-communist democracies . . . – has it proved possible to limn a future that is not only bright but also likely to materialize.[13]

The London-based Foreign Policy Centre echoes Krasner's enthusiasm, arguing that state-building is integral to Europe's political identity: 'if Europe has begun to develop a strategic identity, it is rooted in state-building'.[14] Casting the expansion of the EU in terms of state-building gives us some idea of the extent to which state-building has travelled from humble beginnings in a handful of peripheral, *ad hoc* and over-burdened UN peacekeeping operations in the early 1990s (some of which will be discussed later), to being at the core of international peace and progressive social change today.

State-building as state failure: the task of Sisyphus

Yet, even as state-building has been sanctified and concretized in policy, it has also been bedevilled with problems in implementation. As indicated earlier in this chapter, such problems should be understood largely as a result of the Sisyphean task state-building sets itself. State-building tries to construct political institutions by bringing in a constellation of external agencies and forces. Yet, bringing external power to bear necessarily restricts the political space available for the people whom these institutions are (at least nominally) destined to serve, and limits the exercise of the people's own political creativity. The creation of sovereign, coherent political institutions depends upon engaging the subjectivity of the individuals within the society in question. If people's hopes, interests and desires are mediated through so many external forces, the resulting institutions will be that many more steps removed from the individuals for whom they are established. These institutions, as a consequence, will be less the creations of the people in question, and more products of external interests. Michael Ignatieff points to this when he describes the 'spectacle of disgruntled locals, sitting in cafés, watching earnest young internationals speeding around to important meetings in Toyota Land Cruisers [a spectacle that] has been repeated in every nation-building experiment in the 1990s'.[15] If domestic actors are blocked from exercising power directly, external powers, meanwhile, claim not to be pursuing their own projects, but to be creating institutions for others. Many problems of state-building flow from this basic contradiction between the exercise of external power and the necessity of domestic foundations.

There are many examples of this. For example, since it began in 1999, the United Nations Mission in Kosovo (UNMIK) has explicitly separated the political question of independence for the province from the technical job of institution-building.

In 2003, the UN governor-general of the province, Michael Steiner, launched a policy of 'standards before status', that is, institutional development before resolving Kosovo's ultimate political status, which everyone nonetheless assumes will involve independence from Serbia, where sovereignty still nominally resides. In practice, this political stalemate has been impossible to sever from the task of institution-building. This is reflected in the growing delegitimation of the province's embryonic political institutions, and in Kosovars' alienation from the work of the UN and the EU.[16] Voter turnout in Kosovo has steadily declined. Turnout in the 2000 elections was 79 per cent; but by 2004 it had fallen by over 20 points to 54 per cent.[17] The UN Development Programme has noted that this fall in voter turnout has occurred alongside a shift of electoral support to fringe political parties more openly hostile to UNMIK.[18] The clearest sign of UNMIK failure is the lethal ethnic conflict that has continued since North Atlantic Treaty Organisation (NATO) forces occupied the province in 1999, vividly expressed in the violence of March 2004. This was an example of what Jarat Chopra has termed 'building state failure' through international administration. Evidence of such failure continues in East Timor, until recently a country widely seen as having benefited from a successful UN state-building mission. For Timor, ensuring stability and social peace without international aid has proven elusive. Only a year after UN peacekeepers left, the UN Security Council has backed a new deployment of foreign troops and police from Australia, Malaysia, New Zealand and Portugal, in response to violence that broke out in spring 2006.[19]

Such examples are not restricted to the populations of small territories, such as Kosovo and East Timor, nor to UN administered operations. The EU's absorption of 73 million new citizens in 2004 has come up against similar problems in implementing the *Acquis Communautaire* in new member states (i.e. the corpus of EU rules and regulations that have to be incorporated into the domestic legal systems of member states). In many cases, citizens have repeatedly failed to recognize themselves in the newly imported EU law. In response to the *Acquis* package crafted in Brussels, many citizens of the former Soviet Republic of Estonia have revived what Kristi Raik calls 'Soviet double-think' – the apathetic, sullen response once displayed towards regulations from Moscow. 'When it comes to bureaucracy and over-regulation', writes Raik, 'the image of the EU among Estonians does not differ much from that of the Soviet Union.'[20] In the words of one Estonian columnist quoted by Raik,

> Now, being close, that Europe of a dream rather appears as a boring administrative machinery that produces restrictions and bureaucracy. We must close many more countryside shops and pubs, install thousands of steel basins in school refectories, in order to pass the strict sanitary tests. It's like the army! First delouse the sauna, and only after that you get to wear the gold-starred uniform. First tidiness, then – administrative capacity.[21]

Similar problems were experienced in other candidate countries. In their study of local and regional elites in Hungary, Slovenia and Estonia, Hughes *et al.* have pointed out the shortfall between the incorporation of the *Acquis* into national legislation and people's willingness to actually implement the new regulations. In their view, '[local elites] are highly adept at window-dressing and paying lip-service while also doing the opposite or at the very least doing the minimum'. Non-fulfilment, or poor fulfilment, is, they argue, 'a classic "weapon of the weak," as well as a sign of alienation from the decision-making process elsewhere'.[22] However grudgingly the *Acquis* is observed, it would be wrong to think that it has had no impact on East European countries beyond better sanitation. A prominent feature of the recently completed eastern enlargement was a pronounced strengthening of the executive arm of government in the candidate countries, and a concomitant downgrading of national parliaments to simply rubber stamping EU legislation. Candidate state governments often introduced 'fast-tracking' measures to ensure that laws were pushed through in time to meet EU deadlines.[23] This sidelining of national parliaments belittled the political process of debating and reflecting upon legislation – that is, the very process by which laws become laws, by winning the support of elected representatives in debates. Policy implementation replaces public legislation.

The problems of state-building are so rife that they are impossible not to acknowledge, even among its proponents. Fukuyama, for example, recognizes that a relationship of some kind exists between political processes of accountability and representation, and the development of political institutions. He concedes that 'before you can have democracy, you must have a state, but to have a legitimate and therefore durable state you eventually must have democracy'. He stops here however, concluding with the banal observation that '[democratization and state-building] are intertwined, but the precise sequencing of how and when to build the distinct but interlocking institutions needs very careful thought'.[24] Roland Paris comes to a more determined conclusion in his claim that 'institutionalization' should occur before the introduction of self-government and party political competition.[25] Like Paris, Simon Chesterman argues that 'local ownership' should be introduced at the end of the process of 'capacity-building', after which power can be 'transferred' back to the local population. Chesterman's argument is distinctive in that he locates the difficulties of state-building in the unwillingness of the 'internationals' to fully accept the burden of absolute power. In his words, 'either the international presence exercises quasi-sovereign powers on a temporary basis or it does not . . . in either case, the abiding need is for clarity as to who is in charge'.[26] The problem today is that military occupation and preponderant power are 'now sometimes seen as politically unpalatable, and therefore masked behind the language of ownership'.[27]

But the problem is more than a sentimental attachment to self-determination. If anything, the existence of state-building indicates how weak political belief in the principle of self-determination has become. Nor is the problem a liberal squeamishness about the exercise of power. Jarat Chopra, for example, scathingly speaks of the 'UN's kingdom in East Timor' during the 1999–2002 UN administration over that nation: 'The organizational and juridical status of the UN in East Timor is comparable with that of a pre-constitutional monarch in a sovereign kingdom.'[28] In Bosnia, the High Representative, the appointed official who represents both the international community and the EU, has enjoyed extensive powers and has had few reservations about using them. These powers range from enforcing binding decisions, to taking 'actions against persons holding public office'. Chesterman recounts that, in the years since the Peace Implementation Council agreed to grant the High Representative these so-called Bonn powers, different High Representatives have routinely sacked, suspended or banned over 100 elected officials.[29] Paddy Ashdown used these powers so extensively as to have Bosnia branded a 'European Raj'.[30] Shrugging off these criticisms, Paddy Ashdown claimed that the '*droit de seigneur* was the only thing I didn't have in Bosnia, but if I'd have asked for it, I'd have probably got it...'.[31] Despite the sweeping panoply of powers that the international community has granted to its viceroys in Bosnia, the international presence continues. The extent of this failure has been obscured by subsuming Bosnia within the EU accession process, thereby allowing responsibility for the dependent Bosnian state to be transferred from the Peace Implementation Council to Brussels, buried under the framework of EU incentives and conditionalities. As David Chandler observes, in the shift 'from Dayton to Europe' little has changed. Bosnians remain 'excluded from the transition process and while there is general support for EU membership there has been little discussion of the costs and benefits involved'.[32]

Thus while there is widespread consciousness of these problems, there is little real self-reflection about their origins. The recurring problems, when they are recognized at all, are muted through managerial terms such as calls for 'local ownership', 'bottom-up' approaches and recognizing the dangers of 'capacity sucking-out' and 'crowding-out', whereby domestic institutions may be eroded by the activities of the international administrative apparatus. But this arid analysis transforms a political problem, located in the prevailing understanding of sovereignty, into a technical problem that appears amenable to technical solutions. In response to the practical demands of state-building, analysts have responded by conceptually dismembering sovereignty into smaller, more manageable chunks. Stephen Krasner distinguishes between what he terms 'Westphalian/Vattelian' sovereignty and 'domestic' sovereignty, the former referring to the principle of formal independence and non-intervention, the latter to the capacity to effectively administer a given territory. Krasner advocates the abrogation of the former, in order that state-builders can do their job in restoring 'domestic' sovereignty to weak or 'collapsed' states.[33]

The problem with such approaches is that they advance an understanding of sovereignty as a theory of rule that can be mechanistically isolated from society. Sovereignty is seen as an attribute of the rulers, which can be temporarily waived until domestic 'capacity' is restored. As the first chapter in this book indicates, however, sovereignty is always 'of society'. It is the institution that mediates between individuals and state institutions, between popular will and public power. Part of the confusion arises from the fact that sovereignty is something that necessarily takes the form of being a step removed from society, represented as an independent legal power. But despite the 'detached' form that sovereignty takes, it is still internally related to society. It is only by being abstracted from society that the concept of sovereignty enables people to rise above their immediate interests, and to consider these in relation to the interests of other members of society. In other words, sovereignty is what gives these interests their political, as opposed to purely individuated, character. The process is described by Rousseau as the act of 'transforming each individual, who by himself is a perfect and solitary whole, into a part of a larger whole from which this individual in some way receives his life and his being'.[34]

The fact, therefore, that sovereignty is something abstracted from society does not mean that it can be mechanically severed from society by an external agency, and then grafted back on. To reconstitute sovereignty in this way is to vitiate the entire process by which political will is formed within society. With the intervention of external forces and agencies into the process of shaping state institutions, politics and sovereignty become ever more mediated, more abstract and more distant from the immediate concerns of the members of the society in question. The institution of sovereignty is replaced by an alternative network of internationalized relations in which the liberties and interests of citizens are no longer the essential foundation of political order. One of the most explicit examples of this is the 'Constitutional Framework for Provisional Self-Government' in Kosovo, a document that outlined political arrangements in the province after the 2001 elections. What is remarkable about the 'Framework' is that it is among the first constitutional documents (though tellingly in itself, not a constitution) in modern political history, whose preamble explicitly relegates the 'will of the people' to only one among a number of factors that will be taken into consideration by the UN officials administering the province.[35] To relativize the will of the people in such a way denudes the end products of state-building of their political content; namely, the people as sovereign. It is this external mediation of the process of political creation that gives state-building its fragile and contingent character. State-building is erecting institutions with few social or political foundations. It is unsurprising therefore, that state-building constantly recreates politically dependent administrations, in need of international support to survive. This is the meaning of 'state-building as state failure'.

Having outlined the internal contradictions of contemporary state-building, we must now turn to the historical process through which external support came to be seen as a vital prop to domestic order. A critical examination of the concept of 'state failure' will act as the bridge to cross from the logical analysis of the contradictions of state-building to grasping the historical emergence of state-building in international politics. State-building has emerged as a specific response to a concrete historical phenomenon, namely the exhaustion of post-colonial independence in many developing countries – an issue addressed in the theory of 'state failure'.

Post-colonial states and 'state failure'

The influential idea of 'state failure' is the theoretical epitaph of the progressive, developmental Third World state, written following the defeat of anti-colonial nationalism in the closing decades of the twentieth century. The occasion of political defeat was used by many as retroactive confirmation that there had never been much political substance or progressive force behind anti-imperialist struggles, especially when it came to creating self-sufficient modern states. Philosopher Kwame Anthony Appiah captured this mood of pessimism and disenchantment, observing that 'When the post-colonial rulers inherited the apparatus of the colonial state, they inherited the reins of power; few noticed, at first, that they were not attached to a bit.'[36]

Jackson and Rosberg, in their 1982 analysis of African states, argued that post-colonial African states have been characterized by profound weaknesses in their ability to coerce and tax their populations. These administrative weaknesses, however, were obscured by the legal form of state sovereignty. Anticipating Krasner's taxonomy of different types of sovereignty, this characterization of post-colonial states dissected statehood into 'juridical' and 'empirical' aspects. These African states had 'juridical statehood' – that is, the pomp and circumstance of sovereignty, such as flags, national anthems, membership of the UN, the right to make international treaties and so on – but lacked the 'content' of statehood; in Jackson's words 'the political will, institutional authority and organized power to protect human rights or to provide socio-economic welfare'.[37]

Jackson and Rosberg concluded that weak African states had been allowed to survive by virtue of the legitimacy they were accorded by the benign, indeed misguided, ideals of the post-1945 international order. Whereas in previous periods such weak and fractious communities would have been devoured by their stronger neighbours, the indulgent culture of entitlement and dependence fostered by the ideals of anti-colonialism, equality and self-determination provided external support structures, such as diplomatic recognition and foreign aid, to prop up these hollow shells of sovereign states. These were 'quasi-states', a category popularized by Jackson in his 1990 book *Quasi-States*. Here Jackson conceptually shifted from statehood to sovereignty by characterizing the post-1945 international liberal order as a regime of 'negative sovereignty' embodied in the idea of 'freedom from outside interference'.[38]

Jackson's explicit linkage of sovereignty with the civil strife and continued poverty of many post-colonial states in Africa did much to erode the moral authority traditionally associated with sovereignty and self-determination. Jackson argued that the nominal virtues of sovereignty – independence, dignity and so on – had, in the crucible of anti-colonialism, been twisted into their opposite: 'the same institution [i.e. sovereignty] which provided international recognition, dignity, and independence to all colonized populations could be exploited to deny domestic civility, liberty and welfare to [them] . . . International liberation could therefore be followed by domestic subjugation'.[39] In the end, '[negative sovereignty] usually works in favour of sovereigns against their citizens'.[40] National liberation, in other words, was meaningless.

The influence of Jackson's reading of 'state failure' is difficult to understate; it inaugurated the enormous literature on state failure and state-building. For example, Helman and Ratner, who in 1993 published a seminal article in

Foreign Policy entitled 'Saving failed states', reproduce Jackson's argument in their analysis. In their view, 'the current collapse [of states such as Haiti and Somalia] has its roots in the vast proliferation of nation-states, especially in Africa and Asia, since the end of World War Two'. In particular, in the post-war period, 'self-determination...was given more attention than long-term survivability', and they observe that the principal barrier to more extensive interventions prior to the post-Cold War period was the 'talisman of sovereignty'.[41] This idea that states can fail is obviously the precursor to the idea that states need to be rebuilt. Only after the idea that states could fail had been established was it possible for internationalized state-building to be mooted as an acceptable solution.

But the importance of failed state theory is more than merely being the intellectual precursor to state-building.[42] Jackson's argument also prefigures much of the intellectual and political disdain for sovereignty that is taken for granted today. For example, Jackson used conflict in Africa to give life to the link between sovereignty and barbarism. Moreover, by envisaging sovereignty as an institution that could act *against* society, Jackson laid the ground for seeing sovereignty as something that could be detached *from* society.[43] As we saw in relation to state-building, a crucial presupposition of failed state theory is that the local capacity for political self-creation is regarded as insufficient, potentially even destructive. Hence the necessity of external support to consolidate the process of institution-building; in Jeffrey Herbst's words, we must now 'acknowledge that state consolidation has failed and that external intervention is necessary'.[44] The roots of this idea of political insufficiency can be analysed by interrogating Jackson's analysis of anti-colonialism.

Jackson's disaggregation of sovereignty into 'positive' and 'negative' facets poses a two-fold problem. The first problem is the putative absence of 'positive sovereignty', that is, insufficient administrative capacity to effectively govern a given territory. But Jackson, like many others,[45] reads the historic failure of anti-colonialism backwards into history. In Jackson's reading, the exhaustion of so many post-colonial states is taken as evidence to deny that there was any process of political self-creation involved in the struggle against colonialism. By denying that there was any political weight behind anti-colonial nationalism, Jackson can take the *absence* of highly developed administrative machinery as *evidence* of the absence of any political basis for such institutions. But politics creates institutions, not vice versa. Since Jackson fails to see any political life in these societies, he is logically forced to pose the problem not in political terms, but in technical ones, of the absence of administrative capacity. As we saw from the earlier discussion, this separation of institutional creation from political life has hobbled state-building operations.

Having focused on the domestic side of the theory, dealing with the absence of positive sovereignty, let us now focus on the international dimension of the theory. The second element of this theory put forward the *presence* of negative sovereignty; that is, the rights accorded to states by the liberal international order. For Jackson, colonialism was not destroyed through the efforts of oppressed colonial peoples, but through the simple-minded benevolence of imperial powers, who extended rights of independence to peoples whose political cohesion was so tenuous that they were incapable of exercising these rights. But anti-colonialism did not spring fully formed from the heads of feeble-minded, benevolent colonial administrators. It emerged through a historical process of violent political struggles, from Ireland to Algeria to India and China. These struggles mutually reinforced each other's claims to equality and emancipation throughout the world. The subsequent defeat and demise of anti-colonial nationalism is beyond the scope of this chapter; suffice to say that the prospects of independent statehood were limited by an international economic order still dominated by the metropolitan economies. The main point here is that, by centring the problem on the international regime of 'negative sovereignty', failed state theory implies that the solution can also be found at the international level.

By pointing to the conflicts that raged in nominally self-contained states, and contrasting this with the relative harmony of the international realm, the theory of state failure inverses the traditional concern of IR theory. In their 1982 article, Jackson and Rosberg concluded that 'insofar as our theoretical images follow rather than precede concrete historical change, it is evident that the recent national and international history of Black Africa challenges more than it supports some of the major postulates of international theory'.[46] In a later work, Jackson generalized the conclusions he had earlier drawn about Africa, arguing that 'quasi-states turn Hobbes inside out: the state of nature is domestic, and civil society is international'.[47] Turning international relations theory 'inside-out' was taken forward by the 'state failure' literature, where the single most important international threat is no longer from other states, but from disorder within weak states, as pithily expressed by Ignatieff: 'Chaos has replaced tyranny as the new challenge to human rights in the twenty-first century.'[48]

In counterposing international peace to the putative chaos of domestic society in the developing world, the theory of state failure reflects its historical origins in the waning period of the Cold War. The eclipse of ideological and geopolitical struggle between the USA and USSR had several effects. First, it removed the political and ideological rationale for many struggles in the developing world. Second, the peaceful transition to a post-Cold War world endowed the international order with the patina of world-historic success and progress. Third, it gave international organizations such as the UN a mandate to pursue an expanded agenda, as neutral, benevolent vessels of this very same international progress. The convergence of these three factors can be seen in the proliferation of peace accords in the immediate post-Cold War era, several of which laid the basis for the first UN state-building operations in the post-Cold War period. The end of the Cold War directly undermined the rationale for wars in South East Asia and South West Africa, leading to troop withdrawals, peace agreements and new, 'multidimensional' peacekeeping operations: the United Nations Transitional Authority in Cambodia (UNTAC) and the United Nations Transitional Assistance Group (UNTAG) in Namibia. Most UN field operations had hitherto been restricted to patrolling pre-agreed ceasefire lines; they had no political task, as the political work of agreeing a ceasefire had already been done. In Cambodia and Namibia, however, UN officials found themselves wielding extraordinary powers. Chesterman observes that UNTAG was 'one of the first occasions in which the UN was called upon to exercise quasi-governmental powers'.[49] In fact, while the

> administrative powers exercised by the international actors [in Cambodia] were explicitly limited to ensuring a neutral political environment for the elections – nevertheless they exceeded anything seen since the colonial era and the Allied occupations of Germany and Japan following the Second World War.[50]

One of the most intriguing early case studies in the evolution of state-building is that of Haiti. The significance of this tiny island nation lay, in the words of former UN Secretary-General Boutros Boutros-Ghali, in how far it had fallen from its revolutionary struggle for liberty:

> the first independent republic in Latin America and the first independent black republic anywhere [c]reated by the...revolt of slaves against Napoleon...Ostracised and prey to big powers, Haiti depicted its turbulent history on its flag, which bristles with cannons and banners.[51]

The extremes of Haiti's history, veering between the heroic achievement on which it was founded, and its calamitous post-independence history of international isolation, made Haiti a potent 'symbol of the suffering and the struggle of the third world'.[52] The end of the Cold War gave a glimmer of hope with the election of Jean-Bertrand Aristide in 1990, under the auspices of the United Nations Observer Group for the Verification of the Elections in Haiti (ONUVEH). The presence of ONUVEH produced widespread unease among Haiti's neighbours, who feared establishing a precedent for UN interference in their internal affairs. Haiti's neighbours ensured, therefore, that the presence of ONUVEH was softened by being packaged under the formal aegis of the regional organization, the Organization of American States (OAS).[53]

Aristide was ousted and exiled in a military putsch later that same year, and turned to the UN for aid in restoring democracy to Haiti. In his memoirs, Boutros-Ghali recounts how he 'explained [to Aristide] that UN involvement was limited because the General Assembly...had placed the OAS in charge of the Haitian problem. I advised Aristide to try to gain greater support among the United Nations' member states.' Boutros-Ghali notes how Aristide took his 'recommendation to heart', and describes the effect of the Haitian leader's renowned rhetorical skills when he gave a speech to the General Assembly:

> before a packed hall and in an electric atmosphere, Aristide displayed his dazzling talents...The former seminarian had become a poet-orator: 'I found Haiti, where the roots of liberty set down by Toussaint l'Ouverture endured...diminished, sometimes battered, but never finished'.[54]

A few months later, the speech had its desired effect when the UN adopted a resolution passing effective control of the Haitian question from the OAS to the UN. Boutros-Ghali writes, 'Aristide had won the first round of *his* fight to relegate the OAS to a lesser role' (emphasis added). [55]

Aristide's actions, and the consequences for Haiti, are instructive. The history of intervention in Haiti provides a yardstick by which to measure the evolution of state-building. Today, Aristide is in exile once again, removed this time not by a reactionary putsch, but by a UN-authorized Franco-American military campaign. The latest UN operation in the country, the United Nations Stabilization Mission in Haiti (MINUSTAH), has more than electoral observers in its ranks. At the time of writing, MINUSTAH includes roughly 7,000 troops and 1,000 police officers. Meanwhile, Haiti's Latin American neighbours have cast off their principled objection to interference in each others' affairs, with Latin American states taking the lead in the operation, including Brazil's leftist government under Luiz Inácio Lula da Silva.[56] The operation has been dogged with controversy for mounting counter-insurgency operations against pro-Aristide districts of Haiti's capital, Port-au-Prince, with some MINUSTAH officials' talk of 'collateral damage' making them sound 'more like US generals than UN officials'.[57]

The fate of Haiti under MINUSTAH illustrates the dangers of relying on the caprice of external powers to effect political change within your own society. It is worth re-emphasizing that it was only under the specific conditions of the post-Cold War world that the 'UN solution' could seem to have both legitimacy and efficacy for Aristide's dilemma. More importantly, Aristide's diplomacy illustrates the abandonment of the will to self-determination. Aristide was no petty stooge, isolated in his palace. Yet, despite his immense popularity among Haiti's masses, Aristide decided to rely not on the social power of the Haitian people, but on the international community to restore democracy.

According to Boutros-Ghali, it was of his own free will that Aristide set in motion the relegation of the OAS, which laid the ground for vastly expanded UN intervention in Haitian politics. Aristide's dramatic speech before the General Assembly marked the moment of the involution of the will to self-determination, and with it the demise of a tradition of independence born in slave revolt.

The Haitian experience illustrates historically what we discovered in the theoretical examination of Jackson's work. It also demonstrates how the theory of state failure was born of specific historical circumstances that raised the novel possibility of harnessing the power and moral authority of international organizations to tackle civil conflicts. We have seen that the theory of state failure is not only the precursor to state-building, but also contains, in embryo, the preconceptions and limitations of state-building concepts. Jackson's theory of state failure dismissed anti-colonial nationalism; then it portrayed internal problems as essentially a technical matter of administrative incapacity; and finally it posited the international order as the immanent bearer of peace. This squeezed politics out of the picture, while laying the basic components of bureaucratic state-building theory.

To be sure, in his more recent writings Jackson has retreated from some of the more paternalistic implications of his earlier work. Writing on the return of trusteeship to world politics, Jackson writes, 'Sovereignty is not a political arrangement only for fair weather and good times. It is an arrangement for all political seasons and all kinds of political weather.'[58] Certainly, the value accorded to self-determination has declined in international politics. But this is not just expressed in the revival of outright trusteeship in places like Kosovo. As we have seen, state-building embraces a panoply of intrusive regulatory practices, many of which fall short of trusteeship. Yet at the same time, state-building promotes the form of the independent state as a central feature of international order. To defend self-determination and sovereignty against trusteeship thus misses the extent to which state-building interventions, and the undermining of political autonomy, occur *within* the formal structures of sovereign independence. Ignatieff captures this wider devaluation of autonomy. On the one hand, he claims that 'unlike the empires of the past, the UN administrations are designed to serve and enhance the idea of self-determination, rather than suppress it'.[59] On the other hand, Ignatieff qualifies what he means by sovereignty and self-determination. He describes the aspiration 'for Westphalian sovereignty' as 'a snare and a delusion'.[60] Instead, he urges weak states to build 'partnerships with neighbours and ex-colonial countries in order to strengthen, not their sovereign independence, but their capacities as systems of governance to deliver services and decent economic prospects for their people'. Thus, while invoking the language of self-determination and independence, Ignatieff argues for greater integration of weak states into international structures of regulation and control: 'the more implicated a state is in trade and border agreements and security pacts with other states...the stronger and more efficient as an instrument of governance it becomes.'[61] State-building thus takes the form of 'internationalizing states' – integrating them into the international system of regulation and oversight so as to pacify internal strife.

Stephen Krasner shares Ignatieff's desire for more permanent international systems of political oversight. According to Krasner, missions that are explicitly temporary distort the incentives of local actors to support state-building. In Bosnia, for instance, the transitional administration is failing because 'it is not in the interests of Bosnian political leaders to make it work'.[62] In Krasner's view, it is the finite nature of the transitional administration in Sarajevo that keeps domestic politicians wedded to their ethnic constituents.[63] Note here that the problem for Krasner is what one would normally presume to be the fundamental strength of representative democracy, namely, Bosnian politicians' closeness to their constituents. Krasner's solution is 'shared sovereignty' which 'involve[s] the engagement of external actors in some of the domestic authority structures of the target states for an indefinite period of time'.[64] With more candour than Ignatieff, Krasner recognizes that 'shared sovereignty' is unlikely to appeal to the masses. He suggests that 'for policy purposes', 'it would be best to refer to shared sovereignty as "partnerships"', as this would allow political leaders to pay lip-service to self-determination while signing it away in various international agreements.[65]

'Shared sovereignty' is what existing state-building interventions effectively introduce. For instance, Krasner recommends that in 'badly governed illiberal democracies', political candidates or parties should enter into contracts with the international community as a way of demonstrating their commitment to certain reform strategies. 'Such a political platform could win votes by signalling to the electorate that a politician would make a decisive break with the past by engaging external actors in domestic decision-making.'[66] In fact, this idea of domestic politicians 'binding their hands' through agreements with international agencies has already been practiced for some years in Eastern Europe. In the states of former Yugoslavia, the EU's flagship policy, the Stabilization and Association Process (SAP), formally outlaws authoritarian governments as a condition of signing the agreement. Governments participating in the SAP therefore commit themselves, as parties to a contract, to maintain a plural party political system.[67] But it would be unwise to take this formal commitment to liberal politics at face value. Contracting with an external agency to retain a liberal party system means that the limits on these political systems are now fixed by agreement with parties external to the polity, rather than grounded in a contract between the state and its own society. The polity has renounced its ability to determine, but also its responsibility for maintaining its own institutions. Liberalism in these states is no longer guaranteed by the people, holding their representatives and state institutions to account. Far from strengthening political liberalism, this undermines it, as the institutions of the state are oriented not inwards to their peoples, but outwards to the EU. Again, the factor relegated in this seeming consolidation and extension of liberal democracy is that crucial animus of political life, the 'will of the people'. Understood in this way, we can see that state-building has become the norm in international policy circles: states are to be built not as 'self-standing structures', to use Jackson's phrase, but as nodes integrated into the international system of 'governance'.

Conclusion

This chapter has drawn out the internal inconsistencies of state-building, has situated these within concrete historical developments since the end of the Cold War, and has pointed to the broader implications of state-building interventions for international politics in the twenty-first century. While state-building may aim, at least rhetorically, to rebuild independent states, in practice it is more likely to weaken state institutions, or at the very least to build political structures that are dependent upon international support for their continued existence. The reason for this is that state-building cleaves institution-building from the political life of the society in question.

We have seen how this separation of institution-building from politics is achieved through a reinterpretation of the idea of sovereignty. The relation to which sovereignty normally refers is an organic, internal relation between the state and its own society. Insofar as state-building necessarily involves the partial, and sometimes even the total, assumption of sovereign power by international administration, power relations are reconstituted between international agencies and state institutions, thus bypassing domestic populations. Owing to their integration into global governance networks, target states become increasingly dependent on international patronage rather than relying on the will and passions of their own people, thereby fostering popular withdrawal and disengagement from politics. Instead of representing the centralized authority of a population, internationalized states embody the decentralized power of multiple external agents, making the exercise of power that much less accountable.

The theoretical roots of this vision of state-building lie in the concept of 'state failure'. While denying the capacity of developing countries for self-government was hardly original – it was an argument as old as imperialism itself – Robert Jackson's theory shows what is distinctive about state failure. It portrays sovereignty as something that can be wielded against the interests of its own society. The idea of the 'failed state' has thereby facilitated the dissociation of sovereignty from developing societies, and transformed the political problem of popular politics into a technical one of administrative weakness. Reading the failure of anti-colonial nationalism back into history, Jackson saw no political movement in these societies, and could point to only technical, and not political, problems. In turning states into vectors of international experts and products of external regulation, state-building takes forward this technocratic view of politics. As a consequence, it creates brittle institutions and fragile political regimes, forced to rely on the international arena for moral authority and material sustenance. As we have seen, it was the specific conditions of the post-Cold War world that made international solutions to domestic problems both possible and attractive.

State-building is usually seen as applicable only to the unstable periphery, which reflects its ideological roots in theories of state failure. The theory of state failure has been integral to rolling back the international egalitarianism that was achieved after the destruction of colonial empires. The largely undisputed theory of state failure has succeeded in inverting power relations, suggesting that the greatest threats to humanity emanate not from the strong, but from the 'poorest regions in the world, with limited access to technology and other resources and the least power'. In the words of Frank Füredi, more often than not

> [b]anal commentary regarding the sheer weight of population and the unpredictable character of Eastern fanaticism exhausts the argument. The idea that population and fanaticism cannot pose a formidable challenge to the hi-tech weaponry and industry ... of the West is simply not considered.[68]

However exaggerated the problems posed by 'failed states' may be, it would be a mistake to see them as purely external, 'over there'. Lenin famously characterized the social problems of the developing, colonial world as indicative of the fact that they were the 'weakest links' in the 'chain' of worldwide imperialism.[69] In other words, the turmoil in the periphery expressed in a concentrated form political problems that confronted states the world over, including the metropolitan countries.

A similar point could be made about 'failed states' today. The crisis of government is not restricted to poor and weak countries. The political exhaustion of many post-colonial states, and their subsequent institutional implosion, demonstrates in an acute form a problem that is, to a greater or lesser degree, common to many societies throughout the world, including the industrialized states – as is discussed in Alexander Gourevitch's and James Heartfield's chapters in this volume. Internationalizing state-building is strengthening and consolidating these trends, by replacing the politics of self-determination with bureaucratic rule that is dependent on external power for its survival.

Notes

1 F. Fukuyama, *State-building: Governance and World Order in the Twenty-First Century*, London: Profile, 2004, pp.xi–xii.
2 R.J. Rotberg, 2003, 'Failed States, Collapsed States, Weak States: Causes and Indicators', in R.J. Rotberg (ed.), *State Failure and State Weakness in a Time of Terror*, New York: World Peace Foundation, 2003, p.1.
3 M. Doornbus, *Global Forces and State Restructuring: Dynamics of State Formation and Collapse*, Basingstoke: Palgrave Macmillan, 2006, p.3.
4 P. Martin, 'Lessons from the Americas', *The World in 2005, The Economist*, 2004.
5 W. Pruden, 'No Nation Building but a World Awaits', *Washington Times*, 23 January 2005.
6 C. Rice, 'Transformational Diplomacy', Speech given at Georgetown University, Washington, DC, 18 January 2006. Online. Available at HTTP: <http://www.state.gov/secretary/rm/2006/59306.htm> (accessed 30 May 2006).
7 The citation is from the State Department webpage. Available at HTTP: <http://www.state.gov/s/crs/> (accessed 30 May 2006).
8 See the Post-Conflict Reconstruction Unit webpage. Available at HTTP: <http://www.postconflict.gov.uk/index.asp> (accessed 30 May 2006).
9 K. Annan, 'Addendum Two', *In Larger Freedom: Towards Development, Security and Human-Rights for All*: A/59/2005, 2005. Online. Available at HTTP: <http://www.un.org/largerfreedom/add2.htm> (accessed 30 May 2006).
10 See 'General Assembly, acting concurrently with the Security Council, makes Peacebuilding Commission operational', Department of Public Information, News and Media Division, United Nations. Online. Available at HTTP: <http://www.un.org/News/Press/docs/2005/ga10439.doc.htm> (accessed 30 May 2006).
11 F. Fukuyama, ' "Stateness" First', *Journal of Democracy* 16:1, 2005, p.84.
12 G. Knaus and M. Cox, 'The "Helsinki Moment" in South-Eastern Europe', *Journal for Democracy* 16:1, 2005, pp.39–53. These new members of the European Union as of 2004 are the Czech Republic, Estonia, Hungary, Slovakia, Slovenia, Poland, Latvia and Lithuania.
13 S.D. Krasner, 'The Case for Shared Sovereignty', *Journal of Democracy* 16:1, 2005, p.80.
14 Global Europe, *Report 3: Rescuing the State: Europe's Next Challenge*, London: Foreign Policy Centre, British Council and EU Commission, 2005.
15 M. Ignatieff, 2003, 'State Failure and Nation Building', in J.L. Holzgrefe and R. Keohane (eds), *Humanitarian Intervention: Ethical, Legal, and Political Dilemmas*, Cambridge: Cambridge University Press, 2003, p.321.
16 The UN is responsible for running UNMIK, but the EU has the responsibility for economic development – this is pillar IV, known as the EU pillar. For more information, see the EU's website. Available at HTTP: <http://www.euinkosovo.org/> (accessed 30 May 2006).

17 United Nations Development Programme (UNDP), *UNDP Human Development Report Kosovo. The Rise of the Citizen: Challenges and Choices*, Pristina: UNDP, 2004.
18 Ibid.
19 For more information, see the following reports: S. Donnan and S. Tucker, 'International Peacekeepers Arrive in East Timor', *Financial Times*, 25 May 2006; 'Troops Pour into Unstable E Timor', *BBC News*, 26 May 2006. Online. Available at HTTP: <http://news.bbc.co.uk/1/hi/world/asia-pacific/5018648.stm> (accessed 30 May 2006).
20 K. Raik, 'EU Accession of Central and Eastern European Countries: Democracy and Integration as Conflicting Logics', *East European Politics and Societies* 18:4, 2004, pp.585–586.
21 Ibid., p.586.
22 J. Hughes, G. Sassen and C. Gordon, 'Saying "Maybe" to the Return to Europe', *European Union Politics* 3:3, 2002, p.336.
23 D. Malova and T. Haughton, 'Making Institutions in Central and Eastern Europe, and the Impact of Europe', *Western European Politics* 25:2, 2002, pp.101–120.
24 See J. Chopra, 2003, 'Building State Failure in East Timor', in J. Milliken and K. Krause (eds), *State Failure, Collapse and Reconstruction*, Oxford: Blackwells, 2003, pp.223–244. See also S. Woodward, 'Construire l'État: légitimité internationale contre légitimité nationale?', *Critique Internationale* 28, 2005, pp.139–152.
25 R. Paris, *At War's End; Building Peace After Civil Conflict*, Cambridge: Cambridge University Press, 2004, pp.179–211.
26 S. Chesterman, *You, The People: The United Nations, Transitional Administrations and State-building*, Oxford: Oxford University Press, 2003, p.243.
27 Ibid., p.144.
28 J. Chopra, 'The UN's Kingdom of East Timor', *Survival* 42:3, 2000, p.29.
29 Chesterman, *You, The People*, pp.129–131.
30 G. Knaus and F. Martin, 'Travails of the European Raj', *Journal of Democracy* 14:3, 2003, pp.60–74.
31 P. Ashdown, speech given at St Anthony's College, Oxford, 26 April 2006. Ashdown is referring to the right that the feudal lord had to sleep with any woman in his domain on her wedding night.
32 D. Chandler (ed.), *Peace Without Politics? Ten Years of International State-building in Bosnia*, Abingdon: Routledge, 2006, p.40.
33 S.D. Krasner, 'Sharing Sovereignty: New Institutions for Collapsed and Failing States', *International Security* 29:2, 2005, p.89.
34 Cited in K. Marx, 1844, On the Jewish Question, in J. O'Malley and R.A. Davis (eds), *Marx: Early Political Writings*, Cambridge: Cambridge University Press, 1994, pp.49–50.
35 'Constitutional Framework for Provisional Self-Government', UNMIK/REG/2001/9, 15 May 2001. Online. Available at HTTP: <http://www.unmikonline.org/constframework. htm#preamble> (accessed 30 May 2006).
36 Quoted in Chesterman, *You, the People*, p.236.
37 R.H. Jackson, *Quasi-states: Sovereignty, International Relations and the Third World*, Cambridge: Cambridge University Press, 1990, p.21.
38 Ibid., p.27.
39 Ibid., p.202.
40 K. Booth, 'Human Wrongs and International Relations', *International Affairs* 71:1, 1995, p.116.
41 G.B. Helman and S.R. Ratner, 'Saving Failed States', *Foreign Policy* 89, 1992–93, pp.3, 4, 9.
42 A. Gourevitch, 'Failed State: Failed Concept', paper presented at International Studies Association annual convention. Honolulm, March 2005.

43 Jackson, *Quasi-states*, p.6. A similar argument was first made in 1979 by Charles R. Beitz, see C.R. Beitz, *Political Theory and International Relations*, Oxford: Princeton, 1999.

44 J. Herbst, *States and Power in Africa*, Princeton: Princeton University Press, 2000, p.255.

45 Boutros Boutros-Ghali, for instance, claims that 'theory was *never* matched by reality'. Quoted in Helman and Ratner, 'Saving Failed States', p.10.

46 R.H. Jackson and C.G. Rosberg, 'Why Africa's Weak States Persist: The Empirical and Juridical in Statehood', *World Politics* 35:1, 1982, pp.23–24.

47 Jackson, *Quasi-states*, p.169.

48 Ignatieff, 'State Failure', p.299.

49 Chesterman, *You, the People*, p.58.

50 Ibid., p.24.

51 Boutros Boutros-Ghali, *Unvanquished: A US–UN Saga*, New York: Random House, 1999, p.61.

52 Ibid.

53 Ibid., pp.61–62.

54 Ibid., p.63.

55 Ibid., p.64.

56 See the website of MINUSTAH. Available at HTTP: <http://www.un.org/Depts/dpko/missions/minustah/> (accessed 30 May 2006).

57 A. Diceau, 'Haiti Deserves Better from the United Nations', *Peace Magazine*, 22, 2006 p.16.

58 R. Jackson, *The Global Covenant*, Oxford: Oxford University Press, 2003, p.308.

59 Ignatieff, 'State Failure', p.321.

60 Ibid., p.314.

61 Ibid., p.313.

62 Ibid., p.103.

63 For the contrary argument, see D. Chandler, *Bosnia: Faking Democracy After Dayton*, London: Pluto, 2000.

64 Krasner, 'Case for Shared Sovereignty', p.108.

65 Ibid.

66 Ibid., p.118.

67 See C. Pippan, 'The Rocky Road to Europe: The EU's Stabilization and Association Process for the Western Balkans and the Principle of Conditionality', *European Foreign Affairs Review* 9, 2004, p.238.

68 F. Füredi, *The New Ideology of Imperialism*, London: Pluto Press, 1994, p.3.

69 See N. Harding, *Leninism*, Macmillan: Basingstoke, 1996, especially chapters 5 and 8.

6 Country ownership

The evasion of donor accountability[1]

John Pender

Introduction

The promotion of stronger national ownership of development strategies by aid donors has become a dominant theme within the now ubiquitous Poverty Reduction Strategy (PRS). It was inaugurated in 1999. By June 2005, 49 countries had prepared PRSs, a further 11 had prepared interim PRSs, and another 10 had begun the process towards adoption of the PRS – in total 71 countries, or about a third of all the countries in the world. The 'country ownership' policies promoted by aid donors today stand in stark contrast to the donors' previous approach, the now infamous structural adjustment programme (SAPs). Comprising macroeconomic stabilization, fiscal and monetary austerity, structural adjustment was epitomized by conditionality – that is, legal clauses in loan agreements that insisted on detailed economic reforms, from public expenditure cuts to privatization, as preconditions for the release of loan finance.

Instead of these coercive adjustment policies, PRSs are seen as embodying national autonomy ('country ownership'), with the recipient government at the forefront of a participatory relationship with its own society, and in partnership with its aid donors. As the World Bank and International Monetary Fund (IMF) suggest, the PRS approach calls for 'a fundamental change in the nature of the relationship between developing countries and donors'.[2] Sebastian Mallaby, in his biography of former World Bank President James Wolfensohn, colourfully describes this shift in the Bank's activities. In his words, the World Bank has sought to 'break out of the narrow dialogue with finance-ministry people'. It now tries to 'sell its ideas to NGOs and parliamentarians and journalists', in order to 'build a broad consensus for its economics program', thinking of itself as 'a partner, not a scold'.[3]

This chapter interrogates the switch in development policy from coercion to partnership, and explores what this switch means for sovereignty in the developing world. As the first chapter in this volume makes clear, sovereignty is a political, not an economic concept. While sovereignty does not imply autarky, the concept does involve two components: legitimacy and power. It is this last element, the idea of material capacity to act, which blurs the lines between sovereignty and economics. Power always depends on material strength, and sovereignty has always implied some degree of autonomy from, and control over, economic processes.

Indeed, many of the political struggles of the twentieth century were fought over where to draw the line between the two spheres. For colonized peoples, development was the promise that self-determination offered, in place of imperialist underdevelopment and its lopsided focus on raw materials and cash crops. 'Seek ye first the political kingdom and all else will be added unto you', as the Ghanaian independence leader Kwame Nkrumah famously put it.[4]

If sovereignty and development have always been intertwined, recent shifts in development thinking have blurred the line between politics and economics even further, as we shall see. During the Cold War, aid supplied by capitalist states was bound up with geopolitical rivalry with the USSR. Today, aid is presented as a neutral tool for strengthening the institutions of African states. But as Mark Duffield has argued, aid must still be treated as an integral component of global governance, a 'political project in its own right' that necessitates understanding 'its particular forms of mobilization, justification and reward'.[5] Investigating the changing relationship between sovereignty and development by analysing the politics of aid is my purpose in this chapter.

Mapping these new relationships of power requires navigating through the constellation of 'sinister acronyms', as one philosopher put it, of many different international agencies and policy initiatives.[6] A list of acronyms that are repeated throughout this chapter has been provided to help the reader (see Table 6.1). The empirical focus of the chapter is mostly on Tanzania. There are clearly pitfalls in such restricted selectivity. However, the intensity of the Tanzanian experience in this period is enlightening. At the outset of the period of analysis, Tanzania's relationship with its Western donors was in a profound state of crisis. Since then, that relationship has been fundamentally restructured. Tanzania has now experienced over a decade of concerted external intervention, and has completed an entire cycle of an IMF/World Bank Poverty Reduction and Growth Facility (PRGF). It has received on average over US$1 billion in aid per year for the last 10 years, and has been a major beneficiary of debt relief under the Highly Indebted Poor Countries (HIPC) initiative. Tanzania, therefore, has been at the cutting edge of new forms of international development policy for a considerable period. Not all insights gained from the Tanzanian experience will have a wider relevance, but many will. This notwithstanding, my aim in this chapter is not as ambitious as seeking to distil a series of generalizations. Rather, I am seeking to point the

Table 6.1 List of acronyms

DFID	UK Department for International Development
ESRF	Economics and Social Research Foundation
IMF	International Monetary Fund
NGO	Non-Governmental Organization
PAF	Performance Assessment Framework
PRGF	Poverty Reduction and Growth Facility
PRBS	Poverty Reduction Budget Support
PRS	Poverty Reduction Strategy
PRSP	Poverty Reduction Strategy Paper

discussion about the politics of aid in a new direction, by suggesting a different way of understanding aid–donor relations.

From coercion to partnership

The shift from coercion to partnership involves the renegotiation of key relationships, namely, between the aid-recipient state and aid-donor state, *and* between the aid-recipient state and its own citizens. This renegotiation is driven by an approach to development that is more oriented towards issues of internal governance than the traditional concern with economic growth. The stylized understanding of development that emerged in the mid-twentieth century included a role for the state, but also aimed to unleash the spontaneous forces of civil society – the free movement of labour, goods and capital. It was believed these forces would culminate in industrialization, urbanization and economic diversification, which would enhance a country's capacity to manage external economic shocks.

This understanding of development has been called into question from many different perspectives over the last several decades. These range from defining development in the minimal sense of meeting demands for basic needs, such as 'food security', to more expansive understandings that include life expectancy, education, the natural environment and needs of future generations (sustainable development). These competing ideas have sparked off wide-ranging theoretical and empirical debates over the nature, desirability and feasibility of economic growth. Needless to say, these debates are beyond the scope of this chapter. For my purposes here, there are two things worth stressing. The first is the qualified relegation of growth to the periphery of development concerns. After the Cold War, the devastating effects of structural adjustment could be more widely acknowledged, as this would no longer be seen as strengthening the case for Soviet-style economic models. Michael Hirsch summarized the legacy of SAP thus: 'After a decade of following World Bank advice, living standards in Africa have fallen by 2 per cent annually, unemployment has quadrupled by 100 million and real wages have plunged by a third.'[7] The failure of structural adjustment, and the debt crises of the early 1990s, severely dented faith in the market. With the Bretton Woods institutions adrift, a new generation of economists, spearheaded by Amartya Sen, Joseph Stiglitz and Nicholas Stern, challenged the development orthodoxy. In place of the brute output statistics of economic growth, they stressed other factors, whose common denominator coalesced around the alleviation of extreme poverty in the here and now. The old-fashioned goal of telescoping centuries of industrialization to achieve parity with the West in a few decades has gradually faded, in favour of putatively more immediate and practical goals. The overall effect has been to shunt aside the vision of total social transformation in favour of more piecemeal, manageable change.

The second element is the new-found link between development and governance. As the goal of economic growth has receded, development has expanded laterally to assimilate a variety of other goals and concerns, most conspicuously of all, 'governance' (compare with Christopher Bickerton's chapter in this volume). The acknowledgement of the inequalities caused by growth means that capitalist development is now widely seen as fomenting social fragmentation. Social transformation can no longer be left to the spontaneity of the market, but requires a process of change that is more directly engineered, closely watched and permeates society in a more rigorous and manageable fashion. Or, put another way, markets cannot deliver their benefits if institutions and social networks cannot bear the weight of market forces.[8]

These new components of development thinking mean that countries are singled out for attention based on a lack either of the administrative capacity or the political will to deliver security, good governance and poverty reduction. For example, the coordinating body of aid donors, the Organization for Economic Cooperation and Development – Development Assistance Committee, argues that, 'wherever possible, international actors should work jointly with national reformers in government and civil society to develop a shared analysis of challenges and priorities'.[9] The aim of this partnership should be to build 'legitimate, effective and resilient state institutions',[10] 'building capable, open and responsive states'[11] and 'forging engaged societies.'[12] Goran Hyden draws out the distinction between the imposition of structural adjustment, and the internal reforms of the governance approach, when he observes that 'getting politics right is different from getting policy right in that it calls for a restructuring of the polity itself'. Structural adjustment 'could be pursued by an autocratic government as well as a democratic one'.[13]

Interestingly, a crucial component of this new doctrine of development is the emphasis on harnessing the agency of the poor to this project of social transformation. This striking emphasis on the activity of the poor runs from the micro-level, in discussions about people's 'coping strategies' in times of famine, through to the macro-level, 'country ownership' – poor countries wresting development back from the diktat of the Bretton Woods institutions. This emphasis on agency is evident in the effervescent jargon of the policy documents: 'empowerment', 'partnership', 'responsiveness', 'ownership' and 'engaged societies'. British Chancellor Gordon Brown outlined his vision for Africa in these terms: 'A century ago people talked of "What we could do to Africa". Last century, it was "What can we do for Africa?". Now, in 2006, we must ask what the developing world, empowered, can do for itself.'[14] As Mark Duffield puts it, in this approach the 'poor must be more than victims, they must be capable of volition and action as well'.[15] It seems as if the agency of the poor is elevated in inverse proportion to the declining faith in the transformative capacity of the market. We shall return to the significance of this emphasis on agency later in the chapter.

For aid-recipient countries, the leading donor vehicle for good governance and institution-building has been the aforementioned PRS process. Therefore, the discussion begins with a review of shifting trends in the content of conditionality associated with this process. I will then address in greater detail the PRS process in Tanzania, including the donor-led policy of reconstituting the apparatus of the Tanzanian state. I will highlight how the donors' relationship with Tanzanian society has been re-forged, such that donors exercise enhanced influence over aid-recipient societies. Crucially, the donors' increased influence over Tanzanian society has gone hand-in-hand with less political accountability.

First, let us review some theoretical approaches to the politics of aid. It has become generally accepted since the end of the Cold War that the conventional model of state sovereignty has little bearing on social reality across vast swathes of Africa: 'failed' and 'weak' states are the rule (see Christopher Bickerton's chapter in this volume). In the words of British journalist Jeevan Vasagar,

> In many parts of Africa, the presence of the state is weak. In the refugee camps that dot the borders of conflict-ridden countries, it is the international charities and the UN that sport the trappings of the state: the flags, the shiny cars, and the offices.[16]

As Christopher Clapham has argued, while sovereignty still technically exists when a state formally signs up to, say, an international convention permitting its citizens or multinational corporations to challenge its jurisdiction in an international court, it would be myopic to put too much store by this:

> such [legal] distinctions are not of the first importance: just as an individual who 'chooses' bondage in preference to death can scarcely be said to be free, so a state which accepts the external management of its economy or supervision of its domestic political arrangements, can scarcely be said to be sovereign.[17]

That said, it is far less clear how to conceptualize what has emerged in place of the sovereign state. One particularly interesting approach is Graham Harrison's idea of the 'post-conditionality state'. He suggests that 'rather than conceptualizing donor power as a strong external force on the state, it would be more useful to conceive of donors as part of the state itself'.[18] Harrison clarifies his view as not suggesting that domination has disappeared, but rather that 'external-national distinctions become less useful',[19] and that 'the donor–state relationship is too intimate and interrelated to be understood as a dichotomy. Donors do not just impose conditionality; they also work in a routinized fashion at the centre of policy-making'.[20] The process is better understood as one of the intimate involvement of external actors within poor countries.

A more sanguine approach is that of Thomas Callaghy, who identifies a new dynamic leading to the 'recapture [of] some sovereign space for a few African governments'.[21] This is a result, he argues, of the emergence of 'principled issue networks', composed of actors within Western states, some poor-country governments and non-governmental organizations (NGOs), together with activists and economists. These have 'deployed themselves as an increasingly effective global social movement', prompting changed 'rules and discourse of the debt regime, increased resource flows... new forms of international and local governance... and... strengthened local NGOs'.[22] In short, the new focus on participation and ownership has therefore succeeded in giving borrowers more leverage in the aid and development process.

While Harrison suggests that sovereignty has been superseded by new relations of domination, Callaghy suggests that new relationships of resistance have emerged. Both recognize that something in the aid relationship has changed. They therefore, usefully, do not merely dismiss PRSs as recycled structural adjustment. However, there are important elements that escape both analyses. Against Callaghy, I suggest that the new aid–donor relationship involves more, not less, domination. The rhetoric of participation and ownership is contradicted in practice by the role of international actors at the heart of decision-making in poor countries. Harrison observes this fact, and theorizes it in terms of the effacement of the 'sovereign frontier', an indistinct, grey zone of interaction in place of clearly defined relations between states. But this fails to account for why it is that new forms of intervention are cast in this distinctive language of participatory politics and independence. I shall argue that this paradoxical emphasis on the agency of the poor arises from the evasion of responsibility on the part of the international donors. Unlike structural adjustment, policies of participation and empowerment avoid the language of concrete goals. Country-ownership policies are process-oriented, rather than goal-oriented. The effect is to divorce power from accountability; goals are indistinct, confounding the development of criteria by which to assess development success. Talking up the agency of the poor masks the relations of power, and means that the poor can be held to account for decisions taken on their behalf by donors. This, I argue, is the real significance of country ownership.

Country ownership and conditionality

Let us turn to examine how conditionality has been transformed under the influence of 'country ownership' strategies. The *2005 Review of World Bank Conditionality* assessed all 18,000 conditions and 10,000 benchmarks attached to 695 policy-based loans in the period 1980–2004. It confirms that there has indeed been a reduction in the quantity of conditions attached to the average loan. For the poorest borrowers, the average number of conditions attached to a Bank loan declined from an average of 34 in fiscal year (FY) 1995 to 19 in FY2000 and to 12 in FY2005.[23]

The average number of conditions in PRSs has sharply declined compared to those in SAPs. Nevertheless, a significant residual number of conditions remain. Could it perhaps be that this is the 'pro-poor conditionality' that many NGOs demanded should be linked to development finance released by debt relief? Ann Pettifor, Chairman of the Jubilee 2000 Coalition, insisted that 'a very important condition must be that debt relief must benefit the very poorest sections of society'.[24] The UK Department for International Development (DFID) was itself at the forefront of linking debt relief to poverty reduction, and takes NGO contributions on this issue as 'the starting point of a concept that developed into the [PRS]'.[25] In fact, the notion that residual conditionality is explained by 'pro-poor' conditions is not borne out by the *2005 Review of World Bank Conditionality*. If we compare the conditions applied to loans to the poorest countries between (FY1998 and FY1999) and (FY2004 and FY2005), we see that conditions applied to social sector issues remained virtually static, increasing from 20.6 to 21 per cent of all conditions. In the same period, conditions applied to trade, economic management, financial and private sector development issues declined from 57 to 24 per cent of all conditions.

At the same time, there has been a dramatic increase in conditionality associated with public sector governance. These include conditions on public expenditure management, public financial management (PFM), procurement, the rule of law, accountability and anti-corruption. Conditions linked to public sector governance increased from 20.8 to 49.6 per cent of all conditions.[26] The centrality of governance reform to the poverty reduction approach is also suggested by the HIPC debt relief initiative which 'stressed the need for countries to meet conditions and benchmarks in sixteen PFM areas, and support to accomplish this objective has been both the subject of conditionality and of direct assistance'.[27] In short, an *absolute* fall in the level of conditionality has coincided with a *relative* shift towards the areas of governance and institution-building. While social sector promotion has remained static, governance-related conditionalities have more than *doubled*, to account for around 50 per cent of all conditionalities. As one of the key background papers to the *2005 Review* noted: 'the main finding is that the Bank's programs now place greater emphasis on institution building and governance issues in all areas of intervention'.[28]

How do donors reconcile their commitment to country ownership with the continuance of conditionality? Here we start to see the development of an evasive approach, which at once consolidates external influence while denying aspirations to control. Country ownership is reconciled with residual conditionality by arguing that conditionality should be used to promote country ownership, specifically by stimulating the accountability of the poor country state to both its citizens and to its development partners, and by actively building the capacity of a poor country to fulfil the objectives set out in its PRS. The World Bank emphasizes that 'conditionality is not coercion to undertake reform, and does not prescribe policy content'.[29] Rather, the Bank will use conditionality and benchmarks to promote the 'enhancement of country leadership capacity'.[30] The 'basic tenets' of this approach are: 'a) define the role of the state on the basis of its capacities and b) increase capacity over time by strengthening public institutions'.[31] Conditionality can now be viewed as a 'driver of mutual accountability rather than an instrument of external accountability of governments to their donors'.[32] Thus we see that a striking new aspect of residual conditionality is its justification on the grounds of promoting country ownership. In other words, it is the donors that are enforcing poor countries' 'ownership' of their own development, rather than developing countries claiming it for themselves. The following section traces, in the context of Tanzania, the emergence of the country-ownership theme, and the way in which it has reoriented development and aid strategies, and has seen international actors involve themselves in virtually all aspects of domestic policy-making.

Governance through poverty reduction in Tanzania

The new approach to development in Tanzania emerged out of the crisis of November 1994, precipitated by a suspension of donor aid finance. The political exhaustion and material depletion of the Tanzanian state was vividly described in the Helleiner Report, a donor-sponsored assessment of the crisis:

> In the donors' view, as expressed variously to us, and caricaturing only slightly, the government of Tanzania has lost its momentum and its sense of direction... [It] has little sense of ownership of its major programs, and is unable to exercise fiscal control because of declining administrative capacity and increasing corruption... As one major donor put it to us, 'They seem tired. That fight of earlier years is gone, absolutely gone'... There is a general consensus among donors, senior government officials and well-informed members of the public that the government machinery is at present very weak. Formulation and implementation of government economic policy, and overall economic management, are undoubtedly in disarray.[33]

The crisis was a sobering experience for donors. The Tanzanian government had been fully engaged with structural adjustment since 1986, as well as embarking on the donor-induced introduction of multiparty democracy. Tanzania had been consistently described by the Bank as 'on track', a 'successful adjuster', and – as late as February 1995 – as 'performing better than any other African country'.[34]

The Helleiner Report was scathing in its criticism of donor activity. The Report highlighted the fact that 'many initiatives originate with donors with only limited policy guidance from the [Tanzanian government]'; that economic policy documents were drafted in Washington, with the government relegated to the role of negotiating amendments; that there was 'intrusive donor conditionality at the level of detailed implementation'; that 'each donor has its own aid policies and "agenda," and is anxious to pursue its own objectives even when these are not share[d] by the government'; and that bilateral donors had their own individual agendas and were reluctant to conform to government priorities.[35] The overall impact was to weaken and undermine the state's capacity to coordinate and propel development initiatives. Lack of Tanzanian 'ownership' of the internationally encouraged reforms was identified by the Helleiner Report as the primary underlying cause of the crisis. Ownership, the Report suggested, should involve 'local goals and priorities' being established 'on a genuinely consultative national consensus', where there is 'minimal resort by donors to policy conditionality' and where the final decision rests with government.[36]

The Helleiner Report laid great emphasis on the active role of the Tanzanian state in pushing through the development process, arguing that 'the central coordinating role in all development endeavours ought to be that of the [Tanzanian government]'.[37] Integrated national development was itself undermined by the Tanzanian government's failure to 'have a coherent development program of its own, about which it is enthusiastic or even passionate'. As an alternative, 'a vision that inspires its own population and provides hope for the future' was prescribed, along with efforts to 'foster strong political commitment'.[38] The Helleiner Report also emphasized the role of the state in accommodating the interests of both domestic and international 'stakeholders', emphasizing the need for a mutually agreed development programme, based on 'extensive and early-stage consultation with donor agencies in order to arrive at outcomes which satisfy the objectives of all parties'.[39]

The Helleiner Report proved to be an extremely influential analysis, which inaugurated a major transformation of Tanzanian politics and society. In highlighting the role of donor prescriptiveness in undermining the coherence of the Tanzanian state, and in proposing efforts to build national ownership around a development plan based on the interests of internal and external actors, the Helleiner Report stimulated a range of ground-breaking initiatives in Tanzania and beyond. These initiatives involved three objectives: (1) elite cultivation, (2) building up civil society participation and (3) integrating the role of Tanzania's development partners.

Initiative 1: the dream team approach – cultivating an elite committed to international initiatives

Tanzania, the World Bank notes, 'made a political commitment to increased state effectiveness' relying 'on very senior policymakers and administrators to provide both direction and impetus to reforms'. This is described by the Bank as 'the dream team approach' to achieving 'rapid results'.[40] The key to this approach is nurturing a cadre of Tanzanian policy advisors and civil servants with a strong commitment to international initiatives. These individuals have made their mark in the Offices of the President and Vice-President, the Ministry of Finance, the influential private consultancies REPOA, the Economics and Social Research Foundation (ESRF) and the World Bank office in Dar es Salaam.[41] Donors contrasted the 'pro-reform' outlook of this elite with the former outlook of the Tanzanian elite. Key characteristics of this new outlook included 'skepticism toward local political elites' and 'dissociation from political processes, including those of representative democracy'.[42] The personal commitment and drive of these individuals cannot be doubted. As Holtom notes, the Tanzanian 'pro-reform' economists working at REPOA and ESRF were described as more 'ferocious' than even the Bank's economists.[43]

These 'pro-reform' Tanzanians, were centrally involved in the development of the first PRS Paper (PRSP), whose origin, in turn, was external. As the executive director of REPOA observes: '[T]he PRSP, it is clear... was externally driven, and of course... quite carefully crafted to really become in the end a local initiative. It has local content.'[44] In addition to their own subjective commitment to this project, the 'pro-reform' Tanzanians have received substantial backing in the form of 'capacity building'. The Ministry of Finance is a case in point. In late 1995, at an ESRF capacity-building seminar, the Ministry of Finance was described as 'possibly the agency most lacking capacity in the whole of government'. Since then a 'dramatic capacity development process has taken place', contributing to a 'major process of internal renewal', including training and technical assistance from Sweden, DFID, the Bank, Switzerland, the United Nations Development Programme (UNDP) and Japan.[45]

The Bank, while conceding that it would be 'business unusual for the World Bank', now proposes that capacity development should become one of its core activities, and that 'as the organizing framework for Bank assistance, Country Assistance Strategies should do more to diagnose constraints to capacity development'.[46] Capacity development covers a wide and evolving spectrum of technical assistance, to enable the adoption of internationally recognized techniques and standards. This includes a heavy emphasis on the promotion of transparent reporting, to which we will return. Given that the 'dream team' elites are concentrated in core ministries, the Bank's own criticism of the dream team approach is that it is 'less successful in pushing changes out to the local levels or in sustaining political support'.[47] The Tanzanian government itself accepts that 'there is still a lack of awareness and ownership of the PRS across all levels and sectors of government'. As Peretz and Wangwe highlighted in 2004:

> many ministries continue to view the PRS process as primarily the mandate of the [Vice President's Office], so that even those who are actively implementing the components of the PRS are often unaware that they are doing so – and in some cases unaware of the existence of the PRS.[48]

The remoulding of the Tanzanian state apparatus also involved bypassing Tanzania's parliament – even though donors had pressured Tanzania into multiparty democracy in 1995. As Peretz and Wangwe describe,

> Members of Parliament have up to now generally remained out of the loop except for a few workshops that were organized to inform them about the PRSP and progress reports... the virtual absence until recently of parliamentary interest in the process is particularly striking.[49]

Finally, it should be noted that this 'pro-reform' elite's lack of political roots in Tanzanian society means that it is heavily dependent upon external backing. By the end of the PRGF programme in 2003, Tanzania was benefiting from substantial financial inflows in support of the government's poverty reduction programme. Tanzania had achieved prolonged macroeconomic stability and no longer required IMF support. Despite this, the government chose to renew the PRGF for a further three years. The Economist Intelligence Unit opined that 'the government is probably not confident enough to forgo detailed IMF monitoring', and 'donors may also be reluctant for the monitoring to stop, given that the country is also benefiting substantially from Highly Indebted Poor Country debt relief'.[50] The choice to commit to IMF supervision for a further three years when there was no financial need to borrow, graphically illustrates the pro-reform elite's dependence on external guidance and support. This dependence belies the intended effect; namely, development autonomy. The overall impact of this donor-sponsored nursing of a new elite has been to make the Tanzanian state more open to international initiatives, rather than to strengthen its capacity to implement policies. Country ownership in this sense is domestic 'ownership' of international initiatives.

Initiative 2: civil society – promoting domestic accountability for international initiatives

Donors regard participation as an essential component of governance. 'Societal engagement', suggests the Bank, 'is...both an ends and a means'.[51] Participation is seen as both 'improv[ing] the design and implementation of poverty reduction strategies' and 'as play[ing] an important role in monitoring implementation and strengthening accountability'.[52] With a title invoking the radicalism of Hardt and Negri (*With the Support of Multitudes: Using Strategic Communication to Fight Poverty Through PRSPs*), this joint publication of the World Bank and DFID highlights the key benefits of 'strategic communication'. In their view, informing and soliciting the views of citizens deepens 'a public culture of citizen–government dialogue', helps to build consensus, manages expectations, and helps 'citizens to hold governments to account...by [measuring] progress against promises'.[53]

The Bank and DFID point to Tanzania as a country that is at the cutting edge of these participatory processes. They report that a great deal of donor funding 'has become available for civil society to undertake policy engagement activities and serve as a watchdog on government'. NGOs are seen as 'intermediaries for communication strategies, taking information from the government to their own constituencies and the general public'. They also claim NGOs are 'seen as an effective means of disseminating information downstream, as well as a means to gather feedback from a large rural population'.[54] The highlighted success story of the participation process in Tanzania is the 'phenomenal' success of a booklet called 'Tanzania without Poverty – a plain language guide to Tanzania's poverty reduction strategy paper'. With funding from DFID and the UNDP, 212,000 of these booklets were printed, with publication and distribution subcontracted to the Tanzanian NGO Hakikazi. The publication had a patriotic cover graphic, and became an important tool for rural-based NGOs and local and regional government offices in raising their *own* awareness of the poverty reduction process. Ironically, despite its patriotic cover, it was a donor publication, not a government publication.

While their aim was to raise public awareness of the poverty reduction process, a 2003 survey conducted to measure public awareness of government policy during the PRS period found that the PRS ranked a lowly 9 out of 15. This draws attention to the narrow social basis that NGOs command. In the case of ownership and participation policies, the inclusion of civil society amounts to using NGOs to disseminate information about donor initiatives.[55] Nonetheless, the active engagement of NGOs has been a central feature of the PRS process in Tanzania. NGOs have been involved in many of the key coordinating committees of the PRS process, such as the Participatory Poverty Assessment Implementing Consortium (PPA). The Consortium, for example, is composed of representatives of ESRF, the President's Office, the Ministry of

Finance, the Ministry of Statistics, five national NGOs and five international NGOs.[56] Such groupings are flagged up as transmission belts for public opinion that have the advantage of being outside the political process:

> Key players in and around the PPA see it as a project with a quite explicit political agenda (in the broad sense of the term). Many see the Consortium as an opportunity to promote a coalition of reformists who reject the 'old-style' mode of political participation...Through the assembly of the Consortium and its steering committee, the training of the research teams, and the experience of intensive collaboration in the field, the PPA participants see themselves as involved in mobilizing, sensitizing and building up an *avant garde* of progressive actors linked 'downward' to grassroots communities, and 'upward'...A major outcome of the PPA was to be an enhanced sense of self-awareness [of] non-state advocacy groups as a political force and with a clear strategy for political impact.[57]

The increased NGO focus on advocacy also reflects the greater political role of NGOs in the PRS process. Much external support has been provided for the promotion of 'advocacy' – active campaigning and lobbying on behalf of global policy agendas. Gould and Ojanen note that until around 1998 most international NGOs focused on provision of 'basic services to impoverished citizens'. Now there is a new and significant emphasis on advocacy, with 'the establishment of dedicated policy advocacy positions within these agencies at different levels of the organization'.[58] Specific funding has been made available by bilateral donors to fund advocacy in support of the poverty reduction programme. From 1998, USAID and DFID, among others, began to systematically subcontract to international NGOs including CARE, ActionAid, Save the Children, Oxfam and Concern International to 'build civil society capacity'.[59]

Civil society is thus centrally involved in the rolling out of international initiatives in Tanzania. It works at the heart of the PRS institutions and is the primary vehicle for the domestic promotion of the priorities associated with the PRS process. At the same time, it operates as a 'watchdog' on the new Tanzanian state elite, holding it accountable for the implementation of these international initiatives. Yet, as with the pro-reform state elite, so too Tanzanian civil society is deeply penetrated by international actors, both in terms of its resources and its authority, which derives at least as much from civic actors' relationship with international agencies, as it does with Tanzanian society. Thus despite the appearance of two distinct, complementary and countervailing spheres of Tanzanian politics – civil society and the pro-reform state elite – these two spheres are both separate wings of international influence in Tanzania, playing out a peculiar shadow theatre for the benefit of donors.

Initiative 3: the donors – the creation of 'inside-out' accountability

There is strong donor representation in the committees associated with the coordination and management of the PRS. Representatives of international institutions and donor governments play a routine, intimate part in the regulation and management of the PRS.

> The new partnerships are based on consensus and intimacy among state and donor actors. The management of public finances is based on very close day to day working relations between donor and government technocrats, and a diverse assortment of institutional arrangements (task forces, working groups, ad hoc committees, workshops) through which state and donor actors share responsibility for policy choices and the analysis of their implications.[60]

Donors sit on a multitude of committees covering a vast range of government policy formulation and implementation.[61] However, the most significant innovation in the Tanzanian case is the Performance Assessment Framework (PAF) – the development of a framework of accountability which aims to go beyond the limitations of the prescriptive nature of conditionality. The PAF broke new ground in donor–recipient initiatives. It was 'a first of its kind', providing a 'powerful example'.[62] The PAF is based on two new donor approaches. The first is 'harmonization'. Rather than set different and competing priorities that would allegedly stretch the Tanzanian state thin, donors would come together to act as one in negotiations. Second, the PAF involves conditions and benchmarks being set, based on key targets within the government's development strategy, which itself has been established as the product of negotiation between the government and its donors.

The two PAFs that have been applied to Tanzania involve a variety of 'aims' and 'actions', including improved monitoring of the PRS process; macroeconomic stability; improved delivery of public services; control of resources and improved accountability; reduction of income poverty and environmental sustainability.[63] The PAF has been integrated into the PRS process and has evolved into 'an external accountability framework and a national structure for managing strategic reform processes'.[64] The result is that the 'PRS is ... considered by the Government and civil society, as well as external development partners, as the national framework that guides policy and actions.'[65] Within this accountability framework, there are three separate dimensions of conditionality, based on overall satisfactory progress, assessment of 'prior actions' required for release of Poverty Reduction Support Credit funds, and a separate performance assessment against two criteria for European Union funds. The number of actions being monitored has increased from 28 in FY2002 to 58 in FY2004.[66] Tanzanian officials have been reported as saying that 'the processes of dialogue and conditionality are completely interwoven'. This has two effects. First, it crowds out space for a dispassionate, objective and non-committal sharing of views. Second, it undermines national control because it effectively means that conditionality has no boundaries; that any policy, institutional or administrative issue might be raised as a potential reason for not disbursing PRBS funds.[67]

Donors are thus intimately integrated into the heart of the Tanzanian state, in the management and implementation of the PRS process. The level of this influence, given limited Tanzanian resources, is remarkable. In this sense it is hard to draw any clear lines between the actions of the Tanzanian elite and those of donors. Donors have also established in the PAF a unique framework that makes the Tanzanian elite accountable for the implementation of *international* initiatives to both a domestic *and* an international constituency, establishing a formal separation of accountability. Despite donors' intimate involvement, right through to sitting on committees that implement policy, they actively distance themselves from accountability by shunting formal responsibility to the new Tanzanian elite – an elite that donors themselves have built up across the last decade.

Conclusion: country ownership and the evasion of accountability

The policy of 'country ownership' has continued apace. The 2004 Report to the Government of Tanzania and Development Partners on the PRBS recommended that the PRS be adopted as a national strategy, and that the government of Tanzania should make 'more frequent high level policy statements giving it this status'. It suggested that as part of this process of promoting the PRS as national strategy, the 'Bretton Woods ... nomenclature' should be dropped.[68] The PRS has now ended and the Tanzanian government adopted the advice, replacing the PRS with the 'national Strategy for Growth and the Reduction of Poverty'.[69] Yet this politically correct nomenclature does not change the substance of national development policy, which is still accountable to outside donors through the targets set out in its PAF. The donors also clearly limit the leeway allowed in proposing alternatives, given the need to be 'consistent with the objectives of macroeconomic stability and poverty reduction'.[70] The PRBS report also recommends that the PRS should not 'be subjected to a process that gives the appearance of requiring external approvals by the IMF and World Bank'.[71] However, in the most recent loan agreement between the World Bank-International Development Agency (IDA) and Tanzania, the World Bank-IDA reports that 'the authorities have indicated that they would like some form of Fund involvement with formal Board approval to continue after the current PRGF expires'.[72]

The PRS has been given a local name, the government of Tanzania has signalled its desire to remain under the supervision of the IMF, and the donors are encouraged not to hesitate to impose their own priorities onto Tanzania, while the government is encouraged to repackage external initiatives as nationally owned ones. Such are the paradoxical effects of country ownership. What is the overall outcome?

One of the most telling indictments of the donors' country-ownership agenda is to be found in the donors' own views. In response to a questionnaire evaluating the PRBS, several donors stated that their objective was 'to increase the opportunity for influence over government through participation in policy dialogue'. Interviewers also reported that 'most Development Partners do not yet believe that the forces of democratic accountability are sufficiently strong to hold government to account for its performance'. In other words, donors feel the need to act in place of Tanzania's people in ensuring the accountability of the Tanzanian state.

The report goes on to say that 'neither of these observations is controversial and, indeed the Government of Tanzania for the most part seems to accept these views'.[73] Another analyst argues that, 'Most budget-support donors remain convinced that conditionality – or at least close and regular monitoring of whether agreed policy commitments have been adhered to – still has a vital role to play in ensuring the proper use of funds.'[74]

There is little evidence, at least in the case of Tanzania, that Callaghy's 'principled issue networks' have managed to claw back any domain of 'sovereign space'. On the contrary, the integration of civil society into the PRS framework has helped make Tanzania more permeable to international bodies and external actors. Returning to Harrison's idea of post-conditionality, we do indeed find a heightened, intimate involvement of donors in the Tanzanian state, right through to their representatives sitting on national committees directing policy. However, we also find in the residual conditionality still in place and attached to governance reform something to qualify the idea of 'post-conditionality'. There is a persistent element of coercion, which indicates who still has the last word on setting priorities. Tanzania is by no means idiosyncratic. Finance ministries throughout sub-Saharan Africa have been beachheads for wider international influence.[75] Even Nigeria, Africa's most populous state, and the most powerful state in sub-Saharan Africa after South Africa, has not been immune. In July 2005, the Paris Club of donors redeemed Nigeria's foreign debt in return for international regulation of government spending, in which Nigeria's Millennium Development Committee (which includes representatives of the Bank, IMF, Action Aid and Oxfam), will play a key role.[76]

Let us recapitulate some of the insights that have emerged in the preceding discussion. We have noted the extent to which it is accepted that state sovereignty has become mystifying concept in analysing the international politics of Africa. Certainly, the evidence presented in this chapter of the sociological penetration of the Tanzanian state apparatus means that the idea of the sovereign state as a buffer between domestic society and international relations is erroneous. Given the breadth and depth of Tanzania's relationship with donors, we cannot say that this is a state organically developing in a dynamic relationship with its own society. We have also seen the self-defeating aspect of this state-building, whereby the new Tanzanian elite is still politically dependent on the authority of international agencies, even when the pressing financial dependence has lifted. So the extent of international influence over Tanzanian society only begs the question of why the sovereign state remains the formal unit of political organization. It is here that the question of agency is important.

As we saw earlier in the chapter, country ownership was set up as a response to the devastating legacy of structural adjustment. Yet in some respects, PRS and country ownership is even worse, for the strident emphasis on the agency of the Tanzanian state in the PRS process obscures relationships of power. International agencies and donors dominate the Tanzanian state to the point that it becomes difficult to draw clear lines between donor agencies and the state apparatus itself. International donors exercise all the power and agency, yet there is no way of holding them politically to account for this power; the formal agency remains that of the Tanzanian state. But the more Tanzanian agency is flagged up in PRS and country-ownership programmes, the more it seems to be absent.

In the more explicitly contractual language of structural adjustment, the relationships of subordination and power are relatively clear, as conditionality is plainly a relationship of coercion, externally brought to bear on the sovereign state.[77] At the very least, this means, as David Chandler has argued, that it is possible publicly to confront and to hold to account the proponents of structural adjustment for their destructive legacy. Under 'country ownership', the political clarification of power relationships is more difficult. The report of British Prime Minister Tony Blair's Commission for Africa stresses, for example, the importance of avoiding the adversarial and unpredictable nature of 'specific contracts' in favour of more informal relations of 'mutual respect' and 'solidarity'.[78]

The traditional conception of development involved far-reaching economic transformation that would expand societies' material capacity for the exercise of agency. Today, the content of development policy is little more than the maintenance of macroeconomic stability, accompanied by internationally sponsored anti-poverty initiatives, such as the Millennium Development Goals. The PRS process makes the Tanzanian elite accountable for the implementation of these limited international initiatives, while restricting the development of alternatives and shielding donors from accountability. Most perversely of all, the rhetoric of empowerment places the emphasis on the poor-by definition those with the least material capacity to act, to achieve the benefits of development through sheer effort of will and behavioural change. Should they fail, the fact that they have been 'empowered' means that their failure does not reflect on those making the exhortations: the donor agencies, Western governments, NGOs and international institutions. This is the meaning of replacing sovereignty with country ownership, and development with poverty reduction.

Notes

1 I would like to thank the following people for their critical feedback: the editors, Daniel Ben-Ami, David Chandler, Mark Duffield, Alastair Fraser, Michele Ledda, Tara McCormack and Sanjay Reddy.
2 World Bank and the IMF, *Review of the Poverty Strategy Reduction Approach: Balancing Accountabilities and Scaling Up*, September 2005. Online. Available at HTTP: <http://www.imf.org/external/np/pp/eng/2005/091905p.htm> (accessed 30 May 2006), pp.1–3.
3 S. Mallaby, *The World's Banker: A Story of Failed States, Financial Crises, and the Wealth and Poverty of Nations*, London: Yale University Press, 2005, p.96.
4 K. Nkrumah, *Ghana: The Autobiography of Kwame Nkrumah*, Edinburgh: Thomas Nelson & Sons Ltd., 1957, p.164.
5 M. Duffield, *Global Governance and the New Wars: The Merging of Development and Security*, London: Zed Books, 2002, p.10.
6 The phrase is Jacques Derrida's, from his speech 'Enlightenment Past and to Come', published in *Le Monde Diplomatique*, November 2004.
7 M. Hirsch, 'Orchestrating a revival', *Newsweek*, 9 October 2005, p.44.

8 See for example, D. Rodrik, A. Subramanian and F. Trebbi, 'Institutions Rule: The Primacy of Institutions over Geography and Integration in Economic Development', unpublished, 2002. Online. Available at HTTP: <http://ksghome.harvard.edu/~drodrik/institutionsrule,%205.0.pdf> (accessed 30 May 2006).

9 OECD-DAC, *Principles for Good International Engagement in Fragile States*, 2005, Online. Available at HTTP: <http://www.oecd.org/dataoecd/59/55/34700989.pdf> (accessed 30 May 2006), p.3.

10 Ibid., p.2.

11 World Bank and IMF, *Review of the Poverty Strategy*, p.6.

12 World Bank, *Building Effective States, Forging Engaged Societies: Report of the World Bank Task Force on Capacity Development in Africa*, September 2005, Online. Available at HTTP: <http://web.worldbank.org/WBSITE/EXTERNAL/COUNTRIES/AFRICAEXT/EXTREGINI/EXTAFRDEVOPRTSK/0,,contentMDK:20709126~menuPK:1720354~pagePK:64168445~piPK:64168309~theSitePK:1582018,00.html> (accessed 30 May 2006), p.iii.

13 G. Hyden, 'Sovereignty, Responsibility, and Accountability: Challenges at the National Level in Africa', in F.M. Deng and T. Lyons (eds), *Africa Reckoning: A Quest for Good Governance*, Washington: Brookings Institution, 1998, p.38. On the development of the governance agenda more broadly, see T.G. Weiss, 'Governance, Good Governance and Global Governance: Conceptual and Actual challenges', *Third World Quarterly* 21:5, 2001, pp.795–814.

14 G. Brown, 'Our Final Goal Must be to Offer a Global New Deal', *Guardian*, 11 January 2006.

15 Duffield, *Global Governance*, p.126.

16 J. Vasagar, 'A Failure of Purpose', *Guardian*, 3 January 2006.

17 C. Clapham, 'Sovereignty and the Third World State', *Political Studies* 47:3, 1999, p.536.

18 G. Harrison, *The World Bank and Africa: The Construction of Governance States*, London: Routledge, 2004, pp.87–88.

19 G. Harrison, 'Post-Conditionality Politics and Administrative Reform: Reflections on the Cases of Uganda and Tanzania', *Development and Change* 32:4, 2001, p.657.

20 Ibid., p.671.

21 T. Callaghy, 'Networks and Governance in Africa: Innovation in the Debt Regime', in T. Callaghy, R. Kassimir and R. Latham (eds), *Intervention and Transnationalism in Africa: Global-Local Networks of Power*, Cambridge: Cambridge University Press, 2001, p.116.

22 Ibid., p.146.

23 World Bank, *Review of World Bank Conditionality Background Paper 3: Recent Trends and Practices, Operations Policy and Country Services*, September 2005, p.42.

24 Select Committee on International Development, *Fourth Report 1998–1999: Debt Relief and the Cologne G8 Summit*, London: HMSO, 1999. Response to question no. 99. Online. Available at HTTP: <http://www.publications.parliament.uk/pa/cm199899/cmselect/cmintdev/470/47002.htm> (accessed 30 May 2006).

25 K. Christiansen and I. Hovland , 'The PRSP Initiative: Multilateral Policy Change and the Role of Research', *ODI Working Paper 216*, August 2003. Online. Available at HTTP: <http://www.odi.org.uk/pppg/publications/working_papers/216.html> (accessed 30 May 2006), p.17.

26 World Bank, *Review of World Bank Conditionality Background Paper 3*, p.45.

27 World Bank, *Review of World Bank Conditionality Background Paper 4; Content of Conditionality in World Bank Policy-Based Operations – Public Sector Governance, Privatization, User Fees and Trade*, PREM Group, September 2005, p.5.

28 Ibid., p.1.

29 World Bank, *Review of World Bank Conditionality, Operations Policy and Country Services*, September 2005, p.vi.

30 Ibid., p.28.

31 World Bank, *Review of World Bank Conditionality Background Paper 4*, p.3.
32 World Bank and the IMF, *Review of the Poverty Stragegy*, p.46.
33 G.K. Helleiner, T. Killick, N. Lipumba, B.J. Ndulu and K.E. Svendsen, *Report of the Group of Independent Advisers on Development Cooperation Issues between Tanzania and its Aid Donor* (aka 'Helleiner Report'), Copenhagen: Royal Danish Ministry of Foreign Affairs, 1995, pp.4, 21.
34 Ibid., p.6.
35 Ibid., pp.10–13.
36 Ibid., p.9.
37 Ibid., p.18.
38 Ibid., pp.21, 9.
39 Ibid., p.9.
40 World Bank, *Building Effective States*, p.33.
41 D.R. Holtom, 'Tanzania's Poverty Reduction Strategy: "Everyone Wants a Success Story" – Feedback Report for Interviewees', mimeo, 2002. Holtom notes that REPOA is heavily funded by the Netherlands (p.12) and that the executive director of ESRF openly describes it as a 'baby' of the World Bank (p.9).
42 J. Gould and J. Ojanen, 'Merging the Circle: The Politics of Tanzania's Poverty Reduction Strategy', University of Helsinki, Institute of Development Studies, *Policy Papers 2*, 2003, pp. 67, 15.
43 Holtom, 'Tanzania's Poverty Reduction', p.15.
44 Ibid., p.14.
45 Daimo Associates Ltd and the Overseas Development Institute (ODI), *Joint Evaluation of General Budget Support: Tanzania 1995–2004*, Revised Final Report, Report to the Government of Tanzania and to the Poverty Reduction Budget Support Development Partners, April 2005, pp.37–38, 57–58.
46 World Bank, *Building Effective States*, pp.8–9.
47 Ibid., p.33.
48 D. Peretz and S. Wangwe, *Monitoring Donor IFI Support behind Country-owned Poverty Reduction Strategies in the United Republic of Tanzania*, Report for the Commonwealth Secretariat, London, August 2004. Online. Available at HTTP: <http://www.thecommonwealth.org/shared_asp_files/uploadedfiles/%7B8316FEF5-C6D2–4001-86CE-B70522669A94%7D_Tanzania%20Report%20by%20Peretz%20and%20Wangwe.pdf> (accessed 30 May 2006), pp.8–9.
49 Ibid., p.9.
50 Economist Intelligence Unit (EIU), *Country Report: Tanzania*, August 2003, p.22.
51 World Bank, *Building Effective States*, p.iii.
52 World Bank and IMF, *Review of the Poverty Strategy*, p.26.
53 DFID and World Bank, *With the Support of Multitudes: Using Strategic Communication to Fight Poverty through PRSPs*, Washington, DC: World Bank, 2005, p.9. Hardt and Negri's follow up to *Empire* is called *Multitude: War and Democracy in the Age of Empire*, London: Penguin, 2004.
54 DFID and World Bank, *With the Support of Multitudes*, p.56.
55 See also D. Chandler, *Constructing Global Civil Society: Morality and Power in International Relations*, London: Palgrave, 2004; G. Baker and D. Chandler (eds), *Global Civil Society: Contested Futures*, London: Routledge, 2005.
56 Gould and Ojanen, 'Merging the Circle', p.87.
57 Ibid., p.67.
58 Ibid., p.73.
59 Ibid.
60 Ibid., p.31.
61 To give the reader an idea of the extent of the donor presence on Tanzanian policy committees, Tanzanian/donor forums as of December 2003 included, *inter alia*, Cross-Sectoral Coordination; Poverty Monitoring System Basket Funding Committee;

Poverty Public Expenditure Review Working Group; Public Expenditure Review Macro Group, Local Government Reform Program Consultative Forum and many others. (Peretz & Wangwe, 2004: annex 5.)

62 Daimo Associates and the ODI, *Joint Evaluation*, p.42.

63 Ibid., pp.41–42.

64 Ibid., p.157.

65 Peretz and Wangwe, *Monitoring Donor*, p.10.

66 Daimo Associates and the ODI, *Joint Evaluation*, pp.42–43.

67 Ibid., p.45.

68 Peretz and Wangwe, *Monitoring Donor*, p.ii.

69 This old wine in new bottles is available at website: HTTP: < http://www.tzdac.or.tz/ Mkukuta/Mkukuta%20Page.html> (accessed 30 May 2006).

70 World Bank and IMF, *Monitoring Donor*, p.68.

71 Peretz and Wangwe, *Monitoring Donor*, p.ii.

72 World Bank, 'International Development Association: Program Document for a Proposed Credit in the Amount of SDR103.8 Million ($150 Million) to the United Republic of Tanzania for a Third Poverty Reduction Support Credit', 10 August 2005. Online. Available HTTP: <http://www-wds.worldbank.org/servlet/WDSContentServer/ WDSP/IB/2005/08/18/000090341_20050818111010/Rendered/INDEX/33166.txt> (accessed 30 May 2006), p.11.

73 Daimo Associates and the ODI, *Joint Evaluation*, p.51.

74 D. Booth, 'Poverty Monitoring Systems: An Analysis of Institutional Arrangements in Tanzania', ODI Working Paper 247, March 2005. Online. Available at HTTP: <http://www.odi.org.uk/publications/working_papers/wp247.pdf> (accessed 30 May 2006), p.7.

75 See Harrison, 'Post-Conditionality Politics', p.658.

76 L. Elliot and P. Wintour, 'Biggest African Debt Rescue Saves Nigeria £17.3bn', *Guardian*, 1 July 2005.

77 D. Chandler, 'Africa: "Empowerment" by Imposition', *Spiked-Online*, 7 March 2006. Online. Available at HTTP: <http://www.spiked-online.com/Articles/ 0000000CAFBB.htm> (accessed 30 May 2006).

78 Commission for Africa, *Our Common Interest*, London: Penguin, 2005, p.14.

7 European Union

A process without a subject

James Heartfield

The European Union (EU) is a confusing thing. It often presents the character of a state. It has its own money. It has a parliament. It has laws, a government and a court of justice. It is commonly talked about as a single entity. People will say, 'Europe must reform its agriculture', or 'Europe favours the Kyoto agreement'. Yet, confusingly, the EU still consists of 25 sovereign states: France, Germany, Italy, Belgium, the Netherlands, Luxemburg, the United Kingdom, Ireland, Denmark, Spain, Portugal, Greece, Austria, Finland, Sweden, Latvia, Lithuania, Estonia, Poland, Hungary, Malta, Cyprus, the Czech Republic, Slovenia and Slovakia with Bulgaria and Romania expected to join in 2007. Each of these states also have parliaments, laws, governments and courts, with jurisdiction over the same territory as those of the EU. Not a few of these states, whether Germany or Britain, France or Italy, are considerable powers in their own right, as well as members of the EU. Commonly, the Union is talked of as a 'superstate', implying a great merger of nations, or perhaps something greater still, like an empire (the term was popularized by Margaret Thatcher in September 1988, meaning it derogatorily).[1]

Theoretical approaches to the EU mirror this ambiguity. 'There never has been a governing institution like the European Union', writes Jeremy Rifkin, 'it is not a state, though it acts like one'.[2] Mark Leonard says that, uniquely, it is 'a network rather than a state'.[3] Stephen Haseler thinks that the drive towards super-statehood is 'unstoppable', though not yet attained.[4] Different schools of thought have grown up over the years, with different interpretations of the Union. Functionalists like Ernst Haas and David Mitrany emphasized the processes that led to integration between sovereign states:

> The process in Europe and in the Atlantic areas tends towards the limitation of sovereign independence, the growth of more rather than less formal bonds among national communities and perhaps towards the substitution of a new federal organism for the present national state.[5]

They were impatient with the 'the historical problem of our time, the chief trait of which is the baffling division between the peoples of the world'.[6] They thought that the practical collaboration on uncontroversial administrative 'functions', would spill over into ever-greater integration. Later integrationists such as

Karl Deutsch were less convinced that nation-states would disappear, finding that a plurality of states actually favoured civil integration.[7]

Others, such as Stanley Hoffmann, Robert Keohane, Alan Milward and Andrew Moravcsik have taken issue with the idea that federal organisms might be substituted for the national-state. They have all in different ways analysed the EU by giving methodological primacy to nation-states (or governments, in Moravcsik's case). As Milward has it, the European Economic Community (EEC, predecessor of the EU) represents the 'European rescue of the nation-state'.[8] With almost every single nation of Europe overrun or occupied in the course of the Second World War, the sovereignty of those states was in the balance. As a treaty between mutually recognizing and recognized European nations, the 1957 Treaty of Rome that founded the EEC, guaranteed their independence. Andrew Moravcsik insists that 'intergovernmentalism', not federalism, is the Union's *modus operandi*: 'From its inception the EC has been based on interstate bargains between its member states.'[9] Some International Relations (IR) theorists, such as Alexander Wendt and Barry Buzan, are frustrated with the realist paradigm of the primacy of sovereign states and its implied corollary, a Hobbesian war of all against all at the international level, proposing instead a 'social theory' of international politics. For them, the EU shows that 'some states have managed to form a collective identity' that supersedes the 'anarchy *problematique*'.[10] According to Buzan, as a 'new type of entity' the EU commends itself because it is 'experimenting with a new form both of unit and subsystem structure, where the sharp inside/outside features of the modernist era are blurring into a mixture of the domestic and the international'.[11]

For some, the EU is the supercession of sovereignty, for others its realization. The difference in assessment is striking. Intriguingly, the Union offers up different institutions to affirm different sides of the debate. It has pan-European institutions, pre-eminently the European Commission, whose members swear:

> To perform my duties in complete independence, in the general interests of the communities; in carrying out my duties, neither to seek nor to take instruction from any government or body; to refrain from any action incompatible with my duties.

But it also has the Council of Ministers, the forum for national leaders that is in fact the policy-making body of the Union. Striking too that the order in which these different schools of thought arrived seems to be the reverse of what one might expect. The theorists who emphasized the supercession of sovereignty, the functionalists and integrationists, came *before* the realist reassessment of the primacy of sovereignty. The realists were criticizing what they saw as the functionalist orthodoxy. From the standpoint of today, with such pan-European institutions as the European Central Bank, the Euro, the elected European Parliament, the Common Foreign and Security Policy, and the growth of the body of European law, the *Acquis Communautaire*, all in place, it might seem that there is more evidence of integration, not less. But intellectually, scepticism towards the vaguer pan-European ideals of federalism became stronger, not weaker, as the realist outlook tended to predominate.

According to Moravcsik (though he quarrels with the assessment), it was generally thought that the 1960s 'were the heyday of Commission policy leadership', until nationalistically minded, Gaullist high politics interceded.[12] Donald Puchala suggests that European integration in the 1960s provoked 'two generations of scholars to proliferate abstract explanations of what was happening'. But then 'whatever had been happening in Western Europe apparently stopped happening'. And 'to the intellectual embarrassment of the scholars involved "integration theory" offered no satisfactory explanation'. It was in that climate that 'some suggested that the so-called integration theories were probably not theories at all but post hoc generalizations about current events'. Worse still, 'others suggested [the integration theories] had been little more than moralizations and utopian prescriptions'.[13]

The reemergence of national rivalries in the 1970s underpinned realist scepticism towards European federalism. But their assessments seem less in tune with today's greater degree of pan-European cooperation. A cynic might be tempted to compare the shift in fashion from integration theory to realism as a reaction to changing US assessments of European integration. Whereas the US favoured greater integration in the immediate post-war period (not least to lessen European dependence on American aid[14]) they were increasingly critical of European protectionism after 1973. As America's political leaders found it useful to emphasize the divisions between European states, American academics became more alive to these differences also. It would of course be unfair to reduce the considered arguments of realism to a political interest, but it is also clear that there is today a demand for greater theorization of the integration process in Europe.

At issue: the question of sovereignty, which is to say subjectivity in its national form

Substantially the question at issue is the one of sovereignty, both in fact and in the theoretical analysis. In fact, it is the issue for European national leaders like Jacques Chirac, for whom 'the sovereignty of each state must be defended',[15] or for the German Constitutional Court, which ruled in 1993 that Germany's basic law takes precedence over EU law.[16] Theoretically, the question is whether the EU is an extension (as realists claim) or a moderation of national sovereignty (as argued by functionalists and constructivists).

Sovereignty is a complicated subject. Stephen Krasner breaks it down into four subcategories: domestic sovereignty (the 'organization of public authority in a state'); interdependence sovereignty (the control of borders); international legal sovereignty (the mutual recognition of states); and Westphalian sovereignty (the 'exclusion of external actors from domestic authority configurations').[17] This diremption of the concept seems to help, but it also loses something of the inner vitality of sovereignty, rather like the coroner who unveils the dissected corpse with the phrase, 'behold, your husband'.[18] But then Krasner does warn us of his lack of sympathy for sovereignty with the subtitle of his book, *Sovereignty: Organized Hypocrisy.*

What this analytical approach loses is the vitality of the concept. Sovereignty is something like subjectivity, man's dominion in the world. Specifically, sovereignty is the subjectivity of the Sovereign, or lord, and is for that reason bound up with the idea of territoriality, since lordship is in essence dominion over territory. For us today, the rights of the individual appear to be primary, and the 'rights' of the 'nation' a derivative, or imitating approximation. Historically, of course, subjectivity in the individual is preceded by subjectivity in the sovereign prince. Against expectations, perhaps, the Subject appears in international relations before appearing in social science. Bolshevik jurist Evgeny Pashukanis says that the doctrine of the legal subject in modern law owes more to the Roman *ius gentium* than to the *ius civile*, because the law of nations implies a mutual recognition that is not to be found in the domestic realm.[19] The rights accorded to the stranger in the ancient world are closer to the rights accorded to neighbours in the modern. For Pashukanis, the legal subject, like exchange, first occurs on the margins, between societies, only later penetrating societies (like trade), embracing the towns, and then eventually being generalized in the rights of the people, which finally displace the rights of the sovereign Prince with those of the sovereign people. 'The rights of the untrammelled individual was in fact the democratization of the baroque concept of the despotic Prince', sneers Lewis Mumford, though he should say, 'Renaissance concept of the despotic Prince'.[20] Among intellectuals today, scepticism towards popular sovereignty is high.[21] But the enduring appeal of the slogan 'Power to the People' is something that they ignore at their peril.

Contemporary theorists like Buzan would criticize this account of the emergence of national sovereign states. 'By focusing on how a political system of states developed within Europe over the last 350 years' writes Buzan 'and then using this understanding as a template for what constitutes international relations, the discipline has unnecessarily hampered itself'.[22] Certainly, the temptation one should avoid is to present an idealized development from darkness to light, what Butterfield called the 'Whig interpretation of history'.[23] The actual course of the enlargement of state sovereignty was marked by reversals and compromises that revealed the inner limitations of the concept. At the end of the eighteenth century, Britain's alliance with the reactionary powers of Russia, Prussia and Austria against revolutionary France revealed a pattern of *realpolitik* that subordinated the principle of freedom to pragmatic alliance with despotism, even though the Constitutional law exported to central Europe under the Code Napoleon was much closer to Britain's 'ancient liberties' than Tsarism was. In kind, France's invasion of Portugal pushed Portuguese liberals into alliance with reaction.[24] At its core the concept of sovereignty contains both the universalizing tendency in Enlightenment thinking, the promiscuous expansion of the market, but also the limits of the market, its failure to transform those societies at its margin, therefore pre-eminently its territorial limitations.

If we ask ourselves the question 'why are there nationally-bounded states?', in the first instance it is the *uneven development* of the market system that throws up territorial limits to the extension of the rule of law. Napoleon's armies discovered the territorial limits of constitutional law where there was no middle class of traders to carry it, as in Russia and Egypt. The competitive capitalist logic of attraction and repulsion between hostile brothers also played its role.[25] Revolutionary France was inspired by English ideals of liberty, but under Napoleon France raised tariffs against English goods. The consolidation of state power translated the logic of attraction and repulsion into territorial rivalry. Sovereignty is the territorially truncated form that human subjectivity takes in the concentration of political power. The will of the people is forced into the straitjacket of nationalism.

Realists take the nation-state pursuing its interests to be the irreducible element of international relations, and so set a relatively high store by the concept of state sovereignty. They have been heard to counsel rejecting permanent alliances in favour of a 'balance of power'. By contrast, European federalists and functionalists see cooperation as a principle that trumps sovereignty. They reject the monopoly of states over international relations, pointing to other actors, such as the many non-governmental organizations like Human Rights Watch. They want to see international institutions enforce justice against recalcitrant states. The trouble with trying to understand world politics in these terms is that neither school fully captures the essence of the issue. Rather, both emphasize one sidedly different aspects of international society. The realists are right that as long as political power is not globally unified, states are obliged to compromise with one another, or to go to war. The federalists are right that nations cannot hold onto their own ideals without aspiring to universalize them, by exporting them abroad, at the same time. Both are, in their own way, expressions of the imperfect form of modern society, fragmented into competing nation-states. Any attempt to see through either a wholly realist or wholly internationalist policy will end in confusion.

Europe is the place where sovereignty was born, and it was also the place where the limitations of sovereignty were played out most destructively, in the cycle of world wars from 1914–45. The zero-sum game of national competition accelerated from 'beggar-thy-neighbour' economic policies to total war. In the maelstrom of state-organized violence, there was a genuine attempt to free human subjectivity from its narrow form of national sovereignty into something higher, in the European socialist international. In the event, however, even socialists were seduced by the attraction of recognition in the state to act as recruiting sergeants for national armies, when Europe's social democratic parties voted for war in 1914. Militant internationalism persisted in the mutinies South of Ypres at Christmas 1914, and at Étaples in 1917, and in the revolutions in Ireland (1916), Russia (1917) and Germany (1918). But from Stalin's adoption of the policy of 'Socialism in One Country' in 1926,[26] proletarian internationalism was off the agenda and left-wing politics were constrained within the national framework. Nonetheless, this was still the place where ambitions for self-determination could be given substance, however territorially truncated.

A theory of sovereignty that fails to take cognizance of the underlying structure of subjectivity will fail. Barry Buzan is right that the ahistorical view of international relations put forward by Waltz assimilates essentially distinct eras and events.[27] However, his own attempt to broaden the definition of international relations to embrace all human interactions worldwide seems to be in danger of losing sight of the historical limits of the more narrowly defined field of international relations. To understand the EU we need a conception of sovereignty *and* its modification, that understands the importance of the relationship between sovereignty and subjectivity.

European Union as constrained subjectivity

At least part of the difficulty in understanding the development of the EU is that it is an institution that has performed different tasks at different historical moments. Roughly we can divide these into three definite periods. The first runs from the end of the Second World War, embraces the reconstruction of Europe, and continues right up to the reemergence of West–West rivalries in the mid-1960s. This is the period of consolidation of the EEC, under US tutelage, as a Cold War institution. The second period, reacting to the failure of American leadership, saw the leading European powers attempt to stabilize their own trading system, enlarging the six founding members France, West Germany, Italy, Belgium, Luxembourg and the Netherlands to nine (Britain, Ireland and Denmark) in 1973. This early bid for independence of movement collapsed into 'Euro-sclerosis' as national rivalries limited joint action. The third period, following the failure of the French and Greek attempts to boost their national economies through public spending in the early 1980s, saw a reinvigorated Commission push for greater integration, as witnessed in the Single European Act (1986), the 1992 Maastricht Treaty, and further bouts of enlargement to the north, east and south, culminating most recently in the incorporation of former Soviet bloc states. The different demands of each period regulated the pace and depth of the Union's integrative trends. In the first stage, supranational organization was extensive, less so when national recovery strategies predominated in the 1970s, but from the mid-1980s integration picked up pace again.

What is common to the two latter periods of accelerated integration is not just the high-level of agreement (i.e. between European governments), but also the tendency to demobilize popular nationalism. In contrast to the earlier reaction against national conflict in the form of socialist internationalism, the federalism of the EEC was characterized by its vision of elite, rather than popular, cooperation. The functionalists' approach, which was the approach of the early Commission, was to *depoliticize* aspects of administration, thereby removing them from popular contestation. David Mitrany wrote that the functionalist approach 'should help shift the emphasis from political issues which divide from those social issues in which the interests of the peoples is plainly akin and collective'.[28] In his *The Uniting of Europe*, Ernst Haas justified his concentration upon elites: 'the bureaucratized nature of European organizations of long-standing, in which basic decisions are made by the leadership, sometimes over opposition and usually over the indifference of the general membership'. To reinforce the point, he said 'A further justification for the elite approach to the study of integration lies in the demonstrable difference in attitude held at leadership levels of significant groups, as contrasted with their membership.'[29]

This theoretical attitude corresponded to the practical operation of the EEC. Substantially, the Six were dealing with the problem of demobilizing popular movements, and winding down popular ambitions after the period of mass mobilization during the war. This was most clearly true in Germany, where popular nationalism was actively discouraged under the Allies' de-Nazification policy, and Chancellor Adenauer's recognition of the 'crimes committed in the name of the German people'.[30] In Italy, not just the fascists had to be demobilized, but more importantly, the Committees of National Liberation that had established themselves in the North.[31] In France, the government struggled not only with its Communist deputies, speaking with the authority of their contribution to the resistance, but also with the unfulfilled ambitions of its Gaullists.[32] Interestingly, Dean Acheson dismissed British Foreign Secretary Ernest Bevin's opposition to European integration as 'the old Socialist's difficulty with the problem the Schuman plan [for a Coal and Steel Community] presented to a socialist government of Britain', that is, to meeting the popular expectations mobilized during the war.[33] The rationale of the Coal and Steel Community of 1951 was the removal from national control of those great industrial combines that had, it was thought, accelerated the drive to war. Later, in the EEC, trade and agriculture, both potential weapons of national rivalry, would be contained in a pan-European organization and so put beyond the reach of national policy-making.

Realists have a point when they object that the creation and policy of the EEC remained, throughout, the expression of the will of national governments.[34] The Treaty of Rome was just that, a treaty, or a contract between all parties, from which any one of them could withdraw at any moment. Moreover, incidents like the French veto of British membership, show that, when challenged, national independence seemed to trump integration. However, while the realist approach rests on the question of sovereign states, it tends to leave sovereignty itself unexamined, the notorious 'black box'.[35] The point is that national leaders felt free to 'pool sovereignty' in areas of administration that could be put outside of political contestation, depoliticized. In Europe, where reconstruction of the coal and steel industry meant a generalized economic expansion, the Coal and Steel Community made sense. As regards the Common Agricultural Policy (CAP), Moravcsik's impressive range of references about the input of the agricultural lobbies into the formation of the CAP deceive him.[36] Though farmers' lobbies were an important electoral constituency for centre-right governments, they had been politically defeated during the Second World War, when farming had been reorganized along military lines.[37] In other words, it was the prior depoliticization of the farmers that made the CAP a practical arena for cooperation. Where public expectations were diminished, sovereignty ceased to be so jealously defended, and cooperation made more sense. Pointedly, the one area where cooperation failed definitively was the proposal for a European Defence Community.[38] Though the proposal had originally come from France, it was the hostility of the

French Communist and Socialist deputies to the prospect of German officers commanding French troops that made it untenable.

Rather than being seen as the outcome of rationally choosing subjects (in this case sovereign states), the dynamic towards European integration would be better understood in terms of Althusser's account of history as a process without a subject.[39] It is less the determination of sovereign powers to assert their interests as much as their *own* retreat from sovereignty that has pushed forward the EU. This is not to endorse the federalists' view that it is the entrepreneurship of transnational actors that is the driving force behind the Commission; nor to endorse the equivalently negative Euro-sceptic view that the Commission has suborned the sovereignty of national states. Rather it is the nation-states' retreat from the exercise of their sovereign powers that is decisive. The trend towards European integration over the last 15 years is not for the most part due to the dynamism of the Commission, or the Parliament or the Council of Ministers. Rather it is a negative effect of the decline in the efficacy of national-state institutions. As these institutions lose their authority, a transnational body like the EU comes to the fore, substituting, as it were, for the loss.

This can be demonstrated by observing how policy innovation at the European level is understood in terms of avoiding nationally framed checks or ambitions. Accordingly, elites often speak of 'locking-in' reforms, as in 'Germany's desire to "lock in" a guarantee of low inflation by creating an autonomous European Central Bank'; or the French government 'locking in austerity' by subordinating public spending to the European Monetary System (EMS). So Raymond Barre's government of the late 1970s committed France to 'microeconomic austerity and macroeconomic discipline'. The EMS was a means to 'institutionalize disinflation'.[40] British chancellor Nigel Lawson justified subordinating exchange rates to the European system as an economic policy based on formal rules rather than political discretion.[41] In his words, 'externally imposed exchange rate discipline' would help avoid the 'political pressures for relaxation...as the election approaches'.[42] But one has to ask, from whose point of view does it make sense willingly to give up discretion to a higher authority? The desire to 'lock in' policies indicated divisions *within* nation-states – the desire of one part of the 'national community' to constrain another part.

West European societies in the 1970s had been subject to what the *Financial Times* called 'a revolt of rising expectations'.[43] An overload of social demands upon the state led to what Claus Offe called 'a crisis of legitimation'.[44] The struggle to contain the rising social expectations preoccupied elites throughout the 1970s and 1980s. Over those two decades a variety of national strategies to boost or restrict spending were tried. However, as Moravcsik explains, 'by 1983 national preferences had converged' around 'demands for liberalization'.[45] National economic strategies were shelved, and the traditional instruments of intervention in the economy, such as tariffs and other trade barriers, capital controls, currency and exchange rate manipulation, and central bank policies were successively put beyond use. The crisis of legitimacy of the 1970s was solved by a struggle to contain popular expectations, and demobilize popular movements.

Successful as it was, this was an outcome that created a second problem of legitimacy, the mirror image of the first, due this time not to the growth of popular expectation, but on the contrary, to its decline (compare Alexander Gourevitch's account of the US in this volume).

The loss of national legitimacy in the 1990s

The overriding problem of government in the 1990s was a collapse in popular expectation. The gap between the elite and the masses was palpable. The withdrawal of mass support from the national institutions of public life was marked by a plague of corruption scandals that swept throughout Europe, as ruling parties increasingly came to be seen as venal and self-centred (see Table 7.1).

The EU's own 'Eurobarometer' polling of citizens' attitudes towards their national democratic institutions demonstrates the crisis of legitimacy that lay behind the proliferation of scandals, in particular, the ascendance of dissatisfaction over satisfaction, as seen in Figure 7.1.[46]

Table 7.1 A crisis of legitimacy

Italy, April 1992	Magistrates launch '*Tangentopoli*' investigations, bringing corruption charges against leaders Craxi, Andreotti and Berlusconi
Britain, July 1994–May 1997	'Cash for questions' scandal
Ireland, 1992–94	Beef scandal rocks Haughey's successor Albert Reynolds
France, 1998	Ministerial flats scandal damages Jacques Chirac
Belgium, 1998	Ministerial cover-up in child torture case shakes Jean-Luc Deheane's government
Switzerland, 1998–2000	Sustained campaign over Jewish bank deposits
Germany, 2000	Christian Democratic Union funding scandal

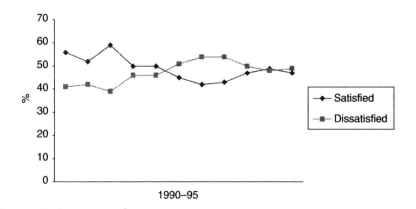

Figure 7.1 Satisfaction and dissatisfaction with national democracy.

Source: Eurobarometer.

This was also the decade of the fringe movements. In 1989, the Green Party won 8 per cent of European votes. In June 1991, the Austrian Freedom Party made its decisive electoral breakthrough. On 26 January 1994 Forza Italia was formed, following the success of the Northern League, to win the elections in March of that year. In 1995, Jean-Marie Le Pen won 15 per cent of the presidential vote (his highest ever, following 14 per cent in 1988, but just 11 per cent in his shock defeat of the Socialists in the first round of the 2002 elections). For the most part, these advances were a reflection of the troubles of the establishment parties.

As the 1980s were characterized by cavalier political leaders such as Margaret Thatcher, François Mitterand, Andreas Papandreou and Mikhail Gorbachev, the 1990s saw the rise of more cautious, technocratic leaders such as John Major, Lionel Jospin, Romano Prodi and Helmut Kohl. While the earlier generation bristled with a jealous, Gaullist sense of their own nation's historic mission, the latter was marked by a preference for moderation (often a preoccupation with crisis management), and, on the diplomatic front, cooperation. The former inspired their people with quixotic gestures, the latter bored and irritated them.

The 1990s saw a sharp up-turn in critical analyses of sovereignty. Among these is *Empire*, by Antonio Negri and Michael Hardt.[47] Their conception of 'Empire' is distinct from the imperialism of nation-states:

> The Passage to Empire emerges from the twilight of modern sovereignty. In contrast to Imperialism, Empire establishes no territorial centre of power ... it is a decentred and deterritorializing apparatus of rule that progressively incorporates the entire global realm ... [48]

French structuralist Louis Althusser was an influence on Negri as indicated in the latter's embrace of Althusser's critique of the Subject in *Empire*.[49] Negri's 'decentred and territorializing apparatus of rule' (though it surely does not exhaust the analysis of world power today) echoes Althusser's 'parallelogram of forces', which 'does not correspond to the consciousness of each will – and at the same time it is a force without a subject, an objective force, but from the outset, nobody's force'.[50] What about European integration as an exemplar of a 'force without a subject'? The complaint of the Euro-sceptics that the original treaty promise of 'ever-deeper union' leads inexorably to a super-state is not entirely convincing. But there is an inexorable process at work. In Pascal Lamy's phrase, the Union is like a bicycle, 'if you don't keep going forward, you fall off'[51]; or as commissioner Roy Jenkins said, European pioneer Jean Monnet 'always taught me to advance along the line of least resistance'.[52] But this process is not best understood in traditional realist terms, as German domination by other means, for example. Rather it is a process without a subject. It operates behind the backs of the actors, as a kind of cunning of reason.

More than that, the Union accrues authority to the extent that national actors eschew it. Blaming Europe for unpopular but 'necessary' changes is a common manoeuvre. Moravcsik argues that politicians can 'reduce the political costs of unpopular policies by "scapegoating" international institutions'.[53] In 1980 the modernization plan for the Belgian Cockerill-Sambre steel works was struck down under the D'Avignon plan to limit output, leading to violent demonstrations: 'One also suspects that the government concerned was delighted to pass the buck to the Commission, and the blame for an unpopular decision thus lay with the "faceless bureaucrats in the Berlaymont" '.[54] In Italy, Giuliano Amato's caretaker government, already paralysed by the emerging corruption scandal, succeeded, where previous governments had failed, to persuade Bruno Trentin of the CGIL union to agree to end the costly inflation indexing of wages, the *Scala Mobile*, on 31 July 1992. Amato did not confront labour directly, via a national referendum, as Andreotti had when reforming the agreement in 1984, but by reference to the 'external constraint' of the EMS. According to Minister Guido Carli's writing in 1993, 'the European Union represented an alternative path for the solution of problems which we were not managing to handle through the normal channels of government and parliament'.[55] In 2005, British Chancellor Gordon Brown's defence of his economic policy ran 'don't blame me, it's the bank' – meaning the Bank of England. In other words, the institution that Brown himself had made independent, in line with Europe's guidelines for a system of European central banks, was to blame for slower growth, rather than his high taxes.[56]

The growing affection for external constraints like the D'Avignon plan, the EMS or independent central banks is inversely related to the fortunes of nationally conceived strategies. In the early 1980s economic plans for national expansion in France (under Mitterand) and in Greece (under Papandreou) proved to be the last of their kind. Both governments responded to the world recession by expanding domestic consumption with programmes of increased public sector employment and minimum wages. 'Extra purchasing power in the French economy tended to be spent on imports rather than home produced goods, unsettling the balance of trade and weakening the currency.'[57] Greeks' extra earning power, too, 'was not translated into overall increases in domestic production, but rather into increased imports'.[58] British economist Will Hutton drew the lesson that 'the old instruments of *dirigisme* and state direction were plainly outmoded'.[59] The French Finance Minister Jacques Delors, who would go on to become the European Commission's most dynamic President, reflected on the limitations of the national solution in October 1983: 'Our only choice is between a United Europe and decline.'[60]

If the left's programme of 'Keynesianism-in-one-country' was defunct, the right's support for sovereignty was not yet dead. Questioned over the propriety of her lobbying on behalf of Cementation (a construction firm in which her son had interests) in Oman, Margaret Thatcher defended herself by saying that she was 'batting for Britain'. However, European Commissioner Leon Brittan contrasted the 'anti-European rhetoric of Margaret Thatcher today to her pro-European actions in government': 'the fact is that she, and indeed virtually the whole of the Conservative Party, both in parliament and in the country, viewed the Single European Act as a great step forward in forcing British-style liberalization further and faster across Continental Europe'.[61] Moravcsik explains how Thatcher, though in agreement with the liberalizing bent of EU policy, was still out of step with its technocratic application: 'in overt opposition to many of her advisors', she 'preferred to disinflate by confronting and conquering rather than circumventing domestic opposition'.[62] As great as their debt to her was, the European leaders that followed preferred to take the politics out of the struggle to restrict spending, by relocating it in Brussels. So though Thatcher was viscerally opposed to British Leyland falling into foreign hands, her successor, John Major actively facilitated its sale to BMW. The British Tory Party's failure to reinvigorate itself through a 'Save the Pound' campaign in the 2001 General Election demonstrated the limited popular appeal of Euro-scepticism. Mark Franklin, one of the wise owls at the Royal Institute of International Affairs had already characterized such scepticism as pathological a decade earlier:

> No amount of explanation that there is nothing new in sharing of sovereignty with other countries has removed the feeling that national control has been lost. No amount of recognition that the watershed was passed when Britain formally joined the Community has reconciled some people to the past. It has only made them more determined to resist further erosion. No amount of ridicule at the fact that the British are clinging to the shadow of sovereignty (e.g. over exchange rates) when economic realities leave them with no option has changed political attitudes, at least in some quarters. No attempt to differentiate the question of sovereignty from that of cultural identity has so far been successful in dispelling the myth that a further pooling of sovereignty in the EC will mean the suppression of the British way of life with all its distinctiveness.[63]

What is interesting here is less the attitudes described but those they express, namely that national independence is an archaism, and an embarrassment. It is noteworthy, too, that Franklin proposes that the aspiration towards British sovereignty could be assuaged with a recognition of the 'cultural identity' of the 'British way of life'. But if identity fills the gap left by sovereignty, what is lost is the principle of self-government, derived from within, replaced by a more passive and bounded cultural or consumption-oriented sense of British-ness. In his essay 'Ideological State Apparatuses' Althusser proposes that ideology interpellates individuals as subjects.[64] He means that the belief that we are self-governing agents is an effect of an ideology that engages us by addressing us as subjects. Franklin's ameliorative substitution of identity for sovereignty really would constitute the British ideologically, as a set of cultural preferences.

If nationally based political programmes were in abeyance in the 1990s, what of the EU, as their reverse image, so to speak? Is there a corresponding rise in the EU's standing? Can we say that integration accelerates as national strategies are moderated? Indeed, attitudes towards the EU also stabilized as disenchantment with national democracy grew, until reported satisfaction with the EU was greater than dissatisfaction over the last decade, as demonstrated in Figure 7.2.

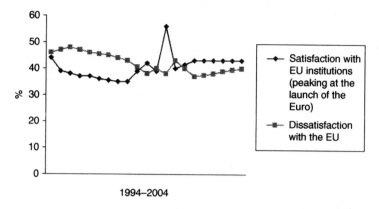

Figure 7.2 Satisfaction and dissatisfaction with the institutions of the EU.
Source: Eurobarometer.

Certainly the Delors presidency (1985–95) is understood to be ground-breaking. The Single European Act (1986), in particular, demonstrated a forward momentum that had been missing in the preceding 10 years, 'a period of "Euro-pessimism" that lasted from the first enlargement to 1985' when the European powers seemed consumed by a zero-sum competition among each other.[65] Delors in particular was adept in building constituencies for the EU among those minority groups who had lost out in the 'first-past-the-post' electoral systems. In 1988, Delors presented Europe's 'Social Dimension' to a sceptical British Trades Union Congress, beginning the process of British Labour's transition from an anti- to pro-European stance. The European Parliament proved to be a tempting platform for national minorities, like the Scottish Nationalists, who tempered the more threatening aspect of their party slogan by campaigning for 'Independence ... in Europe'. The advance climaxed with President Mitterand's support for German reunification, which he offered in exchange for support for a commitment to further integration in the form of a single European currency.[66]

It was German reunification, however, that seemed destined to derail the European train. Specifically, the Bundesbank's tight monetary policy (after Chancellor Kohl's conversion of Ostmarks to Deutschmarks at a rate of one-to-one) was blamed for imposing undue strain on the EMS. As both Britain and Italy were forced out of the Exchange Rate Mechanism, American finance writer Gregory Millman boasted that the 'ERM was decisively vanquished by speculators'.[67] Japanese journalist Noriko Hama wrote a series of apocalyptic articles for the *Mainichi Economist*, published in a collection entitled *Disintegrating Europe: The Twilight of the European Construction* in 1996. Her outsider's perspective probably amplified the tone of the debate, but her report of the pessimism towards European institutions was accurate. On top of frustration over ERM and the high German interest rate, came political opposition to the Maastricht Treaty, which founded the EU. Rejected in a referendum by the Danes in June 1992, and only narrowly supported by the French, it had seemed to summarize the priority of business interests over all else.[68] 'Since the signing of the Maastricht treaty', wrote Stephen Tindale of the British Institute for Public Policy Research, 'the European project has faced its most severe crisis'.[69]

Most impressively, however, the Commission took the failures of 1993 as reasons for further integration, not retreat, culminating in the launch of the single currency in 1999. While Euro-sceptics were organizing the funeral, the integrationists assumed that the ERM's collapse demonstrated the rightness of their cause:

> The significance of this episode lies in the fact that the international capital markets were effectively able to subvert the policies of democratically elected governments in major European countries, despite all the tools and resources available to national governments and despite the monetary cooperation between European countries that had been developed on an inter-governmental basis and through the EU. *This would suggest that there are severe limits to the economic sovereignty of European nation states in the late twentieth century.*[70]

Fundamentally, monetary union was a process of *depoliticizing* a central plank of economic and fiscal administration, the currency. Currency manipulation had assumed an excessive importance as a lever of political control over the economy, as other mechanisms of Keynesian economic management, such as capital controls (abandoned in Britain, Germany and the Netherlands in 1982),[71] had fallen into disfavour. Conditions for entry to the Euro underlined the removal of economic policy from political control, from the enforced independence of central banks, to the three per cent of GDP limitation on budget deficits demanded by the Growth and Stability Pact.

The Commission

The Commission was always intended more as a super civil service than a political directory. Asked who should be proposed as commissioners from France, De Gaulle offered the telling advice 'send the most stupid', meaning that it would be better if the Commission was not so talented that it would become a challenge to the authority of national politicians.[72] For years the Commission was a graveyard for politicians who, if not exactly stupid, were at the end of their careers. This was true right back to its beginning, in fact, when Paul Henri Spaak's 'own personal situation had changed', when he was voted out of government in Belgium: 'The idea of presiding over an international body whose task it would be to create a united Europe appealed to me.'[73] However, in more recent times, setbacks in national politics have proved to be a formative experience, rather than a weakness. When the Mitterand government was forced to abandon its national reflation in 1982, Finance Minister Jacques Delors, on the social Catholic wing of the Socialist Party, was instrumental in persuading the hardliners to accept that the policy could not be defended in the face of international economic pressures. It was a lesson that Delors took with him when he became president of the Commission. 'A high degree of supra-nationality is essential', he told John Ardagh, 'national sovereignty no longer means very much, or has much scope in the modern world economy'.[74]

As we have seen, under Delors the Commission found a new forward momentum, pulled along by the vacuum left as national governments grappled with a loss of legitimacy. A poll of Commission civil servants in 2000 found 91 per cent thought the Commission's influence on the integration process very high.[75] It should be said, though, that this forward momentum also changed the character of the Commission. The Commission was originally conceived of as a stream-lined bureaucracy so that it would not reproduce the efforts of national civil servants, who are generally expected to 'action' EU directives. Even today it only employs 17,000 staff.[76] However, as more policy initiatives develop from the centre, the Commission has extended its reach through the Technical Assistance Offices – *ad hoc* bodies created when the Commission contracts out the administration of its projects. 'The TAO structure clearly operates as a privatized bureaucracy' according to Paul van Buitenen.[77] This decentralized administration, underneath the Commission's permanent civil service, corresponds to the *ad hoc* character of the integration process.

The realists are right to maintain the EU remains, in the last instance, a treaty, a contract from which the contracting parties can nominally withdraw. Over time, of course, the repetition of the agreement becomes routine and formulaic, and the binding nature of the process asserts itself. The right of the state to withdraw from the Union, exemplified in the Council of Ministers' 'unanimity provision', becomes a dead letter. After the 'empty chair' crisis of 1965, when De Gaulle stopped the Council from working by withdrawing representation,[78] to the problems caused by Thatcher's 'veto' threats in the 1980s,[79] the demand that Council resolutions be decided by a majority vote became unavoidable. The Single European Act of 1986 extended 'Qualified Majority Voting', that was taken even further down the road to decision-making by simple majority in the European Constitution (spectacularly rejected in the Dutch and French referendums of 2005). Again, the formal position still remains: any country can withdraw from the Union whenever it likes. But the push away from unanimous voting shows that the process has now established its priority over the contracting parties' immediate rights. The diminished meaning of consent is also demonstrated in the recent enlargement of the Union. The new eastern members of the Union had to accept the totality of EU law into their own legislation, all at once. This can hardly be considered to be a decision that has been reflected upon. The attempt to derive the process of European integration from the interaction of competing national interests, and as a realization of national sovereignty becomes less convincing.

'History', writes Althusser, groping for an account that will not enthrone any singular principle, ' "asserts itself" through the multiform world of the super-structures, from local tradition to international circumstances'.[80] The EU has something of the character of a 'multiform world of superstructures'. Unlike the constitution of a nation-state, its structures have developed without a strong sense of integration, which has always been posed as a goal for the future, belying their imperfect intercorrelation in the present. Different components of the Union – the Council, the Parliament and the Commission – give expression to contrasting elements: the treaty among sovereign states, the still-born European popular will and the tendency towards a depoliticized administration. It often appears to Euro-sceptics that the bureaucratic character of the EU is a top-down imposition upon nation-states. They point, for example, to the fact that over half of British agri-cultural legislation is made to implement decisions taken by ministers in Brussels.[81] On the face of it the enormous body of legislation that comes down from Brussels seems to indicate that the Eurocrats have stolen our democracy. But the truth is that Brussels legislation is incorporated because it is uncontroversial, and is in any event set in train by nationally, rather than Brussels-based elites. More worrying is the hollowing out of national polities, such that the Brussels Eurocrats fill the vacuum that a national political process has left behind.

Conclusion

The process that has driven European cooperation closer over the last 20 years has not been due to a new transnational ethos. Nor has it been due to the prosecution of discrete national interests, masquerading as unity. The difficulty in under-standing the process of European cooperation is that it does not fit into the schema of national interest politics, nor is it a functional coalescence at the elite level – though that does come about as a secondary effect of the process. Driving the coalescence of European elites is the collapse of the internal national dynamic that makes the different national actors into sovereign states. Primarily, this signals the depletion of their national political processes. The movement away from mass political contestation robs nations of the inner life that causes them to formulate national strategies and goals. Political contestation within the domestic sphere is the essential element of self-reflection in modern societies that laid the basis for the formation of national interests. Today's settlement is the outcome of a previous struggle by the elites to reduce public expectations upon the state. But that campaign to demobilize popular expectations was too successful. Today's elites struggle with a different problem from the legitimacy crisis of the 1970s. On the contrary, their problem is the diminution of public aspirations and expec-tations upon government. They struggle with a crisis of legitimacy that comes from the decline in popular voting, participation and involvement in political processes.

All of this would be of interest only to sociologists and political scientists if the relations between nations were not at the same time dependent upon the relations between national leaders and their popular base. In short, sovereignty is an issue only if there is an expectation of sovereignty. But for 20 years elites fought to reduce their populations' expectations that they could influence policy at the national level. This did not lead simply to an elite monopoly on power. On the contrary, it has led to a situation where elites also recoil from responsibility for political decision-making. The best way to understand this development is as the emergence of post-sovereign forms of international relations. We see that sovereignty, as the forceful assertion of national interest and ambitions, is less appropriate to the actual behaviour of today's elites. On the contrary, European integration begins to look somewhat like Althusser's 'process with out a subject'. Sovereignty survives as a performance, but its content is attenuated. Traditional IR theory gives us little insight into the retreat from national sovereignty that we see at work in the EU. A better guide would perhaps be Nietzsche's description of the ideology of self-effacement in his *Genealogy of Morals*, or Marx's account of the unpatriotic bourgeoisie, welcoming the Prussian invader in to discipline the Parisian masses in *On the Paris Commune*. If the outcome of this process is something like the formation of a European political class, it is one that is marked by indecision, rushing to fill the vacuum left by more dynamic national political leaders, rather than one that is jealously stealing power from under our noses.

Notes

1 S. Haseler, *The New Europe and its Challenge to America*, London: I.B. Tauris, 2005, p.89.
2 J. Rifkin, *The European Dream*, Oxford: Polity, 2005, p.197.
3 M. Leonard, *Why Europe Will Run the Twenty-First Century*, London: Fourth Estate, 2005, p.28.
4 Haseler, *New Europe*.
5 E. Haas, *The Uniting of Europe*, London: Stevens and Sons, 1958, p.3.
6 D. Mitrany, *The Functional Theory of Politics*, London: Martin Robertson and Co., 1975, pp.123–124.
7 A. Lijphart, 'Karl Deutsch and the New Paradigm in International Relations', in R. Merrit and B. Russet (eds), *From National Development to Global Community – Essays in Honour of Karl W Deutsch*, London: Allen and Unwin, 1981, pp.237–238.
8 A.S. Milward, *The European Rescue of the Nation State*, London: Routledge, 1992.
9 A. Moravcsik, 'Negotiating the Single European Act: National Interests and Conventional Statecraft in the European Community', in R. Keohane and S. Hoffmann (eds), *The New European Community*, Boulder: Westview, 1991, p.47.
10 A. Wendt, *Social Theory in International Politics*, Cambridge: Cambridge University Press, 1999, pp.242, 307.
11 B. Buzan and R. Little (eds), *International Systems in World History: Remaking the Study of International Relations*, Oxford: Oxford University Press, 2000, p.359.
12 A. Moravcsik, *The Choice for Europe: Social Purpose and State Power from Messina to Maastricht*, London: Routledge, 1998, p.230.
13 D.J. Puchala, 'Integration Studies and the Study of International Relations', in Merrit and Russet, *From National Development*, p.151.
14 See D. Acheson, *Present at the Creation*, New York: Doubleday, 1969.
15 Cited in S.D. Krasner, *Sovereignty: Organized Hypocrisy*, Chichester: Princeton University Press, 1999, p.19.
16 German Constitutional Court, Judgement of 12 October 1993, *Entscheidungen des Bundesverfassungsgericht* (BVerfG) 89, 1993, pp.155–213.
17 Krasner, *Sovereignty*, p.9.
18 See G.W.F. Hegel, *Hegel's Logic, Being Part One of the Encyclopaedia of the Philosophical Sciences*, Oxford: Clarendon Press, 1989, p.63.
19 E. Pashukanis, *Law and Marxism: A General Theory*, London: Pluto, 1989, p.95.
20 L. Mumford, *The City in History*, Hammondsworth: Penguin, 1991, p.510.

21 T. Wright, *Citizens or Subjects*, London: Routledge, 1993; G. Robertson, *Crimes Against Humanity*, London: Allen Lane, 1999; Krasner, *Sovereignty*.
22 Buzan and Little, *International Systems*, p.392.
23 Ibid., p.29.
24 F. McLynn, *Napoleon: A Biography*, London: Pimlico, 1998, p.391.
25 K. Marx, *Capital: A Critique of Political Economy, Vol. III.*, London: Lawrence and Wishart, 1984, pp.209, 253; G.W.F. Hegel, *Science of Logic*, Atlantic Highlands: Humanities International Press, 1991, p.174.
26 J. Stalin, 'The Social-Democratic Deviation in our Party', Report delivered at the Fifteenth All-Union Conference of the CPSU(B), 1 November 1926, in *Stalin on the Opposition*, Peking: Foreign Languages Press, 1974.
27 Buzan and Little, *International Systems*, p.19.
28 Quoted in E. Haas, *Beyond the Nation State, Functionalism and the International Organization*, Stanford: Stanford University Press, 1964, p.7.
29 Haas, *Uniting of Europe*, p.17.
30 E. Barkan, *The Guilt of Nations: Restitution and the Negotiation of Historical Injustices*, New York: W.W. Norton and Company, 2000, p.13.
31 M. Grindrod, *The Rebuilding of Italy*, London: Royal Institute of International Affairs, 1955, p.13.
32 F. Giles, *The Locust Years: The Story of the Fourth French Republic 1946–1958*, London: Secker and Warburg, 1991.
33 Acheson, *Present at the Creation*, p.385.
34 Milward, *European Rescue*; Moravcsik, *Choice for Europe*.
35 Buzan and Little, *International Systems*, p.39.
36 Moravcsik, *Choice for Europe*.
37 A. Sohn-Reuthel, *The Economy and Class Structure of Fascism*, London: Free Association Books, 1987, p.78.
38 Giles, *Locust Years*, p.218.
39 L. Althusser, *The Future Lasts a Long Time*, London: Vintage, 1994, p.217.
40 Moravcsik, *Choice for Europe*, pp.264, 288, 338, 386.
41 N. Lawson, *The View from No. 11*, London: Corgi, 1993, p.1024.
42 Ibid., p.111.
43 G. Brown, *Red Paper on Scotland*, Edinburgh: EUSPB, 1975, p.7.
44 C. Offe, *Contradictions of the Welfare State*, London: Hutchinson, 1974, p.65.
45 Moravcsik, *Choice for Europe*, p.369.
46 Compiled from Eurobarometer sources.
47 M. Hardt and A. Negri, *Empire*, London: Harvard University Press, 2000.
48 Ibid., p.xii.
49 Ibid., p.91.
50 L. Althusser, *For Marx*, Hammondsworth: Penguin, 1966, p.121.
51 P. Lamy, 'The Globalization Process and its Implications for Egypt', Cairo: Council for Foreign Relations at the Diplomatic Club, 5 March 2001.
52 Cited in Moravcsik, *Choice for Europe*, p.295.
53 Ibid., p.74.
54 L. Tsoukalis and R. Strauss, 1987, 'Community Politics and Steel', in Y. Meny and V. Wright (eds), *The Politics of Steel*, New York: de Gruyter, 1987, p.210.
55 Quoted in P. Ginsborg, *Italy and Its Discontents*, London: Allen Lane, 2001, p.243; and see Moravcsik, *Choice for Europe*, pp.74–75.
56 *Guardian*, 9 December 2005.
57 C. Jones, *France: An Illustrated History*, Cambridge: Cambridge University Press, 1994, p.312.
58 M. Spoudalakis, 'The Greek Experience', *Socialist Register*, London: Merlin, 1986, p.252.
59 W. Hutton, *The World We're In*, London: Little Brown and Company, 2002, p.296.

60 C. Grant, *Delors: Inside the House that Jacques Built*, London: Nicholas Brealey, 1994, p.55.
61 L. Brittan, *A Diet of Brussels: The Changing Face of Europe*, London: Little Brown and Company, 2000, p.35.
62 Moravcsik, *Choice for Europe*, p.290.
63 M. Franklin, *Britain's Future in Europe*, London: Royal Institute of International Affairs, 1990, pp.9–10.
64 L. Althusser, 'Ideological State Apparatuses', in S. Žižek (ed.), *Mapping Ideology*, London: Verso, 1994, p.129.
65 R. Baldwin and C. Wyplosz, *The Economics of European Integration*, London: McGraw Hill, 2004, p.17.
66 T. Garton Ash, *In Europe's Name: Germany, and the Divided Continent*, New York: Vintage, 1994, p.390.
67 G. Millman, *Around the World on a Trillion Dollars a Day*, London: Bantam, 1995, p.819.
68 O. Lafontaine, *The Heart Beats on the Left*, Oxford: Polity, 2000, p.30.
69 S. Tindale, 'A People's Europe', in G. Radice (ed.), *What Needs to Change*, London: Harper Collins, 1996, p.231.
70 V. Lintner, 'The European Community – 1958 to the 1990s', in M.-S. Schulze (ed.), *Western Europe: Economic and Social Change since 1945*, London: Longman, 1999, p.153.
71 Hutton, *World We're In*, p.326.
72 A. Menon, 'Send the Most Stupid', *London Review of Books*, 9 December 1999.
73 P.-H. Spaak, *Continuing Battle: Memoirs of a European, 1936–1966*, London: Weidenfield and Nicholson, 1971, p.197.
74 J. Ardagh, *France in the New Century*, London: Penguin, 2000, pp.687–688.
75 A. Topan, 'The Resignation of the Santer Commission: The Impact on "Trust" and "Reputation"', *European Integration Online Papers* (EIoP) 14:6, 2002. Online. Available at HTTP: <http://www.eiop.or.at/eiop/texte/2002–014.htm> (accessed 30 May 2006).
76 P. Van Buitenen, *Blowing the Whistle: One Man's Fight against Fraud in the European Commission*, London: Politicos, 2000, p.138.
77 Van Buitenen, *Blowing the Whistle*, p.12.
78 Spaak, *Continuing Battle*, p.482.
79 See M. Thatcher, *The Downing Street Years*, London: Harper Collins, 1995, pp.78–86.
80 Althusser, *For Marx*, p.112.
81 See Leonard, *Why Europe will Run the Twenty-First Century*, p.14.

8 Deconstructing sovereignty

Constructing global civil society

David Chandler

Introduction

The war on terror has created trepidation among the champions of human rights, international law and 'non-state actors' (such as international organizations and non-governmental organizations, or NGOs). They fear that their past political gains are now being rolled back by a reinvigorated politics of state security, based on military conquest, the trampling of human rights and the subversion of international law and cooperation. One of the leading proponents of global civil society, Mary Kaldor, has poignantly expressed this sentiment:

> Will we look back on the last decade as the 'happy Nineties'? Was it an interregnum between global conflicts when utopian ideas like global civil society, human rights, a global rule of law, or global social justice seemed possible? Or was it, on another interpretation, the moment when global civil society came of age?[1]

However international politics unfolds, we now stand in a position to assess the development of global civil society in the 'happy Nineties' with the benefit of some hindsight. What is more, it would be hasty to consign global civil society to the dustbin of history. However much the war on terror seems to have transformed the landscape of international relations, NGOs and other non-state agents remain key actors in international politics in the early twenty-first century. In fact, much of the energy expended against the international financial institutions in the 1990s has been reinvigorated by and redirected against the United States since the election of President George W. Bush in 2000. This ire has only increased since the 2003 US-led invasion of Iraq; indeed, the anti-war movement flows directly from the anti-capitalist and anti-globalization movements of the 1990s.[2] Therefore it is timely to ask: how viable is the model of politics offered by global civil society? Does it offer a means of transcending state-based politics? This is the question that I shall try to answer in this chapter.

The first problem we encounter in pursuing this question is the peculiarity of the concept of global civil society itself. Even its proponents admit that it is 'fuzzy and contested'.[3] Part of the confusion stems from the fact that global civil society is used both in a descriptive, empirical sense and in a normative, prescriptive sense. Empirically speaking, 'global civil society' refers to the growing numbers of non-state actors that operate beyond the confines of national societies, polities and economies, ranging from NGOs to international social movements and networks. Normatively speaking, global civil society refers to new global values variously ascribed to these actors or derived from their interaction.[4] In this chapter, I shall analyse global civil society by reference to those who focus on building global civil society 'from the bottom-up' – those who see global civil society as an emerging transnational social movement that operates independently of sovereign states.[5]

I shall proceed by presenting the historical development of the ideas at the core of radical 'bottom-up' approaches. The three main elements are (1) the rejection of politics based on formal processes of representation and struggles for state power; the two corollaries of this being (2) the centrality of individual autonomy over social engagement and (3) the expansion of activity into the global arena. The concluding sections dwell on the limitations of this approach, outlining how it slides into a solipsistic, courtier politics of negotiating access to elites. I shall argue that the consequences of legitimizing the individualized politics of global civil society is atomization, and not a more inclusive, democratic form of politics.

The approach of constructing global society 'from below' locates the radical ethics of global civil society in the methods and organization of its members. Advocates of this approach suggest that these radical movements bring politics and ethics together by expanding our sphere of moral concern, and by developing political strategies that bypass state-based constraints on what counts as politics.[6] This 'social movement approach' envisages global civil society as morally progressive in so far as it does not 'seek to replace one form of power with another' but instead has the 'objective of "whittling down" the capacity of concentrated centres of power'.[7] The emphasis is on 'the struggle to reclaim space', on the creation of 'zones of autonomy' and 'counter powers to the state'.[8]

In this outlook, there is a fundamental difficulty in locating political activity at the level of the state. Taking the terms of the state as given tends to legitimize and perpetuate discourses and practices of political regulation that are, in the last instance, built on exclusion and war.[9] For Andrew Linklater, global civil society's aim is to challenge the 'totalising project' of the state, which is based on 'accentuat[ing] the differences between citizens and aliens'. It is this rejection of state-based approaches that marks out the global civil society project as distinct from radical movements of the past. I shall trace the historical development of global civil society from the post-1968 New Left, through the 1980s civic 'oppositionists' of Eastern Europe, right through to the anti-capitalist and anti-war movements of today. Some people have speculated on the dangers of these global civic actors being co-opted by states.[10] But few have interrogated the two key claims of global civil society; first, that it represents an extension of political solidarities beyond the state, and second, its prioritization of individual autonomy over the politics of sovereign representation.

In this chapter, I want to suggest that what appears as a critique of the narrowness of state-based politics subtly shifts registers to become an attack on the very idea of collective political action itself. Despite the promiscuous brandishing of the word 'society' by global civic actors, it is precisely *social* engagement that these actors are resisting by operating in the ethereal realm of 'the global'. This anti-political and elitist stance acquires a radical sheen on the basis of its prior claim, that any state-based political engagement is restrictive. The geographically challenged institutions of the state appear as arbitrary and artificial restrictions on the 'autonomy' of activists to circulate around the globe. But whether activists immerse themselves in indigenous communities many miles from home, or spend their time protesting outside the world summits of global elites, in attacking territorial fetters on political engagement, global civic actors end up rejecting the institutionally grounded responsibility and accountability that is intrinsic to politics itself.

Bypassing the state, undermining sovereignty

In the 1990s, the concept of global civil society was taken up by Western leftists and radicals who saw in civil society an alternative to the exhausted political programmes of the left, as well as a means of checking the power of 'unbridled capitalism' and the state.[11] The idea of global civil society was given impetus by the implosion of many authoritarian regimes at the end of the Cold War, most spectacularly, of course, those of the USSR and Eastern bloc, but also military dictatorships in Latin America. Many people attributed the collapse of these seemingly monolithic states to the activities of handfuls of intellectual dissidents, who drew on international communications and solidarity networks to spread liberal ideas about human rights and democracy. Eastern European dissidents seemed to offer a model of emancipatory politics that could be taken ever further afield. Kaldor, for example, approvingly quotes the dissident and later president of the Czech Republic, Vaclav Havel, in relation to Western political systems:

> It would appear that the traditional parliamentary democracies can offer no fundamental opposition to the automatism of technological civilisation and the industrial-consumer society, for they, too, are being dragged helplessly along. People are manipulated in ways that are infinitely more subtle and refined than the brutal methods used in post-totalitarian societies... In a democracy, human beings may enjoy many personal freedoms... [but] they too are ultimately victims of the same automatism, and are incapable of defending their concerns about their own identity or preventing their superficialisation.[12]

On one level, the appeal of East European dissidents is obvious enough, given that they were commonly held to have had a key role in bringing a totalitarian superpower to its knees. But was there any deeper appeal of East European civil society movements? While the term 'civil society' was used in Poland, more explicit is the title of a book by Hungarian dissident George Konrad: 'anti-politics'.[13] Kaldor, who has not only analysed but also participated in these movements, concurs with Konrad: 'anti-politics is the ethos of civil society'.[14] The individual autonomy claimed by East European dissidents was held to be more thoroughly radical than engagement in political mass movements:

> After 1968, the main form of [East European] opposition was the individual dissident. The dissidents saw themselves not as precursors of a political movement but as individuals who wanted to retain their personal integrity. Dissidence was about the dignity of the individual as much as about politics. It was about the possibility of honest interaction even at a private and personal level, about being able to read, think and discuss freely.[15]

This new form of opposition arose after the defeat of mass uprisings by Soviet tanks in Hungary in 1956, and in Czechoslovakia in 1968. Following these defeats, the dissident elites believed that convincing the masses to overthrow the incumbent regimes, or even to contest their authority, mattered less than the dissidents' individual, ethical stance. Kaldor acknowledges this impulse animating the dissidents: 'They described themselves not as a movement but as a civic initiative, a "small island in a sea of apathy" '.[16] So what is it about the political and social isolation of the Eastern dissidents, and their disillusionment with the 'sea of apathy', that inspires global civil society today? For this, we must look to the origins of global civil society not in Eastern Europe, but in the events of 1968 in Western Europe.

Radical 'autonomy'

The origins of global civil society can be traced back to the first movements that argued for a 'bottom-up' ethics of autonomy over political power, which were called the 'new social movements'. Like the East European dissidents, the origins of these movements lay in the political defeats of 1968. The Soviets crushed the Prague Spring in the east, while the 'old left' in Western Europe – the Communist parties and trade unions – failed spectacularly to capitalize politically on the student turmoil and labour unrest of the late 1960s. This led to a widespread disillusionment with the organized left. But instead of contesting the claims of the old left to represent the collective interests of society at large, the nascent New Left rejected the idea of formalized political representation *tout court*. The disgust with the sclerotic bureaucracies of the Communist parties and trade unions gave the New Left its emphasis on spontaneity, autonomy and its defining mistrust of organization.

The rejection of old forms of mass-based politics had two effects. The first was the search for alternative forms of emancipation that were more individuated, such as the women's movement and the 'autonomy' movements (e.g. the *movement autogestionnaire* in France and the *Alternativbewegung* in Germany). The second effect was the search for alternative oppressed groups, apart from the industrial proletariat, that could act as political agents of social transformation. These were variously found in black power groups, student activists, sexual minorities, women and in the anti-imperialist struggles in Latin America, Africa and Asia.

The political distancing from organized labour went hand-in-hand with a critique of a collective political subject. Leading theorists of the New Left, Ernesto Laclau and Chantal Mouffe, argued that democratic struggles were not necessarily popular struggles requiring sanction through the ballot-box.[17] Laclau and Mouffe denied the idea that politics reaches its peak in the competition among representative parties for control of the state, arguing instead that no one political space should be privileged above another, or considered ontologically prior.[18] For these theorists of 'radical democracy', democratic struggles took place in a 'plurality of political spaces' shaped by their own, relatively autonomous 'ensemble of practices and discourses'.[19] Without a singular concept of 'political space', it became possible to repudiate traditional political practices and methods – such as elections and mass mobilization. The rejection of formal political institutions meant that the key demands of the New Left shifted from political rights (equality and participation) to demands for the recognition of difference and 'autonomy'.[20]

This idea of autonomy gives the new social movements the appearance of being anti-state, though this is less to do with their political views and more to do with their organizational practices. In a path-breaking and favourable analysis of civil society, derived from Eastern European experiences and the new social movements in the West, Jean Cohen and Andrew Arato pointed to the politically constrained character of these civil society movements by characterizing them as 'self-limiting revolutions': 'The self-limiting revolution avoids the total destruction of its enemy, which would inevitably mean putting itself into the place of the sovereign, thereby depriving society of its self-organization and self-defense.'[21] Here, political society (the state), and its operative concept, sovereignty, is a danger, to be warded off by the self-restraint of civil society. This takes the form of demanding that the state restrain itself, but not to the point of actually organizing to seize power directly. They organize to wield indirect influence, not direct power. Cohen and Arato further clarify that this power of influence derives not from the force of numbers that civil society represents, but rather from the ethical power of its ideas:

> Unlike money or power, influence acts on the intentions rather than the situation of other actors, offering the normative value of a desired action (rather than a positive or negative sanction) as its own reward. The actors in the case of influence are oriented not to success or to general consequences but to reaching an understanding with one another.[22]

Civil society, in other words, attempts to shape society and constrain the state not by representing and realizing a popular will, but through moral example. The authority of civil society derives from moral sources, and its conformity with an idealized conception of proper political conduct, rather than from its authorization by expressed wills. The lack of orientation towards 'success or to general consequences', means that civic actors in principle are free to organize at any level of society, in relation to any audience, in any sphere in which it can engage in deliberations. That the groups Cohen and Arato spoke about were sometimes small in number and isolated from wider society, was recast not as a weakness but as a potential strength. Cohen and Arato reasoned that since these groups operated outside the logic of numbers (elections and mass protest), and due to their minority status, they were more vividly aware of the need to use the force of argument and ideas rather than simply impose their will.

If Cohen and Arato theorized new social movements as part of a broader politics of civil society, others pointed to a more radical departure from politics altogether. For the civil society theorist Alberto Melucci, new social movements exist outside the traditional civil society-state nexus. Submerged in everyday life, they 'have created meanings and definitions of identity' that contrast with traditional political definitions.[23] Melucci argues that traditional electoral measures of political success miss the point: 'This is because conflict takes place principally on symbolic ground... The mere existence of a symbolic challenge is in itself a method of unmasking the dominant codes, a different way of perceiving and naming the world.'[24] From this perspective, isolation and the reliance on contacts within 'local communities result in a decentralized strength, rooted in the autonomy of the national and local process'.[25]

The élan of the New Left propelled them beyond the conservative old left, but they too soon ran up against their own limits. First, the claim for recognition on the basis of difference rather than universality inverted the traditional benchmark for assessing political legitimacy. In effect, for the New Left and the new social movements that sprang from it, legitimacy is based on the admission of social isolation (as acknowledged in the demand for 'recognition' of particular claims). This in turn redefined the nature of political activity. In place of unity and common interests that could be represented in formal institutions, the new social movements were forced to define political agency in terms of the spontaneous, immediate interactions among individuals – the only basis on which difference and particularity could be preserved. The lack of any formal political structures of representation made it difficult to integrate people, making it difficult in turn to accumulate social weight behind particular ideological positions, and to sustain political momentum over protracted periods.

Thus well before the end of the Cold War, the new social movements had distanced themselves from the organized labour movement, eschewed struggling for political power through the representation of collective interests, and had reached out for new agents of change in various subaltern groups, both at home and abroad. In addition to claiming the internationalist credentials of the old left, the search for new agents of change predisposed the new social movements to orient themselves externally. The failure to institutionalize themselves politically, and therefore to sink deep roots into their domestic societies, was thus tempered by the chimera of internationalism. Languishing in the margins of domestic politics, adherents often took heart in messages of 'solidarity' or success from other parts of the world, and drew inspiration from the forward march of anti-imperialism in the Third World. Kaldor's own experience of involvement in the waning European peace movements of the 1980s is instructive. Perceiving itself as isolated due to being 'unpatriotic' and 'pro-Soviet', the European Nuclear Disarmament (END) group took the 'Go and live in Russia' slur of its critics literally, decamping to Eastern Europe where its members were fêted as leading radical lights:[26]

> Hundreds of activists travelled to Eastern Europe and identified local groups, individuals, town councils and churches, with whom they could talk and exchange ideas. I have before me as I write a leaflet published by END called 'Go East': 'Forget smoke-filled rooms, this political organisation is asking you to take a holiday – in Eastern Europe.'[27]

Ultimately, however, the new strategy of 'Going East' was less a sign of political dynamism than of having surrendered to domestic political opponents. For the waning new social movements, the international realm was the path of least resistance. The resultant forward momentum was then reinterpreted as a sign of progressive, anti-authoritarian vitality. In Kaldor's words, 'almost all social movements and NGOs...have some kind of transnational relations. Precisely because these groups inhabit a political space outside formal national politics (parties and elections)'.[28] As we shall see, both these limitations of the New Left – its absence of representative politics and the concomitant absence of social engagement – have been carried through into today's global civil society.

New global agency?

The end of the Cold War leant new life to this narcissistic form of internationalism in a number of crucial respects. First, the links with the East European dissidents, who were the immediate beneficiaries of the Stalinist bureaucracies' desperate search for a negotiated regime change, seemed to be a vindication of the internationalist civil society activists and the type of fluid, decentralized politics that they stood for. Furthermore, the end of geopolitical rivalry between the superpowers offered the prospect of greater international cooperation and greater global integration. In short, the end of the Cold War gave impetus to the new social movements, enabling them to diffuse even more widely into the international realm.

In so far as the end of the Cold War belatedly confirmed the rejection of proletarian politics decades earlier, the 'post-Marxist' radicals Michael Hardt and Antonio Negri posed the problem thus: 'The proletariat is not what it used to be.' The task, therefore, was to discover new forms of global agency.[29] Proponents of global civil society 'from below' claim to have discovered these new agents of change. According to the radical guide books advertised in the London *Guardian* and *New Statesman*, a new worldwide revolution is underway, propelled by a global movement for justice, autonomy and civil society, so large and diverse that it has been referred to as a new 'movement of movements'.

Who comprises this 'movement of movements'? Its constituents range from the Zapatistas in Chiapas (often alleged to have founded the new global politics when they started their 12 day 'post-modern revolution' on 1 January 1994), to the farmers protesting against genetically modified crops in Latin America, India, Malaysia and the Philippines. Others include the Narmada Dam protests in India, anti-privatization struggles in South African shanty towns and the struggles of the landless peasantry (*Movimento Sem Terra*) in Brazil. Paul Kingsnorth in his best-selling *One No, Many Yeses*, widely fêted as a 'journey to the heart of the global resistance movement', asks: 'Has a movement this big ever existed before? Has such a diversity of forces, uncontrolled, decentralized, egalitarian, ever existed on a global scale? Has a movement led by the poor, the disenfranchised, the South, ever existed at all?'[30]

This sense of radical global agency is reflected in the leading scholarly treatments. For Hardt and Negri, the plural source of global agency is to be found in disparate forms of resistance, from the 1992 Los Angeles riots, to the Palestinian *Intifada* and the Zapatistas. The local nature of these struggles, Hardt and Negri concede, presents a 'paradox' in so far as it 'makes it extremely difficult to grasp and express the new power posed by the struggles that have emerged'.[31] Because these struggles are isolated, they do not at first sight appear to be particularly powerful. Hardt and Negri contend, however, that this appearance is deceptive, because each one of these struggles challenges different facets of global capitalist domination. For example, the Los Angeles rioters are held to challenge racial and hierarchical forms of 'post-Fordist' social control; the Zapatistas to challenge world markets. The key is that '[p]erhaps precisely because all these struggles are incommunicable and thus blocked from travelling horizontally in the form of a cycle, they are forced instead to leap vertically and touch immediately on the global level'.[32] In other words, these movements spontaneously hook up to the global, precisely because they make no connections with other oppressed groups, and they do not seek to conquer state power.

In the eyes of Hardt and Negri, the strength of these movements is their refusal to be enchained in the claims of sovereign representative politics:

> The entire logical chain of representation might be summarized like this: the people representing the multitude, the nation representing the people, and the state representing the nation. Each link is an attempt to hold in suspension the crisis of modernity. Representation in each case means a further step of abstraction and control.[33]

This critique of the process of political representation is a central theme of global civil society theory and practice. Thus we see the model of political agency championed by Laclau and Mouffe in the 1980s being reapplied in the post-Cold War era to a number of diffuse struggles around the world. However authoritarian any particular sovereign state, sovereignty always entails a representational claim: to represent the people, the general will. To global civil society advocates, this abstract claim to collective representation *itself* is an egregious 'step of abstraction and control', as Hardt and Negri put it.

Thus, one of the unifying themes of these locally oriented struggles is their negative interpretation of traditional politics. They refuse to assimilate their goals and identities into a broader, more universal form. Indeed, we might recall Cohen and Arato's observation that the innovation of civil society's 'self-limiting revolution' is that it self-consciously avoids 'putting itself into the place of the sovereign' because this would 'depriv[e] society of its self-organization and self-defense'.[34] Unity is seen as something imposed from the 'top-down' by the sovereign state, while global civil society draws its identity and authority from the 'bottom-up'. Until the Seattle protests of 2000, the most noted example of global civil society activism 'from below' was the Zapatistas. The Zapatistas' use of the Internet to promote their struggle over land rights was picked up by Western academics, who hailed the Chiapas uprising as a revolutionary 'postmodern social movement'.[35] The example of the Zapatistas is worth dwelling on, as it will help us to draw out the differences between the traditional international linkages of the New Left, and the transnational solidarity of global civil society.

The Zapatistas' message was held to transcend Chiapas. The Zapatistas' leader, former university lecturer Subcomandante Marcos, has promoted the movement as embodying the essence of global civil society. In response to the question 'who is he?' the reply was given:

> Marcos is gay in San Francisco, a black person in South Africa, Asian in Europe, a Jew in Germany . . . a feminist in a political party. In other words, Marcos is a human being in this world. Marcos is every untolerated, oppressed, exploited minority that is beginning to speak and every majority must shut up and listen.[36]

Rather than offering political leadership, the Zapatistas understand themselves as mirroring the struggles of others, which together make up the diverse heterogeneous movements of global civil society.[37] The message is that subaltern subjects should celebrate difference rather than seek integration, for this would be to play the game of power. Gideon Baker, for example, cites Marcos on the need to work outside the framework of the state. Global civil society should operate 'underground', through 'subterranean' forms, eschewing the formal avenues of state-based politics that would only incorporate them as 'losers'.[38]

At its founding congress, the EZLN (Zapatista Army of National Liberation) decreed it would not take part in elections or even allow its members to join political parties. The rejection of all ambition to hold political office became a condition of membership.[39] For all their distance in both time and space, the Zapatistas' approach is strikingly similar to that of the East European movements of the 1980s, in that they accept their weakness vis-à-vis the state and, instead of attempting to overcome it, try to create 'autonomous counter-publics' that allegedly highlight the exclusionary practices of the Mexican state.[40]

In Naomi Klein's view: 'Marcos is convinced that these free spaces, born of reclaimed land, communal agriculture, resistance to privatisation, will eventually create counter-powers to the state simply by existing as alternatives'.[41] Thus, according to Baker, what really makes the Zapatista struggle part of global civil society is not just the rejection of engagement with state-level politics, but the declaration that their struggle is a global one, against 'Power', an all-purpose, unmediated category that serves as convenient shorthand for all the ills and oppression of capitalism at both the global and national levels.[42]

So what is problematic with this new concept of globalization from below? I have already argued that the rejection of formal political representation hampered the New Left, leaving it vulnerable to fragmentation, and pushing it outwards, to find new sources of moral authority in the international realm. In some respects, the model of agency taken for granted in global civil society, and embodied by the Zapatistas, is even more problematic than the New Left's. The concept of representation in global civil society is informal and symbolic rather than formalized and political. When Subcomandante Marcos argues that 'Marcos is every untolerated, oppressed, exploited minority' he does not represent these groups in the sense that he has been elected or in some way authorized by a popular will. Rather, he is a metaphor, and the authority of all other activists and NGOs that claim to speak for the oppressed is similarly predicated on this metaphorical connection.

Having rejected the conventional modes of representation and authority, the global activists explicitly root their authority in the ethical legitimacy predicated on the *absence* of any expressed will. This is what allows human rights advocate Michael Ignatieff to argue that, thanks to global civil society, 'international politics has been democratized', while acknowledging in the same breath that civic actors 'are not elected by the victim groups they represent, and in the nature of things they cannot be'.[43] As Slavoj Žižek notes, the politics of ethical advocacy is based on 'interpassivity', the virtuous activity of a minority that presupposes the passivity of others, who are spoken for.[44] In short, the model of advocacy in global civil society is ethical, not representative.

The dangers in this altruistic, rather than representative advocacy, lie in the fact that we can never be sure that the global civic actors really articulate the interests of the groups they claim to speak for. With no representative links to mediate their mutual relationship, the oppressed groups have no formal means of holding their self-appointed advocates to account. It is revealing of the inner limits of global civil society that its members are so often drawn to the most marginalized groups – indigenous peoples, children, victims of human rights abuses and famines, etc.... – that is to say, precisely those with the least social power to hold the advocates of global civil society to account. Those social groups who are sufficiently organized to mount independent political action and speak for themselves would not, of course, require global civil society.

In the Cold War, the New Left drew succour from organized, militant anti-colonial movements that often had mass support within their own societies, and operated political and military wings. By contrast, today the smaller or more marginal the struggle, the more pregnant with possibility it seems. One wonders whether there is an inverse relationship between the amount of revolutionary potential imputed into these struggles, and their actual strength and influence. A sceptical observer would no doubt suggest that the more marginal an opposition movement is, the more academic commentators can invest it with their own ideas and aspirations. These normative claims can then be used by any institution or individual to promote their own importance and moral legitimacy. Given the enormous moral benefits that can be gained from plugging into global civil society, with little political costs and dangers (there are no elections, after all), it seems probable that if it did not already exist, global civil society would have to be invented.

Second, the meaning of 'global' is worth drawing out here. The sense of 'global' deployed here is not positive, in the sense that it refers to a substantive agency or organized political power capable of acting systematically across borders. Rather, the sense of global is negative, in the sense that it refers to the act of *refusing* to operate within the political logic of the state. Global agency essentially means non-state agency, which in turn collapses into meaning unmediated politics, in the sense that any set of informal, temporary links can be established between groups located anywhere, so long as they are not institutionalized as an attempt to create a new global unity. It is impossible to ignore the fact that the rhetoric of global resistance coexists with a striking failure of the Zapatistas to achieve any relief from the abject poverty that afflicts Chiapas' peoples. More than a decade after the 12 day uprising of the EZLN, the Zapatistas' demands are still ignored by the Mexican government. The EZLN have rationalized this by arguing that their failure to deliver resources is only of secondary importance, since they 'know their "dignity" is worth more than any government development project'.[45]

This contrast between the grandiose claims made by global civic actors, and the reality of their limited and transient impact, was clear in the anti-globalization conference, held at the same time as the World Trade Organization (WTO) talks in Cancún in September 2003. Meeting in Cancún beneath pictures of Ché Guevara and Emiliano Zapata, WTO protestors could allege they represented 100 million peasant farmers (who would have been there but could not afford to come). Radical Western publishers launched their new books to an audience of Western spokespeople who talked-up the event. Peter Rossett, from US think-tank Food First, argued that the Cancún meeting demonstrated the strength of new social movements: 'These movements are growing fast, everywhere. For the first time you have global alliances forming.'[46] Barry Coates, of the World Development Movement, concurred: 'What we are seeing is the emergence of mass movements from across the spectrum of the developing world.'[47] The highlight of the counter-conference was a message of international support from Zapatista leaders, their first international message for 4 years.

But, as the New Left relied on links with anti-imperialist movements to compensate for its absence of domestic political authority, so the putative 'interconnectedness' between diverse local struggles is, I argue, the flip-side of domestic political isolation: 'Air travel and the Internet create new horizontal communities of people, who perhaps have more in common, than with those who live close by.'[48] What these 'citizen pilgrims' have in common is not only the financial ability to travel, but also isolation from and rejection of their own political spheres. It is this rejection of their domestic circumstances, rather than the richness of their international ties, that sustains their project. As we have seen, such transnational links are always contingent and never institutionalized. Rather than be exposed through a formal struggle to win the argument with people in a genuine debate, isolated activists are drawn to the forums of international financial and interstate institutions where there is no democratic discussion and they have no formal rights or responsibilities. Protesting outside meetings of the WTO or the G8 does not involve winning any arguments. At best, it is a matter of 'courtier politics', or elite lobbying, shortcutting any attempt to win popular support. At worst, it is a justification for a retreat into solipsism.

Before we turn to examine the limits of courtier politics, it is instructive to flag up the differences between global civil society and past internationalist movements. Indeed, today's global movement for emancipation 'from below' could be read as a product of the end of any genuine transnational struggle. In his book-length study *International Civil Society*, Alejandro Colás makes the point that advocates of 'globalisation from below' lack historical awareness of movements that have gone before them.[49] In the nineteenth and twentieth centuries the main political currents, whether they were conservatives, communists, anarchists, socialists, pacifists, feminists or even nationalists were in fact internationally – as much as nationally – orientated. For example, the People's International League, a cross-European association of nationalists, was established by Giuseppe Mazzini in 1847; Marx's and Engels' International Working Men's Association (the first International) was formed in 1864; and the International Congress of Women was established in 1888.[50] Compared to these historical examples, transnational political activism today appears to be not so much on the rise as diminished. Historical international social movements had the independence of aim and capacity to effect meaningful political change at both domestic *and* international levels, without relying on states to act on their behalf or, at the other extreme, avoiding any engagement with formal, domestic politics for fear of undermining their 'autonomy'. Contemporary global civil society movements have not proven their power in any comparable way. Instead, they have chosen to cast off the politics of a domestic sphere in which they are relatively weak.

Courtier politics

As we have seen, in adopting an unelected form of representation, activists tend to seek out those groups least likely to complain about Western advocates claiming to represent and lead them.[51] This leads to the de facto political exploitation or instrumentalization of marginal groups. The second consequence of the search for new political avenues that do not rely on representational legitimacy is talking up the importance of international institutional gatherings that previously attracted little interest. Pianta argues, for example, that 'the new power of summits of states and inter-governmental organisations' needs to be confronted through the invention of parallel summits.[52] Having no constituent interests to represent, global civic actors are forced to latch on to the ready-made agenda provided by international institutions. It is increasingly apparent that what little coherence these otherwise eclectic and fragmented radical movements have was given to them by the timetable of G8, WTO and Davos meetings.

Ironically, rather than bringing pressure to bear on these institutions, global civic actors are more often than not seen as making a positive contribution to the global agenda of these institutions. The IMF and the World Bank have invited lobby groups such as Global Exchange, Jobs with Justice, 50 Years is Enough and Essential Action to engage in public debate. Guy Verhofstadt, former Prime Minister of Belgium and President of the European Union at the time of the 2001 G8 summit in Genoa, wrote an open letter to the anti-globalization movement, published it in major national newspapers around the world, and collected the responses. French Prime Minister Lionel Jospin welcomed 'the emergence of a citizen's movement at the planetary level'.[53] Two years later, French President Jacques Chirac, then hosting the G8 summit in Evian, France, granted a delegation from the anti-capitalist counter-summit quasi-official status by meeting with them.[54]

As highlighted by US President George W. Bush's relationship with U2 rock star Bono, or British Prime Minister Tony Blair's cosy relationship with aging Live Eight rocker Bob Geldof, elites, governments and international institutions can only gain from their association with radical advocates.[55] The reason for the positive response of the establishment lies in the fact that the elites hope that the moral authority of global civic actors can rub off on them. The minimal effort of opening the doors of high-level meetings to NGO representatives can be passed off as turning an attentive ear to the oppressed, whom the NGOs supposedly represent.[56] But the activists need the ear of the elites even more than the elites need them. The absence of any representative, institutional links between oppressed groups and civic actors makes it difficult to amass any genuine social weight behind them, leaving activists politically weak. Having so little independent authority entails that the activists' actual power can *only* derive from their access to governing elites. Of course, this ultimately leaves control in the hands of the powerful, while having the bonus of offering the appearance of 'openness', 'transparency' and 'accountability'.[57] Under these circumstances, the more 'radical' global civic actors have become, the more the doors of global summits have opened up to them.[58]

Despite the hopes and aspirations of many critical theorists, there is little to suggest that operating outside the formal political sphere of electoral representation contributes much to challenging existing hierarchies of power. Compared to social movements of the past, new social movements based on advocacy pose much less of a threat to the status quo.[59] The activists may have declared themselves to constitute a 'global movement', but what distinguishes contemporary global civic activism is its individualized and unrepresentative form. This contrasts with the collective, mass character of the great anti-capitalist movements of the last two centuries, which fought for and occasionally achieved revolution.

The anti-globalization movement, for example, draws disparate groups and organizations together that have in common the privilege of global lobbying and advocacy politics over the struggle for democratic legitimacy at the national level. The rejection of the mass politics of democracy is repackaged as a radical claim to be operating on a higher ethical level, that of making common cause with the social groups most marginalized by the global economy. Ethical advocates who take it upon themselves to provide ' "interpretations" for a select number of marginalized groups, in a language suited to the global context',[60] are thus free to lobby for their political ends without the thorny questions of democratic accountability and representation. Rather than expand the horizon of democratic politics, this is a form of politics which is neither 'democratic' nor 'inclusive'.[61] It is focused around the 'freedoms' of the individual advocate who engages in courtier politics and elite lobbying. This highly individualized approach is described by Kaldor: 'I develop my own definition of civil society as the medium through which social contracts or bargains between the *individual* and centres of political and economic power are negotiated, discussed and mediated.'[62] We have moved on from forging the 'social contract' made through collective and egalitarian political engagement, to a period when civil society is the space in which individuals negotiate their own, unmediated, access to political power and decision-making.

Living in truth

In line with the courtier politics of elite advocates, we have also seen the rise of a new type of individuated activism. Ann Mische highlights the fact that this is a 'type of civic participation in which human subjectivity is not sacrificed to politics'.[63] In other words, the individual subject is opposed to the collective one. This follows Baker's suggestion that personal ethics should be the basis of public resistance to power. This blurring of the private and the public is central to the promise of post-political activism: 'This holds out the hope of both personal and political autonomy, in short, of self-rule.'[64] But, as we have seen, this individuated ethos is a product of political isolation from the domestic context in which the activist could build a representative organization. Ken Nichols O'Keefe, leading the volunteer mission of human shields during the 2003 Iraq war, is a prime example of the new breed of transnational activists. According to O'Keefe 'we the "citizens" are responsible for the actions of "our" governments . . . we are collectively guilty for what we allow to be done in our name'.[65] For this reason O'Keefe has renounced his US citizenship and would 'invite everybody to join me in declaring themselves not citizens of nations but world citizens prepared to act in solidarity with the most wretched on our planet and to join us'.[66] O'Keefe would 'rather die in defence of justice and peace than "prosper" in complicity with mass murder and war'.[67] Noble sentiments perhaps, but there is nothing particularly necessary or logical about *which* 'wretched' cause is adopted. This is because the legitimacy of the act stems from the rejection of one's *own* political situation. The irony of this is that it actually produces indifference to the 'wretched', whose existence is acknowledged only to the extent that they validate the activists' claims.

The need to make a moral statement is itself a response not to the specificities of the political situation of the weak, but aimed at the country of origin. The motivation of those acting as human shields and 'witnesses' in Iraq and the West Bank generally has less to do with the politics of these conflicts and more to do with their own personal need to make a moral statement.[68] Kate Edwards, a community worker from Manchester, explained why she joined the International Solidarity Movement in the occupied Palestinian territories: 'I wanted to challenge myself to see if I could cope working in a place like this. I have good friends and a comfortable life. I wanted to do something for those who were not as fortunate as me.'[69] But rather than donate to the International Red Cross or another professionally trained organization, Kate felt the need to put her own life at risk, suffering severe internal injuries from bullet wounds in Bethlehem, after refusing to follow Israeli troops' orders to halt.

It is at this end of the spectrum that the parallel between radical international activists and more violent, but equally individuated, global jihadists comes into focus. As Olivier Roy has pointed out, jihad is not a political relationship, but a devotional one. For all the hysteria that jihad evokes, it is not even primarily directed at the non-believing enemy. First and foremost, jihad is about the relationship between the believer and God, with the jihadi actions aimed at demonstrating the strength of the individual's devotion to God. Actually overcoming the political opponent is secondary to the fate of one's eternal soul.[70] Faisal Devji argues further that contemporary jihadism is 'more ethical than political in nature' because it inverts the traditional means-ends calculation, making the spectacular symbolism of the act its central purpose rather than any broader aim it furthers.[71] The demonstrative nature of postmodern jihad lends itself to exhibitionism rather than achieving political change – actions that are similar in form, if not content, to that of the global civic activists.

Conclusion

Global civil society theorists focus their ire on what they understand to be the narrow, exclusionary bias of the sovereign state. In turn, they view a wide constellation of transnational actors, from the global mega-NGOs to local farming cooperatives, as representing a radical alternative that opens up the space for new kinds of political organization and activity. In fact, what the celebration of 'bottom-up' politics and the critique of the state really express is a deep disenchantment with mass society and the demands of formal accountability that go along with representative democracy.[72] A consequence of rejecting the political sphere is that it leaves political struggles isolated from any shared framework of meaning or from any formal processes of democratic accountability. The quest for individual autonomy and the claim for the recognition of separate 'political spaces' and the 'incommunicability' of political causes, each demonstrate the limits of these radical claims for the normative project of global civil society 'from below'. Far from reflecting the emergence of new global political forces, the global civil society, by virtue of its social isolation, is marked by political weakness. As such, the only strategy left to it is a retreat into elite lobbying and individualized ethical postures.

It is important to stress that I am not claiming that the key problem with radical global civil society approaches is their rejection of formal engagement per se in existing political institutions and established parties. The point I am making here is that the rejection of state-based politics, which forces the individual to engage with and account for the views of other members of society, reflects a deeper problem – an unwillingness to engage in political contestation per se. Proponents of global civil society 'from below' therefore seek to legitimize their views as the *prior* moral claims of others. This has the effect of transforming global civic actors into the advocates of those unable to make moral claims themselves. Alternatively, they put themselves in harm's way and would lead by inarticulate example. What they avoid doing is pursuing their own interests or seeking to build political solidarity around shared interests. What can actually be achieved through their chosen methods is limited. Radical lobbying and calls for recognition may in some cases precipitate a generational turnover in the establishment. However, the rejection of social engagement is more likely to lead to a further shrinking of the political sphere, reducing it to a small circle of increasingly unaccountable elites. If the only alternative to the political 'game' is to threaten to 'take our ball home' – the anti-politics of rejectionism – the powers that be can sleep peacefully in their beds.

Notes

1 Mary Kaldor quoted in M. Jacques, 'Divided We Stand', *Guardian*, 3 March 2004.
2 J. Heartfield, 'Capitalism and Anti-Capitalism', *Interventions* 5:2, 2003, pp.271–289.
3 A. Giddens, 2001, 'Foreword', in H. Anheier, M. Glasius and M. Kaldor (eds), *Global Civil Society 2001*, Oxford: Oxford University Press, 2003, p.iii.
4 H. Anheier, M. Glasius and M. Kaldor, 2001, 'Introducing Global Civil Society', in Anheier, Glasius and Kaldor, *Global Civil Society 2001*, pp.3–22.
5 Note that, for many authors, these approaches are not necessarily mutually exclusive. For more on this distinction see G. Baker, 'Problems in the Theorisation of Global Civil Society', *Political Studies* 50:5, 2002, pp.928–943.
6 For example, M. Pianta, 2003, 'Democracy vs Globalisation: The Growth of Parallel Summits and Global Movements', in D. Archibugi (ed.), *Debating Cosmopolitics*, London: Verso, 2003, p.237.
7 For example, in the work of cosmopolitan democracy theorists, such as David Held, Daniele Archibugi and Richard Falk. See Archibugi, *Debating Cosmopolitics*.
8 See for example, N. Klein, *Fences and Windows: Dispatches from the Front Lines of the Globalisation Debate*, London: Flamingo, 2002, p.220.
9 M. Foucault, *Society Must Be Defended: Lectures at the Collège De France, 1975–76*, London: Allen Lane/Penguin, 2003, pp.98–99.
10 See for example, N. Chandhoke, 2002, 'The Limits of Global Civil Society', in Anheier, Glasius and Kaldor, *Global Civil Society 2001*, pp.35–53.
11 M. Kaldor, *Global Civil Society: An Answer to War*, Cambridge: Polity, 2003, p.21.
12 Ibid., p.21.
13 G. Konrad, *Anti-Politics: An Essay*, New York: Harcourt, Brace and Janovich, 1984.

14 Kaldor, *Global Civil Society*, p.57.
15 Ibid., p.53.
16 Ibid., p.56.
17 E. Laclau and C. Mouffe, *Hegemony and Socialist Strategy: Towards a Radical Democratic Politics,* 2nd Ed., London: Verso, 2001.
18 Ibid. Also B. Jessop, *State Theory: Putting Capitalist States in Their Place*, Cambridge: Polity Press, 1990.
19 Laclau and Mouffe, *Hegemony and Socialist Strategy*, p.132.
20 Ibid., p.184.
21 J.L. Cohen and A. Arato, *Civil Society and Political Theory*, Cambridge: MIT Press, 1994, p.74.
22 Ibid., p.486.
23 A. Melucci, 'Social Movements and the Democratization of Everyday Life', in John Keane (ed.), *Civil Society and the State: New European Perspectives*, London: Verso, 1988, p.247.
24 Ibid., p.248.
25 S. Patel, J. Bolnick and M. Mitlin, 2001, 'Squatting on the Global Highway: Community Exchanges for Urban Transformation', in M. Edwards and J. Gaventa (eds), *Global Citizen Action*, London: Earthscan, 2001, p.244.
26 Kaldor, *Global Civil Society*, p.48.
27 Ibid., p.64.
28 Ibid., p.82.
29 M. Hardt and A. Negri, *Empire*, London: Harvard University Press, 2000, p.53.
30 P. Kingsnorth, *One No, Many Yeses: A Journey to the Heart of the Global Resistance Movement*, London: Free Press, 2004, p.329.
31 Hardt and Negri, *Empire*, p.54.
32 Ibid., p.56.
33 Ibid., p.134.
34 Cohen and Arato, *Civil Society*, p.74.
35 R. Debray, 'A Guerrilla with a Difference', *New Left Review* 218, 1996, pp.128–137.
36 Cited in M. Giles and K. Stokke, 'Participatory Development and Empowerment: The Dangers of Localism', *Third World Quarterly* 21:2, 2000, pp.247–258.
37 Klein, *Fences and Windows*, pp.210–212.
38 Baker, *Problems in the Theorisation*, p.941.
39 P. Cunninghame and B.C. Corona, 'A Rainbow at Midnight: Zapatistas and Autonomy', *Capital and Class* 66, 1998, p.16.
40 G. Baker, *Civil Society and Democratic Theory: Alternative Voices*, London: Routledge, 2002, p.140.
41 Klein, *Fences and Windows*, p.220.
42 Baker, *Civil Society*, pp.142–143.
43 M. Ignatieff, 2001, 'Human Rights as Politics and Idolatry', in Amy Gutmann (ed.), *Human Rights as Politics and Idolatry*, Princeton, NJ: Princeton University Press, 2001, pp.10–11.
44 S. Žižek, 'The Interpassive Subject', 20 May 2003. Online. Available at HTTP: http://www.lacan.com/interpass.htm (accessed 30 May 2006).
45 J. Tuckman, 'Zapatistas Go Back to the Grassroots', *Guardian*, 27 December 2003.
46 Cited in J. Vidal, 'Peasant Farmers Show Strength in Cauldron of Grassroots Politics', *Guardian*, 10 September 2003.
47 Ibid.
48 Kaldor, *Global Civil Society*, pp.111–112.
49 A. Colás, *International Civil Society: Social Movements in World Politics*, Cambridge: Polity Press, 2002.
50 Ibid., pp.55–57.

51 Of course, this does not mean that there is no local opposition to some 'social movements'. Trevor Ngwane says such movements 'consist of nothing more than an office and a big grant from somewhere or other' and 'call a workshop, pay people to attend, give them a nice meal and then write up a good report' but 'build nothing on the ground'. 'Sparks in the Township', in Tom Mertes (ed.), *A Movement of Movements: Is Another World Really Possible?*, London: Verso, 2004, pp.111–135.

52 Pianta, 'Democracy vs Globalisation', p.238.

53 Kaldor, *Global Civil Society*, p.103.

54 For details on Jacques Chirac's 'extended dialogue' at the G8 summit in June 2003, see the editorial comment, 'Le G8 de M. Chirac', *Le Monde*, 1–2 June 2003. For details on the parallel/counter G8 summit held in Annemasse, France, see 'Les Milles Visages de l'Altermondialisme', *Le Monde*, 1–2 June 2003.

55 J. Vidal, 'Odd Couple's African Tour Highlights Battle over Debt', *Guardian*, 22 May 2002.

56 J. Heartfield, 2004, 'Contextualising the "Anti-Capitalism" Movement in Global Civil Society', in G. Baker and D. Chandler (eds), *Global Civil Society: Contested Futures*, London: Routledge, 2004, pp.85–99.

57 As Steve Charnovitz notes, the power to appoint non-state actors and lobby groups to advisory committees ensures that states control the policy process through determining which groups should be 'recognised'. 'NGOs and International Governance', *Michigan Journal of International Law* 18, 1997, p.283.

58 V. Heins, 2004, 'Global Civil Society as the Politics of Faith', in Baker and Chandler, *Global Civil Society*, pp.186–201.

59 There is a growing number of critical studies considering the limits of NGO and non-state actor engagement in evolving mechanisms of global governance, see for example, A.C. Hudock, *NGOs and Civil Society: Democracy by Proxy?*, Cambridge: Polity, 1999; J. Hearn, 'Aiding Democracy? Donors and Civil Society in South Africa', *Third World Quarterly* 21:5, 2000, pp.815–830.

60 Kaldor, *Global Civil Society*, p.95.

61 R. Lipschutz, 2004, 'Global Civil Society and Global Governmentality: Resistance, Reform and Resignation?', in Baker and Chandler, *Global Civil Society*, pp.171–185.

62 Kaldor, *Global Civil Society*, p.12.

63 A. Mische, 'Post-Communism's "Lost Treasure": Subjectivity and Gender in a Shifting Public Place', *Praxis International* 13:3, 1993, p.245.

64 Baker, *Civil Society*, p.149.

65 K.N. O'Keefe, 'Back to Iraq as a Human Shield', *Observer Comment Extra*, 29 December 2002.

66 Ibid.

67 Ibid.

68 I. Hazboun, 'Volunteers Act as Human Shields', *Associated Press*, 2 August 2001.

69 P. Beaumont and M. Wainwright, 'I Never Thought They Would Fire Live Rounds', *Guardian*, 3 April 2002.

70 O. Roy, *Globalised Islam: The Search For a New Ummah*, London: Hurst and Co., 2004, p.296.

71 F. Devji, *Landscapes of the Jihad: Militancy, Morality, Modernity*, Ithaca: Cornell University Press, 2005, p.3.

72 See for example, W.E. Connolly, 'Democracy and Totality', *Millennium* 20:3, 1991, p.479.

9 Legalizing politics and politicizing law

The changing relationship between sovereignty and international law

Michael Savage

Introduction

The relationship between international politics and international law is being renegotiated. Politics is more concerned with law. The Kyoto Protocol has been a focal point for criticism of the US. The argument in Britain over the British role in the 2003 invasion of Iraq concentrated obsessively on the legality of the invasion, picking over the detail of the legal advice given to the British government. But the way we view international law is also changing, with law becoming more politicized. The reach of law is being extended, and its derivation from the will of sovereign states is being challenged. Some argue that law has a greater independence from states than might previously have been the case, or at least more so than was recognized. Others claim that law is no more than a cover for the imposition of force by the American Empire. Neither side accepts international law as something made and remade by sovereigns. In this chapter I argue that the intermingling of law and politics that is taking place is bad for law and bad for politics.

Systems of law change slowly. Constitutions are amended from time to time, but rarely get rewritten (notwithstanding France). So too with international law. William G. Grewe outlines the Spanish, French, British, American and Cold War 'systems' of international relations, each of which corresponded to a different legal order.[1] Gerry Simpson takes the Congress of Vienna (1815), the Second Hague Peace Conference (1907) and the United Nations (UN) Charter (1945) as key formative moments in the development of international law.[2] Change has come from time to time, usually through slow evolution, sometimes accelerated by war. Now things seem to be changing again. Superficially, more law is being made, especially in the areas of trade and the environment.[3] And international law is extending its reach, considering individuals as well as states to be subject to it. There are some excellent critiques of this tendency in specific fields, such as human rights.[4] But it is when we step back from what is happening at the level of individual laws that the novelty of the current situation becomes apparent.

First, some context for the debate. When the modern state system emerged in the sixteenth and seventeenth centuries, and state interaction was more sporadic than today, international law was unambiguously the product of states. States made treaties and agreements that were consented to by states, and which to a greater or lesser extent bound states to the obligations that they had entered into. The difference between national and international law was perhaps less marked in this period, because when states emerged national laws were also less comprehensive and less enforceable. Just as international agreements were more likely to succeed if they were backed by a great power and corresponded to the balance of power, domestic laws often relied on local dynastic powers rather than centralized authority.

By the time of the Cold War this system was dramatically different. First, in national law the idea of competing authorities, or legal relationships outside a national framework of law, was now impossible. Indeed, even by the nineteenth century John Austin considered law to be nothing more than sovereign commands backed by force. This influential approach pushed aside the study of international law, because it was held that the absence of any authoritative power to enforce it meant that it could not be considered law at all. Nonetheless, at the international level something analogous was happening that paralleled developments in the domestic sphere. A structure of international law was emerging that effectively bound states in certain respects. Most striking in the Cold War period was the UN, created by states and reflecting power imbalances between them to be sure, but nevertheless providing a framework of international law. In a famous 1944 essay, Hans Kelsen, a critic of Austinian jurisprudence and an intellectual wellspring of the UN Charter, celebrated the Charter for its ability to bring all states under the same regulatory framework.[5] Even when the Charter was disregarded, no state ever proposed a different legal framework. International lawyers no longer regarded the right to make war as the sovereign's prerogative. In the discipline of International Relations (IR), on the other hand, the ascendant realist school put the state's ability to make war at the heart of their analysis. Today the two disciplines, which went down separate paths during the Cold War, are once more engaged in dialogue. Central to this dialogue is a view that the web of norms and obligations in the international system are constitutive of a society at the international level.

In the European Union (EU), new entrants are formally required to accede to the *Acquis Communautaire*, the body of existing EU law. This formalizes what is assumed to happen at the international level. The depth and breadth of international law means that any new state will be bound to it from its appearance on the world stage. New states are not free to pick and choose. The cost of agreeing is often low (particularly given patchy enforcement), which together with states' desire to be seen as legitimate 'good international citizens', means that states are generally happy to agree.[6] Some have drawn the conclusion that law might therefore be constitutive of states, which is the exact reversal of the classical account, where sovereign states contract to make law. This has enabled a shift from 'equal sovereignty', in which all states are equally free to pursue their interests, to 'sovereign equality', in which all states are equal before a law that constitutes their sovereign rights and liberties (see further Philip Cunliffe's chapter in this volume).[7] I shall propose that this argument has deleterious consequences for the way that we view both international politics and international law.

My argument requires that I clarify what is specific about politics and law, such that they can be separated. But I do not propose to offer an account of what politics and law 'essentially' are. This is a fool's errand that has trapped many people, not all of whom are fools. But I do want to flag some distinctions that matter, if only on the practical and pragmatic grounds that the invocation of law signals greater authority and obligation to obey than a political position, irrespective of the power and influence of the political actor. Law is a sphere where interests are pursued within a framework of agreed rules. When we turn to law to resolve a dispute, we are submitting ourselves to the law's authority; the parties are, at least implicitly, handing over the resolution to a higher authority. This consent is not necessarily explicit, and a legal judgement does not necessarily signal the final resolution of a conflict, but if we did not acknowledge the legitimacy of law, the process would be unworkable.

It therefore requires our consent, and the framework of laws needs to be reasonably stable and settled. Given all this, the relative absence of fundamental ideological disagreement between powerful international actors is particularly important, because it makes technical coordination easier, and accounts for a good deal of the recent expansion in the sheer volume of international law. One area of difference between politics and law that is essential for my argument is that political disputes involve more fundamental disagreement – disagreement that is not susceptible to resolution through an agreed framework. For example, a debate might be conducted within the framework of constitutional law, and a law passed. But the political essence at stake in the debate is not necessarily resolved by the process of making a law. In other words, the legal sphere can take us to the point of decision, but the political debate runs on. Legal judgements require assessment of a problem in the framework of agreed rules. Political judgements require assessments of interests, power and norms.

In the first section I discuss the qualitative expansion of international law, which intrudes on areas that would ordinarily be regarded as political. In effect, controversial political claims are borrowing the authority of law. This narrows the scope of politics and makes it harder to change existing arrangements. The second section reverses the perspective, by looking at how the politicization of law has been to the detriment of law. There are two distinct parts to this argument. First, I look at how some scholars have denied the derivation of law from the will of subjects, preferring a much more substantive conception of law where authority derives from its normative content, not the consent given to it. The second way in which law has been undermined is by a surfeit of cynicism about the law, emanating from both radicals and (neo)conservatives – cynicism that derives its force from the actual changes that have taken place in international law.

In the third section I clarify the argument that I am making about what is distinctive about contemporary international law. Discussions of international law have historically been pulled between a utopian pole that disdains politics, and a realist pole that disdains law. The utopians have promoted the international rule of law as a path to peace, notwithstanding the political obstacles to achieving it. Realists have been sceptical about international law, because in the absence of a generally acknowledged sovereign power, force trumps law and state interests override all else. We can discern this heritage in recent discussions of law. But I suggest that something more fundamental is happening, and sticking to the old paradigm hinders our appreciation of recent developments. There is now, I argue, a more explicit hostility to politics – not merely a desire to overcome political barriers, but a desire to resolve issues without recourse to politics at all. On the other hand, there is also a direct attack on the foundations of international law. These twin movements are central to understanding the direction of international law today.

In conclusion, I step back from the debate in IR. In this chapter I write as if law and politics are two self-contained realms polluting one another. This is a useful trope for developing my normative claim about their mutual degradation, but it is limited as a way of understanding the world. Politics and law are not two separate, water-tight compartments. They are becoming more alike not because they are seeping into each other, diluting some Platonic ideal of politics and law, but because of dynamics common to both realms. The expansion of law into politics is predicated on the vacuum that results from strong defenders of state sovereignty vacating the political field. As James Heartfield shows in his chapter in this volume, the EU has developed as states have avoided sovereign political responsibilities. As Christopher Bickerton and Philip Cunliffe discuss in their chapters, the anti-imperialist nationalism of the Third World, which once drew succour from the USSR's promotion of national self-determination, has fallen away with its sponsor. And, as Alex Gourevitch shows in his chapter in this volume, even the USA, that seemingly bold defender of its national interest, is not what it seems. Therefore, the degradation of law that I describe is predicated on weaker sovereigns, who are less inclined to pursue their claims vigorously. My conclusion, which makes the case for upholding the integrity of both politics and law, should be read in this light. Mine is an instrumental defence that upholds what I consider to be of crucial normative value – the claim that the unencumbered subjective desires of both individuals and their collective representatives in sovereign states should be pursued as freely as possible.

International law and the colonization of the political sphere

The discussion of international law has suffered from a surfeit of rather obscure scholarship. To clarify what is at stake, and to provide an accessible entry to the debate, consider the question, what does it mean to have a right to democracy? Inside the state, the demand for democracy means first that governments are chosen by the people rather than imposed, selected arbitrarily, or inherited. Democracy means the people staking a claim on their polity and their future, rather than having it determined externally. Second, it means that all of the people choose; that is, that every individual is the formal equal of every other individual in the polity. These principles are enshrined in varying ways and to differing extents in the constitutional laws and practices of many individual states. But what could it mean to extend this principle to international law?

Thomas Franck offers the most comprehensive argument for recognizing an emerging right to democracy in international law. Franck distinguishes the internal and external legitimacy of governments, and claims that legitimacy increasingly requires that states adhere to standards and norms of international society.[8] He notes that although it is not yet accepted as law, there is an emerging international right to democracy. But the consequences of recognizing such a right would be close to the opposite of this right in the national context. Instead of a liberating, internally generated demand for self-determination and equality, it would be a demand that individual states must live up to standards determined externally.

The post-Cold War wave of democratization is welcomed by Franck, but his reasons are chilling: 'what began as review by politicised, anticolonial committees of the General Assembly and by the Trusteeship Council may be expected to become a judicious process of principled rule interpretation by independent experts'.[9] Here, Franck is castigating the Third World assault on the anti-democratic nature of colonialism, on the grounds that it was a 'politicised' attack, thereby implying that politics was brought to the issue from the outside, rather than being intrinsically bound up with questions of democracy. It follows from Franck's recommendations that we need a world administered by impartial experts as in the old days, because this would protect the important issues from being polluted by politics. In practice of course, 'impartial' administrators have an inherent vested interest in the status quo (see Christopher Bickerton's chapter in this volume). But issues become politicized precisely because people are not happy with the status quo. Franck's account describes law expanding to fill the political sphere, where alternative political arrangements are potentially stigmatized as illegal.

Franck approaches the relationship between law and politics from a legal background. Friedrich Kratochwil approaches the question from a political perspective, and he appears to offer an alternative to the dreary technocracy espoused by Franck. Kratochwil defines law as the application of existing norms to a controversy by a third party.[10] Law is, in Kratochwil's reading, 'better understood as a particular style of reasoning with rules'.[11] He thus opens the floodgates to consider a whole host of relationships at the global level as forms of law. Rather than being a body of agreements between sovereigns, law can also encompass informal understandings, regimes and norms. The consequence of this is that law becomes the arena in which norms should be contested. Sovereignty is constituted through law, through the recognition of internal legitimacy by other international actors. Internal order, therefore, is justified by the external legitimization of sovereignty.

Kratochwil's and Franck's analyses are confusing because such seemingly distinct spheres – law and politics – are thrown together. More importantly there are also normative problems with this reading of international law, which become apparent from Kratochwil's conclusion, where he argues that

> [i]t would be a legalism of the worst kind to reduce the problem of compliance to the technical problem of ensuring norm-conformity at the least cost

through the elaboration of repressive techniques, while leaving the issue of justifying actions in terms of broader principles, demands for justice, and pleas for peaceful change to history and philosophy.[12]

Kratochwil is arguing that it would be a vacuous conception of law that only dealt with issues of compliance, and did not reflect on more substantive issues of peace and justice. But this noble sentiment is almost tautological in the context of his earlier remarks. On the one hand, Kratochwil defines law expansively as a particular style of reasoning; on the other, he argues that law proper must be expanded to cover more substantive issues. A narrow understanding of law could quite legitimately indulge in the kind of 'legalism' that he criticizes, adopting a purely instrumental approach to enforcing decisions that have been made in another sphere. This is defensible if we allow that 'broader principles, demands for justice and pleas for peaceful change' can all be made at a level of decision-making that is political; that is, separated from the legal process. However, once all agreements are held to be law, and once law becomes a *form* of reasoning rather than a *body* of rules and agreements, then political principles inescapably become part of the legal process itself. In other words, Kratochwil's argument presupposes the illegitimacy of any autonomous political sphere.

Consequently, international politics is identified at a high level with international law. If this were merely a matter of semantics it would not be worth challenging. But these scholars were not inspired to write by a desire to call things by different names, but rather because calling things law has consequences in terms of how we perceive issues and how we act on them. If we are reduced to arguing not about the legitimacy of a norm, but the extent to which it has become universally recognized, then political debate is impoverished. And if something is a legal requirement, then those implementing it are excused from the requirement to justify themselves. They can cast an expression of their particular will as an already existing consensus. This is a forlorn and limited conception of international politics.

The narrowness of this vision is clear in Christian Reus-Smit, who defends international law as something better than the cut and thrust of politics, which is tainted by self-interest:

> the principles of self-legislation eventually conjoined politics and law in the practice of multilateralism. The two have been attenuated, however, in the field of issue definition, and quarantined in the realms of interpretation and adjudication. It matters to international actors whether a problem or issue is defined as political or legal, and while power and self-interest are at play in the politics of definition, the framework of existing legal norms, and the modes of argument that enliven them, discipline that play. Once it has been commonly acknowledged that a problem or issue is legal, in the sense of being governed by a pre-existing set of norms, the narrowly defined politics of power and self-interest [is] delegitimised and communicative action is empowered.[13]

The key move here is in the last sentence. Reus-Smit suggests that communicative, political action is opened up, and the political sphere widened, when a problem or issue is defined as legal – meaning that it is governed by pre-existing norms. There is a sleight of hand in the presentation, because there is easy agreement that the politics of power and self-interest is narrow and negative. But no case is made for regarding the application of existing norms as empowering. Indeed, the more obvious assumption would be that this is limiting, because taking norms for granted restricts actors' freedom of manoeuvre. It is revealing that this capacious approach to international law assumes so often that existing norms are right and appropriate, thereby taking them in an extremely conservative and uncritical direction. Against this foil, the 'grubby' politics of power and self-interest seem decidedly liberating.

The immediate question about the right to democracy has quickly taken us into deep theoretical discussions. Approaching the same questions at a different level, a number of scholars offer rich accounts of what international politics looks like if we treat political debates as legal issues.

Implementing the new international law: regimes and networks

In the 1980s many in the discipline of IR were studying regimes, which are 'principles, norms, rules, and decision-making procedures around which actor expectations converge in a given issue-area'.[14] Regime theory forms a neat bridge between the liberal and functionalist analysis of the 1970s, and the new developments in international law of the 1980s and 1990s. Regimes are about areas of agreement that are not necessarily formally legislated – much like the understanding of international law put forward by Kratochwil and Franck. The contribution of regime theory to understanding international relations was in part to pull away from the obsessive focus on conflict that characterized the discipline in the 1980s. But today these insights have been pushed much further, and form the basis for a holistic account of international politics.

According to Anne-Marie Slaughter, state functions have been disaggregated. World order is built up not from states, but from parts of states.[15] International institutions therefore have to ' "borrow" the coercive power of domestic government officials to implement supranational rules and decisions'.[16] It is a view of enforcement that focuses solely on the application of power, and not on its source. Whereas classical theories of international relations emphasized the derivation of power from human social relations, Slaughter abstracts from this to show only the coercive functionality of power.[17] Power is something that was an attribute of states, but, for some reason that is left unexplained, it can now somehow be shifted around between other actors to achieve broader policy goals.

A useful illustration is provided by her discussion of the opportunity created in Iraq:

> regulators and other executive officials of every stripe could help to rebuild basic government services, from policing to banking regulation. In all these

cases the experts and targeted technical assistance would be readily available; the rebuilding efforts would be multilateral and sustainable; and the new Iraqi officials would have a continuing source of technical, political, and moral support.[18]

The idea of providing 'moral' support is merely patronizing. Technical support is no doubt welcome, although most of the challenges that she discusses are political and administrative, not technical (banking regulation is intensely political, particularly in American politics). In effect, she denies by fiat the possibility of fundamental political disagreement. The claim to provide support around technical issues is insidious, because it is around precisely these issues that Iraqis could reasonably be expected to want to assert political autonomy. While no one in Iraq is in a position at the moment to offer an alternative political theory or ideology, credible opposition to the external agenda might reasonably be expected to coalesce around issues such as government services, policing, industrial regulation and federalism.[19] The absence of any reference to the oil industry in Iraq is telling, because while it is one of the main industries needing regulation, it is also the most clearly political.

For Slaughter, the principle is not 'global equality' but 'global deliberative equality'.[20] Any form of substantive equality is subsumed under the technocratic impulse that drives towards better regulation. Provided everyone can be involved in deliberation, justice has been done. Indeed, the main argument against the vision of the world that she sketches is the likelihood that more powerful actors, and actors with a particular interest in any one area of governance, would have an effective preponderance of power because they have access to more information and better lawyers. But Slaughter dismisses this argument quickly, because the Internet supposedly demonstrates how easily small groups can challenge the monopoly on information that larger actors enjoy. Slaughter's New World Order is a world order defined by technical problems and run by experts, not by political subjects. International law is made by technocrats, and all of the other actors who are welcomed into the dialogue are welcomed only insofar as they can engage on technical problems. The questions that really matter to political subjects are ignored in this approach – such as: what are the issue areas that are candidates for regulation, who determines them, who ultimately takes the decisions and at what point does the 'deliberative equality' get resolved in favour of one party and against the other? It is only when these questions are raised in concrete political contexts that Slaughter's world order begins to unravel.

Martti Koskenniemi offers a perceptive critique:

> The language of 'governance' (in contrast to government), of the management of 'regimes', of ensuring 'compliance', that has become rooted in much American writing about international law, is the language of a powerful and a confident actor with an enviable amount of resources to back up its policies.[21]

Koskenniemi is cleverly reversing the positive claims that are made on behalf of governance networks by Slaughter and others, and pointing to their underbelly – that where there is in practice a great preponderance of power, formalistic changes towards a more open model of 'governance' cannot avoid reflecting the will of the mighty. He points towards the profoundly apologetic power of Slaughter's case, because it reflects so perfectly the actuality of American power. The import of Koskenniemi's claim is that he is bringing politics back in, revealing the dishonesty at the heart of 'network law' and regimes, because they reflect the interests of specific political actors rather than the consent of subjects in international law.

The political subversion of international law

The expansion of law into the space of politics transforms law as well as politics. The identification of international law with the law of nations seems to miss the depth and range of legal relations prevalent in international relations today, and is certainly narrower than the expansive conceptions of law developed by Slaughter and Kratochwil. The idea that international law derives from the will of states is generally established with reference to a long tradition of contractarian thinking. This background is not necessary, however. An important recent book derives the same argument from rational choice theory:

> The usual view is that international law is a check on state interests, causing a state to behave in a way contrary to its interests. In our view, the causal relationship between international law and state interests runs in the opposite direction. International law emerges from states' pursuit of self-interested policies on the international stage.[22]

This is my position also. Laws are social relationships that require a level of consent. If international laws had no consent at all, they could not function. Law would be an empty shell not corresponding to actual practice. On the other hand, if it were just imposed by force, we would not recognize it as law. It would just be the arbitrary deployment of power. There is, however, a valid question about the level at which our consent may be presumed. In a national polity we assume a social contract, and there is a body of constitutional law telling us what is and is not law, and how to make laws. The actual body of law binding individual citizens is far removed from immediate, conscious consent. But as citizens we can be presumed to have agreed to surrender our absolute autonomy in return for protection under law, and accountability to law, notwithstanding the absurdity or injustice of any individual laws.

In international relations there is something analogous to this, especially in the UN, and in the Vienna Convention on the Law of Treaties. The question is to what extent there is an international society that allows us to presuppose the consent of international actors to law, in either the narrow conventional sense, or the expanded sense of Kratochwil *et al.* discussed earlier. Utopians have argued that such a society is emerging, or will emerge if we take the right actions. Today, it is more common simply to assert that it is upon us, and that state sovereignty should be regarded as bounded by legal rules. Allen Buchanan has developed perhaps the most thorough and systematic assault on the idea that sovereignty confers unassailable rights. He writes:

> The choice to recognize or not recognize has moral implications and can be made rightly or wrongly. To recognize an entity as a state is to acknowledge that it has an internal legal right of territorial integrity and this in turn lends strong presumptive support to its territorial claims and thereby presumes the illegitimacy of claims on its territory that others may make. For the same reason, simply continuing the current practice of recognizing the legitimacy of existing states is not a morally neutral activity. Recognizing an entity as a legitimate state empowers certain persons, those who constitute its government, to wield coercive powers over others, for better or worse ... To participate without protest in a practice of recognition that empowers governments that engage in systematic violations of human rights is to be an accomplice to injustice.[23]

The import of this is clear when we contrast it with the established idea that international law derives from the will of states. Buchanan would deny states admission to the international system if they fail to conform to the right norms. His proselytizing zeal is evident throughout:

> The fiction that international law is or ought to be a system of equal sovereignty states founded on state consent, is a distraction from the daunting task of developing and implementing a genuinely more democratic form of global governance in which those who make, apply and enforce international law are accountable to individuals and non-state groups, not only, or even primarily, to states.[24]

Here, sovereignty is understood as evasion. Different levels of social organization are collapsed and all are to be held accountable to the same standards. Sovereignty cannot have a privileged place in this universalist ethical system, where norms are trumps.

This argument is remarkably parallel to that of sixteenth century Catholic natural law theorists, as Giorgio Agamben recognized when he wrote of the 'tacit confusion of ethical categories and juridical categories (or worse, of juridical categories and theological categories), ... [which] gives rise to a new theodicy'.[25] For example, Grewe characterizes Francisco Suarez's approach:

> certain rules so evidently corresponded to the natural order of international life that they were spontaneously recognised by all and consequently and without difficulty attracted the consensus of the will of States. However, the content of international legal rules could not be derived *per conclusionem* by way of logical inference from general principles, but only *per determinationem*, through the detailed expression of political power. Rules derived in the latter way were, however, only binding in so far as they were in accordance with justice.[26]

In the case of both Buchanan and Suarez, moral norms are set outside the legal and political framework, and are used to hold political actors accountable. But the differences are instructive. Implicit in Suarez is a sense of the divine, the community of Christendom, which provides an anchor against which to judge political action. It is a transcendent and eternal standard capable of inspiring people and cohering institutions. But for Buchanan, there are norms such as democracy and human rights, which are good in their own terms, and there are states that are not respecting these norms. The conclusion is that these norms must be elevated over states' claims to be sovereigns over their territory. But these norms are as ethereal as the divine – they have no institutional existence except inasmuch as they are codified in treaties. So while these norms can be used as battering rams against states' rights, they cannot fill the void that sovereigns vacate when they submit to international norms, as Christendom could conceivably have once done, through the coherent ideology and institutional form of the Catholic Church.

The will of sovereigns is removed in favour of universal accountability to norms. The truly daunting question here is, by what authority? States continue, by and large, to have the monopoly on legitimate violence. But what sort of laws can be drawn out from these norms if they are not enforced? The argument here veers towards anarchy because there is no concrete alternative – either established in the world or proposed by Buchanan – to make and enforce laws. We may be left with something much more arbitrary as a result, with putative 'laws' being enforced on the whim of great powers. One answer to these questions is that international law is just a reflection of power. But, as I will now argue, this would be to underestimate the value of international law.

The myth of international law: power and law in IR

There is a venerable tradition of thinking in international relations that holds international law to be mythical, or at best a pale shadow of 'real' law. Carl Schmitt's question is central: 'in a conflict, who removes doubts and resolves differences of opinion?'.[27] Ultimately it is power that decides, he argues. These arguments are widespread among conservative realists and radical critics. Both believe that force trumps law to such an extent that there cannot be any properly legal relationships between states. The realist arguments are longstanding; Goldsmith and Posner's *The Limits of International Law* (2005) is an important recent treatment that engages directly with contemporary debates. However, it is the radicals who are often more vociferous today in their criticisms of international law.

Particularly noteworthy are Michael Hardt and Antonio Negri, whose two major collaborative books, *Empire* (2001) and *Multitude* (2004) focus on the ways in which law has escaped the sovereign state in the formation of Empire. They claim that:

> The importance of the Gulf War derives ... from the fact that it presented the United States as the only power able to manage international justice, not as a function of its own national motives but in the name of global right ... The U.S. world police acts not in imperialist interest but in imperial interest.[28]

So, the US acts not as a great power against other powers, but as a universal power operating on behalf of Empire. On the understanding of international law as agreement between sovereign states, international law could not exist under these circumstances, because the US represents the interests of all while disavowing its individual interest. According to Hardt and Negri, power now presents itself directly: 'with the appearance of Empire, we are confronted no longer with the local mediations of the universal but with a concrete universal itself'.[29] What is not investigated by Hardt and Negri is what this power is actually for, what is the purpose of this power. They are right to recognize that posturing between, for example, the US and the EU does not amount to a struggle of alternative visions. But taking this into account, why would any state (or every state) have any incentive to remake law so consciously? There is, as Hardt and Negri recognize, no incentive in terms of the structure of international politics.

Whether the argument is made by realists or radicals, the existence of mediating links between power and its object are denied when the legal sphere is collapsed into a pure expression of power. They claim that because powerful actors can circumvent law, law is a dead letter. In practice, though, once institutions are created they take on a life of their own. This much we can take from constructivists such as Kratochwil and Reus-Smit. In a practical sense, once a law has been effected, the powerful actor that promoted it is bound by it. There is never complete freedom to make and remake law. Indeed, great powers are often stronger when they can mobilize other states behind them, rather than when they are forced to rule by force alone. This is the traditional argument for why one of the greatest powers of the sovereign is to *make* law, and not, as Schmitt would have it, merely to break it. Moreover, within limits, these institutions can provide real succour to the less powerful, and be used to hold the powerful to account. While constructivists often take this argument too far in denying the political space outside existing institutions, appeal to law and to legal principles can still provide some bulwark against power.

The realist argument that international law is pure power is one sided. While powerful states have certainly disregarded international law, and there has never been an absolute authority to enforce international law, there have been norms that have generally been respected. It is notable, for example, that the most egregious offenders against international law historically have not been the most established states, but the upstart powers such as Germany. The critics of the realist approach to international law, however, have also been guilty of a certain one sidedness in their tendency to take the universalism of international law too much at face value, as a reflection of something above nation-states. In fact, the central consideration of international law that has acted as a restraining force in the modern era has been grafted from domestic law, and from political struggles largely internal to nation-states. This is the principle of legal equality, which applies to legal persons within states, and to sovereign states in international relations. Sovereignty – our theme – is the overarching legal principle exemplifying this. Of course, as the Introduction and Chapter 1 in this volume make clear, sovereignty is more than a legal principle. But the point here is that the status of states as free and equal has often been invoked against the deployment of power. The effect is generally limited, and interventions do not cease because law has been invoked. Yet the legal framework centred on sovereignty does nevertheless provide a basis to oppose intervention, and a shared vocabulary that forces the intervening powers onto the defensive.

Explaining international law

In this section I criticize my false friends – those scholars making arguments close to mine. I clarify and refine my argument by showing how I differ from them.

The focus on sovereignty as the source of the troubles in international order seems eccentric in the recent context. As Sir Robert Jennings has written, 'The basic problem in the big trouble spots of this present time – Somalia, Rwanda, Bosnia, Sierra Leone, East Timor and the like – has been above all the lack of a government with real sovereign power.'[30] But recognizing the need for sovereign power is not the same as appreciating the value of sovereign right. In this respect, Jennings can be compared to the state-builders discussed in Christopher Bickerton's contribution to this volume. They want functioning states, but hold back from granting these states the right to determine their own way in the world. However, in the context of international law, sovereignty refers to rights-bearing states, not states with certain capacities. Yet the two are not altogether divorced, and the links between them become apparent when we look at the more enthusiastic defenders of sovereignty.

Jon Holbrook defends sovereignty thus: 'sovereign equality is a vital legal principle that enables power to be exercised fairly, accountably and legitimately'.[31] But he is asking too much of a legal principle when he expects it to put so many controls on power – controls of fairness, accountability and legitimacy. *Fair* use of power is certainly not implied in the idea of sovereign equality. *Accountability* is partially implied, because the principle of sovereignty sets a standard against which to judge power. But it does not establish, nor imply, that there is a body competent to make that judgement. *Legitimacy*, on the other hand, is certainly present in the idea of sovereignty. But its desirability in this context is questionable, and legitimacy is generally a domestic not international question to begin with. The point to draw out from this is that the assertion of a right, and even the general acceptance of a right, is not sufficient. Capacity is also required. Collapsed states cannot bear rights. For example, Somalia – entirely without functioning government for a while – is the only state other than the US not to have signed the UN Convention on the Rights of the Child. America has reservations. Somalia had no one to sign for it. Moreover, great powers have often gained influence through proxy states that exist only through their sponsorship, which is again distinct from sovereignty.

My defence of sovereignty differs from others because it is more modest and more instrumental. The nature of my defence can be seen in relation to a few exceptional scholars who have kicked against the tendency to see the expansion of international law as inaugurating a glittering new era of global justice. Martti Koskenniemi, William Grewe and Gerry Simpson have all offered accounts of the development of international law that challenge the sweeping ambitions of contemporary 'boosters'. We can draw an enormous amount from their careful historical studies. However, as critique they rely too much on the characterization of current developments as the reassertion of idealism. Grewe's description of the doctrine of state sovereignty is to the point:

> National sovereignty could not tolerate superior authority – except a collective security alliance restricted to mutual protection. Each obligation of the State could only be based on its own free will. All of the law of nations therefore had to rest on an agreement of wills among States.[32]

As a description of the ideal, this is an excellent summary, because it emphasizes the absolute, non-contingent nature of the claim to autonomy that is represented by the ideal of sovereignty.

In a brilliant analysis of the failings of conventional approaches, Martti Koskenniemi takes matters a step further. After surveying a range of contemporary writing on international law, Koskenniemi notes that:

> Few of these writings sustain a concept of international law that would be other than an idiosyncratic technique for studying either what works (instrumentalism) or what would be good if it should work (normativism), in other words, a special kind of sociology or morality of the international. The two aspects of the argument are indissociable:...instrumentalism and normativism complement each other in a necessary, yet profoundly ambivalent way.[33]

He further notes that the proposed control on instrumentalist abuses of power is democracy and liberalism.[34] So the result, he concludes, is that for mainstream liberalism as well as constructivism, international law becomes an instrumental tool for advancing normative ends. And the weakness – as noted earlier in relation to constructivism – is that the ends are unexamined.

However, these writers do not provide a satisfactory analysis of what is new today, and how it has arisen. Koskenniemi makes a convincing parallel between Hersch Lauterpacht and more recent American approaches in the way that Lauterpacht denies any clear separation of politics and law.[35] However, Lauterpacht's approach is more akin to bracketing out the problem for pragmatic reasons, because we cannot reach an agreement on where the line can be drawn, and then turning to address the role of lawyers in society.[36] More recent constructivists are more confident, and attack the problem head on with precisely the intent of establishing consensus on the relationship between law and politics, which, as we have seen, is to intermingle them to the detriment of both. The relationship between law and international politics is expressed explicitly by Grewe, who writes that

> a legal order is not primarily a logical system of precisely interacting rules without gaps and contradictions. It is much more the normative image of a natural state of order. The totality of diverse legal rules deserves to be called

a legal order if it deals with the totality of facts needing to be regulated legally in a manner which corresponds to the specific intellectual, cultural, social and political situation in question and establishes directions for existing in this situation.[37]

In other words, a legal order is not just an agglomeration of random laws. Nor is it a perfectly consistent system. Instead, international law becomes a legal order inasmuch as it is a reflection of the international society prevalent at the time. Perhaps the point now is that time is out of joint. Accounting for this is a difficulty that Grewe, Simpson and Koskenniemi face.

Simpson abstracts historical processes from the historical circumstances that give rise to, and sustain, the processes. For Simpson, 'The crises concerning Iraq, weapons of mass destruction and terrorism have exaggerated trends largely discernible but sometimes dormant since 1815.'[38] So, from 1815 (and perhaps earlier) trends have been ongoing, punctuated by transient events, but reasserting themselves again and again. The tension that he describes is inscribed in the very function of the system. But this is to miss what is new about recent changes in international law, which are more fundamental because they issue such an explicit challenge to the autonomy and relative objectivity of law.

Grewe comes much closer to accounting for this, in his tantalizing but undeveloped comment that, 'for a century the ideas of the [1789 French] Revolution concerning the law of nations contributed next to nothing to this order; only in 1919 did they experience a rebirth'.[39] What we can take from this is that the idea that sovereignty derives from the bundle of Enlightenment ideas that were realized – albeit partially and unsatisfactorily – in the French Revolution. But, in the aftermath of the French Revolution, the balance of power decisively shifted as a result of Europe's wars with Napoleonic France. The stable and durable order of the Congress of Vienna was the result, which held back the application of these ideas. Indeed, even the demand for sovereignty as a popular radical slogan was attenuated as attention shifted to domestic reforms across Europe. Only with Versailles did these ideas return, due in no small part to the Russian Revolution which once again brought popular sovereignty onto the agenda. I think that this is what Grewe was pointing towards, but he was hampered by the context of Nazi censorship when he was writing.

There are two weaknesses in Simpson's and Koskenniemi's accounts of international law. First, both downplay or ignore pressures exogenous to the international system itself. Above all there is democratic pressure, which, especially in the form of anti-colonial struggles, I argue has been important in the formulation of the classical modern right to sovereignty. Second, there is minimal recognition in their argument of the way that law does not only change itself, but exists in a dynamic relationship to power and international affairs more broadly. For example, the debates about Spanish colonialism in the sixteenth century were conducted by lawyers in the language of natural law. Today, again, political events in international relations are being discussed in legal terms, such as the legality of the war in Iraq. However, at other times questions of legality have been of little importance. The Cold War in particular was a time when legality was distinctly subordinated to pragmatism.

What must be explained today is not only why international law is changing – which requires only an understanding of the changing political context – but also why law is becoming a much more important part of international relations, especially by detaching itself from the anchor of the sovereign state. I would relate this back to my first criticism, and see the answer in the retreat from politics at different levels – from the disengagement of the public from national politics right up to the attenuated rivalry between great powers. Gopal Balakrishnan describes this well:

> the proposition that the political itself is on the wane might be confusing, as there has obviously been no decrease in politics per se. What is meant is an eclipse of 'high politics', of arms races between nations and classes in which the structure of society is at stake.[40]

But the wane of 'high politics' is no reason simply to jettison what remains of politics, in favour of a bland legalized order ruled over by lawyers and technocrats.

Conclusion

This chapter has tried to clarify what is at stake in debates about international politics and international law, and it has tried to defend politics and law as separate spheres of human action, each important in its own right. I have teased out these points from a number of obfuscatory debates, and it is now time boldly to summarize my claims.

Politics has come to be associated by some with all that is worst about society – the unseemly scramble for resources, narrow self-interest, corruption and violence. Law appears by contrast a calmer, more rational respite. The promotion of international law has thus sometimes acquired a particular argumentative bent against the political sphere. David Kennedy, a sceptical humanitarian, writes of the 'turn to law in flight from economic analysis and political choice' and warns that, 'rules of private law . . . allocate resources and authority toward some and away from others'.[41] Slaughter's idea of the network expresses perfectly the self-image of the new international law theorists. Networks do not have centres. They are about links more than about nodes, about processes more than about subjects. But the allocation of resources and authority continues apace, even if it does not speak its name. Anyone wanting to intervene and seize resources and authority, for whatever purpose, needs to push against these tendencies. I summarize the challenge in three ways: first, we need to understand better what is happening. Second, politics must be defended as a practice that resists the closure of law. Third, law must be reclaimed from those who ask too much of it.

Analytic clarity

The simple plea for clarity is easily confused with a philistine disdain for complexity. My point is rather that if, as most of the scholars discussed here agree, law and politics are both human creations, then at the most elemental level our analysis needs to derive from human subjectivity. We then face a question of levels of analysis. Our freedom to act is mediated by existing institutions, ideas and arrangements, with sovereignty being the highest existing form for expressing political subjectivity in the international sphere. But to throw every social relationship together and say that they are mutually constitutive is intellectually evasive. We can distinguish day and night despite the existence of dusk. So, even when categories are fuzzy, their distinctive core often remains valuable for understanding society, and indeed for identifying where changes are desirable. In IR, our categories of politics, law and sovereignty remain valuable in all these ways.

In defence of politics

The expanded notion of law serves not to democratize the legal process but rather to legalize the political process. When controversial questions that have engaged the passions of millions are treated as settled legal norms, the space for politics is squeezed. And when a norm is absolutely settled, it does not need to be codified as law. There are no great debates or global rivalries in international politics today, or at least none that measure up to the Cold War, or the periods of French and British ascendancy. It is in this context – where actors have retreated from the political sphere – that law has begun to colonize the political realm. This is precisely why it should be resisted. The further the tendency to blur the boundaries between law and politics, the more the current impoverished state of politics will be entrenched. Consenting to the legal principle of sovereignty provides a secure basis for international relations to be conducted, including but not limited to international law-making. This allows for political disputes within and across states about the proper form of human social organization – subsidiarity, superstates, world government, autonomous collectives – but a minimum is settled to allow for the world to work as it is now. The problem with international law today is that people who have a particular vision for how the world should be organized – such as the right to democracy – try to inscribe it in law directly, rather than seeing it as a debate that needs to win supporters in the cut and thrust of politics.

In defence of law

Law cannot do all that is asked of it. When norms that are still widely contested are held to be a part of international law, the whole edifice of international law loses legitimacy, because it is seen as an instrument for the advancement of particular political agendas. Subjective consent cannot be inferred for 'politicized' international law, which means that these laws have the character of enforced rules rather than laws, bolstering the case of those who would dispense with all international law as nothing more than imperialism. Instead, I claim that international law is worth defending. It is some small solace in a world of power politics. The claim of sovereign rights, for example, means that weak states have, or at least had, a recognized vocabulary with which to assert their independence. This also means that defending law means resisting the temptation to separate law from its anchor in sovereignty. It is only as the outcome of consent among sovereign states that law retains its character as the product of acting and interacting collective subjects.

Notes

1 W.G. Grewe, *The Epochs of International Law*, trans. M. Byers (ed.), Berlin: Walter de Gruyter, 2000.
2 G. Simpson, *Great Powers and Outlaw States*, Cambridge: Cambridge University Press, 2004.
3 M.N. Shaw, *International Law*, 5th Ed., Cambridge: Cambridge University Press, 2003, ch.3.
4 D. Chandler, *From Kosovo to Kabul: Human Rights and International Interventions*, London: Pluto, 2002.
5 H. Kelsen, 'The Principle of Sovereign Equality of States as a Basis for International Organization', *The Yale Law Journal* 53, 1944, p.53.
6 J.L. Goldsmith and E.A. Posner, *The Limits of International Law*, Oxford: Oxford University Press, 2005.
7 B. Fassbender, 2003, 'Sovereignty and Constitutionalism in International Law', in N. Walker (ed.), *Sovereignty in Transition*, Oxford: Oxford University Press, 2003, pp.55–87.
8 T.M. Franck, 'The Emerging Right to Democratic Governance', *The American Journal of International Law* 86:1, 1992, p.50.
9 Ibid., p.60.
10 F.V. Kratochwil, *Rules, Norms and Decisions: On the Conditions of Practical and Legal Reasoning in International Relations and Domestic Affairs*, Cambridge: Cambridge University Press, 1989, p.210.
11 Ibid., p.211.
12 Ibid., p.256.
13 C. Reus-Smit (ed.), *The Politics of International Law*, Cambridge: Cambridge University Press, 2004, pp.37–38.
14 S.D. Krasner, *Sovereignty: Organized Hypocrisy*, Princeton: Princeton University Press, 1999, p.1.
15 A. Slaughter, *A New World Order*, Princeton: Princeton University Press, 2004, p.6.
16 Ibid., p.21.
17 I will simplify. Earlier scholars have suffered from inadequate accounts of social power. But the extent to which IR has drawn directly or indirectly on sophisticated political and social theories of power is especially striking in contrast to today.
18 Slaughter, *New World Over*, p.26.
19 Regarding the limited political potential of Islamism, see O. Roy, *The Failure of Political Islam* , Trans. Carol Volk, London: IB Tauris, 1994.
20 Slaughter, *New World Over*, p.29.
21 M. Koskenniemi, *The Gentle Civilizer of Nations: The Rise and Fall of International Law 1870–1960*, Cambridge: Cambridge University Press, 2001, p.480.
22 Goldsmith and Posner, *Limits of International Law*, p.13.

23 A. Buchanan, *Justice, Legitimacy and Self-Determination: Moral Foundations of International Law*, Oxford: Oxford University Press, 2003, p.3.

24 Ibid., pp.289–290.

25 G. Agamben, *Remnants of Auschwitz: The Witness and the Archive*, trans. Daniel Heller-Roazen, New York: Zone, 1999, p.18.

26 Grewe, *Epochs of International Law*, p.191.

27 C. Schmitt, *Legality and Legitimacy*, trans. Jeffrey Seitzer, Durham: Duke University Press, 2004, p.34.

28 M. Hardt and A. Negri, *Empire*, Cambridge: Harvard University Press, 2001, p.180.

29 Ibid., p.19.

30 Sir R. Jennings, 2002, 'Sovereignty and International Law', in G. Kreijin (ed.), *State, Sovereignty and International Governance*, Oxford: Oxford University Press, 2002, p.30.

31 J. Holbrook, 'Humanitarian Intervention and the Recasting of International Law', in D. Chandler (ed.), *Rethinking Human Rights*, New York: Palgrave, 2003, p.136.

32 Grewe, *Epochs of International Law*, p.416.

33 Koskenniemi, *Gentle Civilizer*, p.485.

34 Ibid., p.488.

35 M. Koskenniemi, *From Apology To Utopia*, Cambridge: Cambridge University Press, 2006, pp.35–38; Koskenniemi, *Gentle Civilizer*, pp.368–369.

36 There are suggestive parallels here with political and philosophical developments of this period, including American philosophical pragmatism, Vienna Circle positivism, German hermeneutics and even existentialism. It is to Koskenniemi's detriment that he focuses on developments in international law, neglecting the rich political and intellectual context.

37 Grewe, *Epochs of International Law*, p.32.

38 Simpson, *Great Powers*, p.353.

39 Grewe, *Epochs of International Law*, p.424.

40 G. Balakrishnan, 'Future Unknown: Machiavelli for the Twenty-First Century', *New Left Review* 32, 2005, p.8.

41 D. Kennedy, *The Dark Sides of Virtue: Reassessing International Humanitarianism*, Princeton: Princeton University Press, 2004, p.153.

10 How should sovereignty be defended?

James Der Derian, Michael W. Doyle,
Jack L. Snyder and David Kennedy

This chapter is a transcription of a round table discussion that took place at a conference at Columbia University, New York, on 2 December 2005. The discussion was chaired by Alexander Gourevitch. The discussion has been edited for the sake of brevity and clarity.

ALEXANDER GOUREVITCH: During the 1990s, the central question was how to reconceptualize, redefine, limit or otherwise curtail sovereignty. It was presumed that whatever positive one could say about sovereignty, the old absolutist conception had to go. The question, then, was always – how should sovereignty be criticized? It is therefore worth asking the question from the other direction – how should sovereignty be defended?

DAVID KENNEDY: Juridically, sovereignty has never been absolute. It's had a history of being, at once, a formal and an anti-formal conception; of being a unified idea and, at the same time, a bundle of rights to be parcelled out in a whole bunch of different directions. I would say, in the critical tradition of thinking about law, in which I would situate myself, there has been a sharing of disillusionment with the '90s project of eliminating or reducing sovereignty. Why might one want sovereignty back, after having spent all of the '90s getting rid of it? There are a series of desires that echo in that aspiration. And I'm sceptical, myself, about them. First, it's the desire for public capacity, as opposed to private capacity. Another would be the desire for local or national authority and autonomy against the forces of globalization, in particular, for national autonomy in the Third World against the forces of neoliberal globalization. Public capacity in the Third World against global forces of private economic activity. And then, finally, comes the desire for a place for politics as opposed to ethics, which we heard discussed this morning. We might hope sovereignty could return us to ideology and contestation and whatever politics is – a distribution or interest, instead of a discussion in the vocabulary of ethics that seemed much more the rage in the late '90s.

Now, if you said – quick, do you prefer the public to the private? The local to the global? Politics to ethics? I'd say – yeah, absolutely. And from that point of view, sovereignty would be great to bring back if it could bring back local public politics. But once one understands sovereignty as a much more open-ended juridical and institutional form, it's less clear that its resurrection would be an easy path towards the public from the private. Sovereignty, also, is that which defines and protects the private; and has been for a long time, the source of not only national and local authority, but also, the vehicle through which globalization has occurred. It's not just a vehicle for politics, but also a vehicle for the definition of personhood in the ethical. So from that point of view, it's all mixed up. And it's less certain that getting rid of it or bringing it back is the way to redeem what one might find politically attractive. And the last thing that I'll say before we open it up to discussion is – so if sovereignty is not a good mark for how to get more public/local politics, and how to have less private/global/ethical denunciation, how might we proceed?

Here I have my own pet project. My own sense is that we actually don't have a very good map of our global governance system. We don't have an idea of how we're constituted, as a polity internationally – either legally or politically. Domestically, we think we're constituted by our constitution, which always struck me as an absurd idea; as a description of how our politics is actually constituted. But internationally, we don't even have that as a kind of basic description. And in trying to develop a map, I have been tinkering around with the idea that background norms and institutions, as well as the activities of experts in a variety of locations, are far more important than we have given them credit for being. The way things get done is there are actual people in actual institutions, organized into actual knowledge disciplines that make decisions that they experience. And you can tell by their expertise that such people allocate resources among people. One could, as a lawyer, as a political scientist, try to map who gets to decide what for whom, and who ends up getting the stuff and who doesn't – as a result of the decisions of which individuals and which institutions. If one focused on the actual activity of people making choices in institutions – whether it be economists or political scientists and so forth – rather than what the diplomats do, we might downgrade diplomacy and being the President to just being one of a whole bunch of different expert professions – probably not the most important one, and not the most important site for political activity. Redeeming public capacity and making testability of decisions real would mean entering into the terrain of institutional experts, a relatively old idea in both political science and sociology, to try to figure out how the experience in those institutions could be opened up to contestability.

Here, my own thought is that we go down the wrong road when we try to redeem sovereignty by investing those sites with the attributes we traditionally wanted to invest a nation-state with – namely, accountability and a politics of representation in voting. I'm all for having a public policy jury that decides everything, randomly selected; and they decide whether to go to war. And one could do a lot of things to open up the framework for decisions. But I'm much more interested in the whole decisionist tradition through

Nietzsche, Kierkegaard, Schmitt, Weber which might encourage us to seek ways to get these experts to experience politics as their vocation, in the Weberian sense. And therefore to experience themselves to be exercising responsible human freedom. To experience themselves as deciding in the exception or deciding as an exercise in discretion – rather than deciding out of their expertise. So for me, the question of redeeming sovereignty is redeeming the experience for experts located in professions across the globe, of deciding responsibly in human freedom. Rather than deciding as an exercise of their knowledge. Redeeming that experience and making it more available, would seem to me to be the policy proposal I would put on the table for those who are hoping sovereignty could be rebuilt.

MICHAEL DOYLE: The question is sovereignty. Can it be defended? My bottom line is that it should be and it probably can be. But I'd like to focus on what values are served by sovereign independence. Why would rational, informed individuals with the set of values that I'm going to mention in a moment, choose to establish a sovereign nation-state?

I liked the description of sovereignty that David just gave us. The shorthand that I would use is sovereignty as the idea that the state has the authority to determine its own competence – the traditional kompetenz/kompetenz definition. States thus choose, to some degree and over time, whether they autarkic are or autonomous, on the one hand, or interdependent and codetermining, on the other. The process of choice is the essence of sovereignty.

Three major values are served by sovereignty that would induce rational individuals to choose sovereign national states. I draw upon old-fashioned thinkers like Mazzini, Mill and Weber, modern thinkers like Walzer and Lipsey, and some of my own earlier work. I want to combine normative and practical considerations, looking at interests that fit both. First, there are the expressive values that sovereignty can serve. Second, there are protective values. And third, there are material productive values. In short: identity, safety and wealth. My conclusion is that these are all interdependent, codetermining. There is a dynamic equilibrium among them and there is no simple choice, whether in one category or another.

With regard to expressive identity, I focus on the old slogan – to each nation its own state. The sovereign state, historically, has provided the mechanism that – for example, through compulsory education and public monuments – allows peoples to perpetuate their cultural identity. Empires have sometimes been tolerant, particularly if you think of the Ottomans. But the state has been a better guarantee – that is, if it's your own state – for promoting and preserving your culture. States, reciprocally, cultivate political culture. They do so by creating national or hegemonic churches and national or hegemonic languages. The French state instituted and the Academy regulated the *langue d'oïl*. Ireland, once independent, struggled to establish Erse. When the Croats, more recently, created a state, they set about creating a Croatian language out of what was very recently before the Serbo-Croatian shared by all of Yugoslavia.

Mill once suggested that a singular national identity helps to stabilize states and serves as a foundation for democratic government. Mazzini famously said that when each nation is satisfied with its own state, international relations would tend to be more stable too. That's the good news for the expressive foundations of the nation state. The bad news, from the standpoint of expression, is that there are about 6,000 spoken languages still existing in the world. There are about 190 states. Clearly, if language remains a powerful font of identity, there's a dangerous gap in the equation of one nation, one state. Fifty-two per cent of these languages are spoken by fewer than 10,000 persons; so we might forget about them. But that still leaves us a very troublesome 2,600 currently unsatisfied, potential claimants on statehood. That's a serious problem. Maybe, as Michael Walzer suggested, rather than completing the project of 'one nation, one state,' we could try to complicate it through tolerance and institutional guarantee of self-administration – as sometimes has been achieved for religions.

The second is safety, the protective function. States protect nations from conquest and sometimes from destruction. Walzer has also speculated that if, in the first half of the twentieth century, the Armenians and the Jews had had their own states, those peoples would have been much safer. There's clearly something to that argument, even though we would have to acknowledge that independence per se is no absolute guarantee against genocide, one of the famous classical cases being the Athenians' destruction of the Melians, where all the men were killed and the women and children were enslaved. The Rwandans had a state; it fell into murderous hands. Some political societies have served as better forms of protecting sovereign independence than have others. We call the ones that fail, 'peripheries', in imperial historiography. Those that succeed in conquering them we have called 'metropoles.'

There appear to be systematic differences among them. Drawing on Weberian insights, in my book *Empires* I found that tribal societies and patrimonial societies tend to be very unsuccessful in defending themselves when they come in contact with metropolitan societies. Even though they are highly integrated – that is, they share local values – tribal societies tend to have an undifferentiated social structure which is a weak environment for advanced technology. It's also a weak foundation for cooperation amongst various tribes. Patrimonial societies are differentiated in terms of class. But they lack an integrated common identity. It's easy for them to collaborate. Again following Weber's argument, these kinds of societies are systematically vulnerable to failures of national sovereignty.

The states that tend to take them over are the metropoles, which are societies that are both integrated and differentiated and that, most importantly, have central states. These states are capable of mobilizing power in ways that are effective, at least compared to the tribal societies and the patrimonial societies. Motivated by interests in commerce, investments and religion, empires expand to fulfil those interests.

Empires can achieve a stable peace. Gibbon once waxed poetic about the *Pax Romana* from the times of the Flavians to the Antonines. Those were good times to live – if you were an aristocrat with a large number of slaves. Empires did provide a degree of peace. On the other hand, we know they were bloody in their formation and very bloody as they fell apart.

Nation-states seem to have done a better job in protecting sovereign independence for a larger number of peoples. That's the good news connected with them. The bad news, of course, is that a system of nation-states is a system of anarchy, a potential state of war. That is dangerous; but under special conditions it need not be an actual condition of war. If Mazzini is right, nations can remain at peace if they are satisfied with their state boundaries; when, and if our defence theorists are right, defence technologies are dominant and distinguishable; and when liberal republics establish a separate peace among themselves.

Let me turn to the production of wealth, the third value. Rational producers and consumers would also want a national sovereign state. It has long been recognized that the state provides important foundations for economies. It establishes and regulates money. It helps enforce contracts, allowing for the better realization of exchange value. It legislates property rights, so that producers will try to become owners. It creates limited liability, so shareholders will invest. It creates 'entity liability' so that creditors will lend. States can also realize public goods, under normal schemes of administration: street lamps, police, schools, et cetera. Putting these things all together is conducive to efficiency and growth.

Other economic values are not as friendly to nation-states. Your standard rational producers and consumers will want as few rent-seeking states as possible – perhaps, ideally, just one global state. For Lipsey, customs unions were second best entities, second best to multilateral free trade and flexible exchange rates. Thomas Friedman has announced that we are increasingly living in a flat world. But our expressive and protective selves do not allow us to live in a Friedmanesque world, in one world or even on a flat world. So the question then – for the political economist, and not the simple economist – is what is the most productive order that takes into account the kind of world that will, inevitably, have numerous sovereigns?

In a dangerous world where security is scarce, defence economics will mandate secure access to raw materials, protected markets, and thus tend toward continental-sized economies, with *Grossraum* states to match. In a much more peaceful world, on the other hand, with liberal peace or stable defensive technologies and where transportation is cheap, smaller national economies can be productive because free trading and investing are likely to be permitted. Our producers and consumers in these safe circumstances may still want their states to amalgamate economies into customs unions but only when the trade-creating effects outweigh the trade-diverting effects; and when firms can take advantage of the dynamic possibilities of growth in a slightly larger market for both goods and factors. This tends to occur when two countries have equivalent technologies and roughly similar legal institutions and, yet, have different factor endowments and tastes. When economics and security go hand in hand, as in Europe during the Cold War, we will see an acceptance of a degree of amalgamation. But still probably far short of anything like a global state.

So let me conclude with three messages drawn from this very simple, first cut, at the analytics of national sovereignty. Statically, state sovereignty is useful for individuals who have the fears, interests and values that I've described. Dynamically, state structures interact with expressive, protective and productive interests, and vice versa for each. They are mutually constitutive. And thirdly, comparatively, political structures have changed over time. The nation-state or state sovereign is not a perpetual institution. The current regime of national sovereignty, however, is deeply embedded in the modern condition and not likely to disappear until it is replaceable.

JAMES DER DERIAN: I'm going to follow Michael Doyle's precedent here, put my cards on the table and hopefully open up some space for dialogue: I think that sovereignty is indefensible, and yet, as a contradiction, it remains indispensable.

My remarks will be framed by this contradiction as well as the belief that sovereignty is an illusion whose illusionary nature we've forgotten – which also happens to be Nietzsche's definition of the truth. Sovereignty is currently one of the most powerful truths out there, and I think we've right now invested a surplus of illusory beliefs in sovereignty. We believe sovereignty can keep us safe. We have national borders, armies, homeland security, bureaucracies, and technologies. All these instruments of sovereignty are empowered and legitimated by the assumption that just off shore is a turbulent world where anarchy lurks.

But this turbulence also comes from within, with the threat of global terrorism taking the place of the whole idea of a fifth column during the Cold War. But I would argue that this parochial worldview of the realists has recently taken some very hard knocks. Prior to 9/11, national borders were thought necessary and sufficient to keep enemies at bay; prior to our incursion into Baghdad we thought a triumphalist intervention was going to help bring peace and democracy not only to the Middle East, but also maintain and further our own sovereignty. And when we look at sovereignty in terms of its internal implications, we see a failure to protect and further the well-being of a population. We vividly saw how, in the case of Hurricane Katrina, emergency preparedness and all the intricate systems of protection failed to keep New Orleans safe and dry.

We need to recognize just how disastrous our faith in sovereignty can be. 9/11 is a disaster. Katrina is a disaster. Baghdad is a disaster. I think what we see in the unexpected and unprecedented nature of these events is that sovereignty really fails to deliver on its promise. And I think what we have to recognize is the likelihood that local events will continue to be exacerbated, magnified, and amplified because of the interconnectedness of the current international global reality. It's going to be very hard to isolate dangers as they might once have been, and it's going to be very hard to keep on considering sovereignty as sacrosanct. Sovereignty cannot really cope with the global event. And of course, we haven't really discussed the role of an unblinking global media in all this. The spatial is losing out to the temporal. The accelerated transmission of information by multiple media means that distance has been shrunken by time.

This means that the protections implied by sovereignty – a spatial and temporal security – are also being reduced. So in the final analysis sovereignty is indefensible. I believe that the national accoutrements of sovereignty – especially the planning and preparation for worst-case scenarios – are actually contributing to the insecurities of the moment. I'm not talking about the classic security dilemma on which we all cut our teeth. But rather, the force-five hurricane, the terrorist attack, pandemic disease. We see this when the Homeland Security Director comes on national television and says the reason we couldn't adequately deal with these disasters is because they are 'ultra-catastrophes'. When people start to use these types of metaphors, it's a sign that the sovereignty of language itself is no longer adequate. Nietzsche somewhere calls language the prison house of reality; in this regard we see here how realism has become the 'supermax' penitentiary of reality.

Our realist planning can only accommodate the expected, the local, the imaginable, and, in turn, we see an atrophy of other important human capabilities for dealing with the unexpected, the unplanned, the unimaginable. We put too much faith in sovereignty and its instruments of power. We see the stultification of an intelligence agency still working within the idea of impermeable borders. We see the lack of imagination in our war gaming, and the hubris of the revolution in military affairs that says you can do 'quick-in, quick-out' interventions. So I see sovereignty now as part of the problem, not the solution.

The problem is compounded because so many of the effects of global events can't be measured in the ways of causality and rationality upon which sovereignty is based. According to complexity theory, the flapping of a butterfly's wings somewhere in the southern hemisphere can create a force-five hurricane. Sovereignty cannot keep apace of new global threats that operate in a nonlinear fashion and produce quantum effects. It's old, antiquated machinery trying to keep up with new immaterial effects. How can sovereignty deal with the CNN-effect, let alone the Al Jazeera-effect that we see operating in Baghdad? Or the Nokia-effect, as we saw operating in the 7/7 London terrorist attack?

What we see in operation is what organizational theories call negative synergy. Sovereignty actually contributes to the negative synergy of complex networks: the very solution that is supposed to stop the cascading effects actually acts as a force multiplier. It creates a negative synergy of automated bungling, like we witnessed in Baghdad and with Katrina. Every new complex technology and network produces its own form of accident. And in the interconnectedness that's been created by an information revolution, we cannot depend upon sovereignty to keep us protected. Global events defy sovereign management. And indeed, if anything, sovereignty – in the way that organizational theorists talk about normal accidents – contributes to what I call 'planned disasters'.

So that's my view of sovereignty. And in response to something that came up in the last discussion, the final reason I think why sovereignty is not up to global tasks is because we are not in a unipolar world. I think the bi-polar days, despite what Ken Waltz would like us to believe, are long gone. And we are not moving towards a multi-polar world. I think we are moving towards a configuration that most closely resembles a 'hetero-polar' world. And by 'hetero-', as opposed to 'multi-', what I want to accentuate is the difference of actors operating in a complex matrix rather than a competitive system. This new configuration of power is based on the capability of super-empowered actors to utilize new networks to multiply their impact. So the notion of a sovereignty based on the management of symmetrical threats – or at least formally-comparable threats in a state-bounded form – is antiquated. I think that we have to reassess global dangers in light of new actors and drivers that gain advantage through networked technologies. So, my final statement is that sovereignty has become a disaster waiting to happen.

JACK SNYDER: If Karl Marx were invited to our panel today, he would have reiterated what he was already saying in the 1840s: that the state is all washed up as a system for organizing politics. As the neo-Marxist Eric Hobsbawm wrote, in a good but poorly timed book on nationalism that came out in 1990 just as Yugoslavia was breaking up in a fit of nationalist violence, in a highly-interdependent, globalized world, nationalism is washed up because it's obsolete.

Yet, as we've learned since 1990, we've had the rise of many state-seeking nationalist movements. Everybody wants a state. Now, why is that? The simple answer is that states are the most effective organizational form for providing social order, security and an institutional context in which economic growth can occur. Current social science shows that the quality of state institutions are crucial for providing these things that everyone wants. If Steve Krasner were here, one of the things that he might say about sovereignty in the era of interdependence globally – and he has said it in print – is that strong states are needed to create effective international institutions, to make global interdependence work. In other words, strong states that have effective institutions for state-to-state cooperation are needed to make the world 'flat', as Thomas Friedman's recent book title puts it. If my colleague, Al Stepan were here he might say, as he does from time to time, 'no state, no democracy'. Finally, if I were here, I might talk about my research with my colleague, Ed Mansfield, on the increased probability of war when transitions to democracy happen in places that have weak state institutions.

I recently attended a conference convened by a group of constructivist international relations scholars on the topic of failed states and state building. The conference asked why the international community is trying to build states in places where it's been shown that states just don't work. In places where state institutions are either weak or nonexistent, there are all sorts of non-state networks and actors, ranging from drug lords to NGOs, that are the real stuff of politics and economics in these regions. So the question that was posed was – why not focus on such networks as the basis for political order rather than building the state? At the end of two days of discussion, no one in the room had been able to show how this might work. We all left the room convinced that the solution is to try to build strong and effective states.

There is, however, a danger in propping up failing states. Ann Hironaka has just published a book from Princeton University Press, *Neverending Wars*, which shows how the sovereignty system props up weak states that would have otherwise been eliminated. Since 1945, there's been a very strong norm against conquest. As a result, there's been a low rate of state death. There have been relatively few international wars and even fewer conquests. This has propped up states that would otherwise have been driven out of business. We have, as a result, more failed states and more civil wars.

Despite this, my prescription is not to get rid of the sovereignty system. Instead, it is to use humanitarian intervention and neo-trusteeship when necessary, until strong and effective states can be built in the areas where they are now lacking.

ALEXANDER GOUREVITCH: I'd like to open up for questions. I'm sure there are many, as there are many interesting issues on the table.

AUDIENCE MEMBER: [Professor Kennedy] in your book, you make a very good point about international law in a political context. But it seems to me that the rule of experts and expertise that you're talking about, actually would do exactly the same thing. And perhaps going back to sovereignty, as the question suggested, might be a more effective way of addressing the point that you raised in the book.

DAVID KENNEDY: I think we have a couple of different conversations going on here. One is the question of whether the existing governmental apparatus, administrative outfit, the modern, well-developed state is a good idea or not. Should we be trying to generalize it over the whole world? And it seems to me that Jack has got to be right – that the answer is, a lot of times it is a good idea. Especially when it's functional to one of the purposes that Michael was putting on the table. It seems to me, the answer to that has to be 'sometimes'. Sometimes it is and sometimes it's not. It's hard to figure out. It requires a great deal of context-specific political analysis; and also, of course, knowing what you're in favour of. So for some people in some groups, having a state that can bring about, that can meet, those functions would be really useful. For others, having those functions met won't be what they had in mind; and for them, it would actually be a bad idea to have a state that is efficient in providing them. So that's going to be a classic question of, it seems to me, politics and constitutional design.

Then there's a second conversation that gets mixed up with the same word, which is – is some general concept like sovereignty a good general conceptual description of our overall international system? And here, I agree with James Der Derian, that the system has no central logic anymore. If there ever was a central system where there is central sovereignty logic, there is no such central logic at the moment.

I think where I differ with James in that part of the conversation is about how we might interpret wacko post-modern theory for international relations. The part of your presentation that I would like you to comment further on is the part where the effort to describe what was going on turns super-metaphorical. It's a fluid, hetero-normative plural, atmospheric generality. And I'm all for that. That sounds right to me. Compared to the well-organized, formal structure that you could put on a chart, that sounds right. But I think what's elided in that is the actual work of actual people who put that together. And from inside the law, everything is some whacked-out, bizarro, fluid thing. So a corporation is not a Chevron. Chevron is nowhere. Chevron is a trademark that's been licensed here, and a mine that's been parcelled out this way. A set of shares that have been sold here, and a set of risk obligations that have been mortgaged over there.

So the idea that the entity is a fragmented, fluid set of capacities and per-missions and prohibitions is something that's very familiar in our economic order. And it's also very familiar in our political order. And it's something whose structure can be studied and mapped and where people in Chevron decide things about whether they're going to pay taxes in Nigeria or whether they're put all the losses from their fleet in Nigeria, so they don't have to pay taxes. Those kinds of decisions, it seems to me, focusing on them as moments of global governance. So the people who are governing, it seems to me, are the experts in all of those locations. We can ask them what they're doing. We can ask them why they thought it was a good idea. And we can study the process by which they shift responsibility from one to another, so that they all imagine that they are not the place where responsibility happens. That's a very useful kind of sociology of the actual decision making. So the answer to the question – how would I map it? I would map it that way – by going into the locations where people decide things with consequences for other people. And ask them why they thought they had the power to do that. Why they thought that was the right way to decide it. And why they didn't experience themselves as ethically responsible for the consequences.

MICHAEL DOYLE: States tend to be the dominant entity in international society not because every individual wants his or her own state, or every single group its own state; but instead, because states are the residual, default form of effective protection against other states. And even though you might not want to create your own state, it's very difficult to achieve security if you're just a free-floating member of civil society in some geographic spot.

It's not as if states are good and perfect. We know all of their flaws. States are the entities that commit genocide, exploit, and disrespect. It's just that other institutional forms that have been developed through history or that are available today – like large criminal enterprises, or churches or other forms of enterprises – don't do key things that many individuals, at least collectively, want to have done for them, which are to protect their sense of identity and provide physical protection from threats and to provide a framework in which they can engage in productive activities that are sufficiently reliable, that over the long term it will produce growth.

Nor is it the case that states will always be with us. There's no reason why we shouldn't imagine that some day, through vast improvements in communications – maybe through an identity that really is transnational, maybe through innovations in institutional design that we haven't fully taken on board – we will get a better system. It's just that it's very difficult to see right now, what that better system would be that would meet the kinds of threats and dangers that we experience today. So I don't want to defend a nation-state as a good thing. All I would want to say is that we can imagine much less secure, protective and productive institutions.

JAMES DER DERIAN: I think I'll try to respond to David Kennedy's point because I think there's this conceit, and sometimes a riposte, that if there are no subjects, in the sense of sovereign states or individuals, there can be no rights. Without the sovereign state there can be no human rights, or any protections granted to groups of people with a common identity. That's the world being invoked here, as opposed to my metaphorical language about it. And yet, simultaneously we hear about the virtualization of the corporation. We hear about the virtualization of war. We hear about the virtualization of the economy.

Everything solid seems – to go back to Karl Marx – to be melting into thin air, because of globalization and because of other virtualizing forces at work. And yet, we cling to sovereignty as a principle that stands outside of this reality. Well, if this is true, I think reality is a nice place to visit, but I'm not sure we can live there. I believe that there is a disconnect, between all of these virtualizations and our need to cling to these hard and fast notions of sovereign subjects. It just doesn't correspond to reality. This does beg the question: where are your ethics? Well, ethics is not some sort of set of principles or commands that exist outside of subjectivity. They are prior to and part of the construction of our own subjectivities. In that sense, it's an ethics of care. It's an ethics of responding to the other that gives us the means to live together – without reliance upon a sovereign authority. So there is an ethics, a code of responsiveness that is as much a part of the constitution of our identities as it is a means of existing peacefully through differences.

And how would you map this? Go to our website[1] at the Watson Institute. We have created a visual, analytical tool where we disaggregated security. We have human security, group security, national security, international security, global security as the horizontal axis. In the vertical we have basically proliferated the notion of what constitutes a threat, to take us outside of the narrow realist purview. And the threats shift according to what level of analysis you're operating from. It's a visual, analytical, and metaphorical tool. It's very much a beta-product and we're looking for people to respond on our Watsonblog about it. It's a work in progress, but it's our attempt to visualize a hetero-polar matrix.

JACK SNYDER: I think the realist justifications for the sovereignty system are mostly dead. Namely that the sovereignty system is needed to regulate competition among states. I think the real core in justifying the sovereignty system nowadays has to be liberal pragmatism, namely the view that the only effective institution for guaranteeing democracy, rule of law, and human rights is a well-ordered state. Some might argue that the International Criminal Court, Human Rights Watch, the Ban The Landmine campaign, the World Trade Organisation, or enlightened multinational corporations can somehow guarantee these things that we value. But I think that's empirically wrong in the present and the foreseeable future. So, that's why I say – two cheers for the sovereignty system.

AUDIENCE MEMBER: I was surprised to hear such a focus on the panel on questions of nationalism, and the question of the extent to which every nation should have a state or not. It seems to me, that nationalism is one force that is absent in contemporary international relations, at least compared to the historical past. It seems like there was a brief upsurge, a nationalist moment at the end of the Cold War, and the disintegration of some states. But beyond that, there doesn't seem to be any nationalism the way it existed in the past.

JACK SNYDER: It was asked, why should we be talking about nationalism here? In my view, nationalism is not the cause of all the conflicts in the world. Some are opportunist conflicts driven by the availability of resources that can be plundered in weakly governed environments. That qualification aside, nationalism is one of the major causes of the conflicts that we are seeing right now. Three of the four most recent nuclear-proliferating states wanted nuclear weapons mainly for reasons associated with nationalism. Nationalism is also implicated in suicide terrorism. Robert Pape tells us that suicide terrorism happens when an elected regime is occupying the national territory of some other group, and opponents of the occupation come to believe that suicide terrorist attacks are the most effective means to get the occupying power off their back. That sounds like a form of nationalism to me.

Nationalism drives not only the post-communist wars. In addition, ethnic dominance struggles between Hutu and Tutsi are about nationalism: which ethnic group controls the coercive power of the state. We've seen ethnic autonomy movements. We've even seen a World War I style conflict between Ethiopia and Eritrea, which was in part about consolidating the nationalisms of those states. So the question is, can the sovereignty system manage nationalism? One could take the view that it is an inherent flaw of the sovereignty system that nations are often mismatched with state boundaries. In this view, the only solution is to come up with some other system of governance that doesn't depend on somehow getting a match between the governance unit and the cultural unit, between the state and the nation.

But no one has offered a plausible proposal to accomplish that. Consequently, the best strategy for the time being is to try to tinker with the way the sovereignty system works in order to head off nationalist conflicts. One technique is to build strong, impartial states that can administer their territory in ways that guarantee the rights of the national minorities on their territories. Another is for strong, wealthy democratic states to continue to do what the European Union has been doing – namely, create incentives for other states to moderate their treatment of nationalities as a condition for getting the benefits of membership or trade.

JAMES DER DERIAN: First, one clarification – I never said that the world was too complex to understand. My point was that the world is getting too complex and too interdependent for any single rational actor or a single sovereign state to manage this state of affairs on its own. It was an argument for multi-lateral action, to get beyond the notion of unilateral actor or even a coalition of the willing. We need multidisciplinary approaches just as we need multilateral actions to cope with global issues. On the relationship between justice and sovereignty, I think this is a key question. I was schooled by Hedley Bull to historicize this as a relationship between justice and order. Can you have order without justice? Justice without order? You quickly learn that there were other formal organizations of power that provided justice before the sovereign state claimed to have a monopoly on it. Now, by trying to cure the disease of 'global terrorism' through sovereign actions, we've produced a worse effect, an auto-immune response that will be remembered by historians long after the initial attack of 9/11 has been forgotten. Historians will remember the tragic consequences of the Patriot Act, the war in Iraq, the erosion of civil liberties and the promotion of fear. And of course, they will remember the incredible loss of standing of the United States in the world community.

MICHAEL DOYLE: On nationalism, I would agree with the points that Jack has made about the developing world. But I would also say that even though nationalism takes different forms, it still has a strong resonance in the developed world. American politics in recent years has reflected a form of nationalism. We saw an exultation in the successes of American troops, which is most importantly understandable, but on the other hand, reflective of a desperate identification that had much to do with some of the harder forms of nationalism in the past. So, despite the salience of broad principles of human rights and democratic institutions and free markets, there remains a nationalist underlay, even though it takes this civic form that I think is still very powerful in the United States. And we shouldn't underestimate it.

In Europe, there has been more attenuation of those nationalist fires. But when Europeans were pressed to decide on the European constitution, there was pushback from the European – that is, French, Belgian, Dutch – peoples that made the new constitutional project unviable. Now, it may have been just that it was poorly explained and poorly designed. But there looked as if there was a pushback of nationalism on the European side. So, together with the nationalisms that we see very powerfully in the developing world, nationalism is not an absent phenomenon, even in the developed world.

With regard to justice and sovereignty – sovereignty is both a condition and an obstacle to justice. Sovereignty helps achieve domestic justice. It's a condition, but not a guarantee. Sovereignty can help, also, to shield genocide. But it can be the condition that avoids free riding, and assures that taxes are paid and distributed in a way that pursues genuine public purposes. The very success of domestic sovereignty is the reason why we don't have global law and order, global sovereignty. This is why the poor in a rich country can be taken care of, with all the problems we know still, but the global poor remain without the hope of genuine assistance even though they are more disadvantaged than the domestic poor within any society. Indeed, the international system is structured in a way that even the rules of fair play, with regard to trade and others, are systematically biased in favour of the rich. So, state sovereignty is a condition, I think, of domestic justice, though not a guarantee, by any means. But it's also a condition of international injustice.

DAVID KENNEDY: Alex, I think a pragmatic defence of sovereignty is the only kind that really makes sense. So, yeah, I'm not interested in a theoretical defence of whatever it would mean – sovereignty on the moon, or some other society than we actually live in, in some time other than the one we're actually in. But that doesn't mean that in defending it, one should adopt the viewpoint that there is a particular nation taken for granted, and a particular general will taken for granted, whose purposes we can assess in relationship to the efficacy of sovereignty.

If you look at the history of sovereignty over the last 150 years, it's a mixed story. There was something emancipatory about getting everybody jammed into a nation-state with a passport. And there was something that was really terrible about it. And it was quite different for people in different locations. So my own assessment, looking at the Third World at the moment of decolonization was that the idea of self-determination and that what they should have is sovereignty – was a disaster. And it was a disaster in part because it made them and us imagine that there was a divorce between public and private authority, and between here and there responsibility. The idea of separation that was brought about was a kind of ideological crippling of our capacity for moral and political imagination over the last fifty years that has made global poverty more intractable and difficult to deal with. So from that point of view, it seems to me the idea is 'all right, let's think of some new form that it could have'. And here, I find the analogies from property and its fluid reorganization helpful. Imagine that if sovereignty were a thing that you could parcel out in a lot of different ways, where there was a standard openness to buy in. So, imagine, if you wanted a global politics that was more inclusive. Here are some concrete examples of what one could do. You could say – the European Union should make a standing offer of admission. So they have changed regimes all over the place, in Eastern and Central Europe, one could argue about whether or not that was imperialistic or well done, or poorly done. But if I wanted to change the regime in Iraq, I would much rather the Europeans did it by membership in the European Union. It would have cost about the same amount – than when we did it, in the way that we seem to typically do it. And so, a standing offer of admission to the European Union – for Egypt, for Palestine, for Israel, for Morocco.

Or maybe Massachusetts could do a deal with Canada, or Brazil. One could do this without getting rid of sovereignty. Or imagine if everybody was issued not a passport and a citizenship, but a one-time, anywhere-in-the-world five-year residency visa that went with it – exercisable anywhere. You could regulate it, but still, the idea would be – one could imagine the citizenship dimension of sovereignty that we talked very little about, in a way that put much more emphasis on mobility and fluidity. Or imagine, as one does in the suburban context, if every citizen of a suburb around New York had three votes that they could cast in any election in the metropolitan area that they cared about. Then you would have people who were working in the city, but living in the suburbs, able to have some role in urban politics. Imagine that globally. Everybody gets three votes that they can cast in any election around the world that they care about. There are lots of things one could do, within this context, that would be far more radical and upending, and would expose far more the processes of decision-making than the discussions that we have been able to imagine within the framework of sovereignty as we know it now.

AUDIENCE MEMBER: My thoughts to the panel – cheer up. There is an overwhelming sense of the horrors of the world. I was really struck by the last defence of sovereignty, that seems to be the community of the at-risk, the solidarity of the victims. I wonder what happens to the solidarity of the public good? And how could that exist, really, without the capacity for self-reflection and consideration that is political life? And that could exist in a global world.

But at the moment, that's on the moon. I think, right now, actual political public goods can only be really estimated within existing polities. And I'm interested in the future, in the year 8000. But right now I'm looking at the year 2005.

JAMES DER DERIAN: I'd like to address the question about cheering up. Well, let's face it, we're in an academic setting. We are here to be pessimists of the intellect, not optimists of the will, as Gramsci put it. I am sure that we all, in our own lives and in other ways try to combine the two. I know, for instance, that the people on these panels wear two hats, working with the United Nations or doing pro bono work in international law. Some even are in the business of nation-building. I think that our assigned task was to cast a bit of pallor over sovereignty. I don't feel bad about it. That said, I think sovereignty is ethically indefensible, but I act on the premise that it is pragmatically indispensable at this moment. So we're all, in this regard, realists of the intellect, idealists of the will. But I think you must, in the absence of any sort of robust imaginaries in current political discourse, use metaphor, use language, use whatever means possible to form alternatives from past historical examples or future possibilities. Finally, I want to put on the table a peculiar character of sovereignty that we haven't really plumbed. In my mind, sovereignty is like a George Romero film. It's got the quality of the undead. I feel like it's been dead for a long time, but doesn't know it. It's got this vampire quality and I just don't know how to kill it. I don't know where the wooden stake is.

MICHAEL DOYLE: With regard to the issue of the minorities. The grim scenario is that every nation demands its own state, which means that revolution is not over, even in Europe. But that's obviously a grim scenario. A better scenario involves federalism, as has been suggested by the questioner. The hope is that, by having a federal structure where we complicate the world rather than complete the world of nation states (the phrase comes from Michael Walzer) we will provide various forms of effective protection short of secession that recognize multiple identities. That is the hope for the Catalans, for Germans in Northern Italy, for East and West Germans; the creation of a broader identity so that one identity doesn't have to fully merge.

European success is not readily replicable. The horrible circumstances of World War II, the U.S. Cold War protectorate over Europe, Europe's highly-advanced technological structure, its shared inter-dependent history – all played a role. It's not clear that this can be repeated around the world. Their success does not reach all the nationalities. It's not yet sure for European Turks.

David also raised interesting questions about identity at the national level. I certainly wouldn't want to celebrate it as any kind of a harmony that doesn't exist. James, most eloquently, brought up the Katrina example. And that gives us two messages. Number one – when the police force disappeared, looters came out. Communal solidarity was weaker than some thought. Some of the looters stole for survival; they had to feed their family. Others saw it as an opportunity. That the state broke down temporarily, in New Orleans, is a bad sign. You take away the police, and you discover there's no unity. Number two, I thought it was very interesting that the press called the individuals who fled and were taken out of New Orleans, 'refugees'. But they insisted upon being re-labelled as 'evacuees'. Even populations that have been neglected, in some cases exploited – demand that their national membership be recognized, that they deserved better, that they were part of a national community, and yet they weren't receiving what was due to a member over and above the protection that international law awards to foreign refugees.

JACK SNYDER: On the question of whether there can be some preferred alternatives to propping up the sovereign state systems, one possibility would be some kind of a solution that doesn't rely on the territorial administration and control of territory. And I think that that's a non-starter because there has to be a monopoly of violence for any good thing to follow. So if you're going to have territorial administration, who's going to do it? A sovereign state? Or should we return to some kind of permanent direct rule by emissaries from the international community such as colonialism or permanent trusteeship? That didn't work so well when we did this in the past. And it's not likely to return, because the kinds of places that once were colonized now have nationalism, literacy, the diffusion of small arms, which raises the costs of doing it, so that nobody wants to do it. Direct colonial-style rule is also less attractive because we now have free trade, and there are ways to extract resources from these parts of the world without occupying the territory and running it politically. Some might argue that terrorism increases the motive to go back to permanent direct rule, but as we have learned in Iraq, attempting direct rule abroad simply gives rise to terrorism, rather than preventing it.

DAVID KENNEDY: On Katrina – I think that we in the Northeast really don't understand the extent to which people see the government's failure in New Orleans as another reason not to have government, and to cut taxes even further. I think we just don't get the fact that government ineptitude is, in part, the reason that people want to build down the government and not respond by building it up. We are living in the wrong-colour state to get it, in some way.

I want to just return to a couple of ideas about sovereignty. I think the sovereignty we need to understand is a sovereignty that's both associated with the separation of public and private life, and with their interaction and inter-mediation. That's associated both with the idea of 'I'm a citizen of Germany' and also with the idea that we know how to have foreigners living in our midst, Turks who are part this and part that. That's associated both with the idea of national, territorial integrity and autonomy; and with the idea that there are a whole series of ways in which the authorities over different territories overlap. And we constantly want to forget that, and remember only the side of sovereignty that's associated with we are us and you are them, we have territorial authority and we are public capacity. Sovereignty is also about mixing and matching. And so, to understand the forms of life that create bad results in the world, we have to understand and map out the ways in which, in a system that's both clear and murky at the same time, power is exercised by people.

Note

1 The website James Der Derian is referring to can be accessed at HTTP:

Index